A
WAY OF
LIFE

A
WAY OF
LIFE

Over 30 years of blood, sweat and tears

REG KRAY

PAN BOOKS

First published 2000 by Sidgwick & Jackson

This edition published 2001 by Pan Books
an imprint of Macmillan Publishers Ltd
25 Eccleston Place, London SW1W 9NF
Basingstoke and Oxford
Associated companies throughout the world
www.macmillan.com

ISBN 0 330 48511 3

1 3 5 7 9 8 6 4 2

A CIP catalogue record for this book is available from
the British Library.

Typeset by SetSystems Ltd, Saffron Walden, Essex
Printed and bound in Great Britain by
Mackays of Chatham plc, Chatham, Kent

To the young of the world . . . the Bradleys, Pauls, Kevins, Billys, Joes, and all the rest – in the hope I have taken you through this journey to save you the trip. Take it easy . . . because I care.
God Bless,
Reg Kray

Acknowledgements

Many thanks to my wife Roberta for all her hard work and encouragement. Thanks as well to Bill Taylor.

'If you travel the same route as everybody else,
all you will see is what they have already seen.'
– Iain Banks

Contents

INTRODUCTION

This book is a recollection of all my prison years. Included are memories of love, loyalty, friendship, intrigue, betrayal, treachery, violence, laughter and tears – not necessarily in that order. This story is of a journey, a journey that takes place over a period of more than thirty years ... and which still remains unfinished.

My brother Ron and I were arrested on 8 May 1968 at my mother's flat in Braithwaite House, Bunhill Row, Old Street, London. We were later charged with murder, extortion, fraud, bonds charges and grievous bodily harm. Those charges led to us sitting in a cell in Brixton where we remained on remand until we were sentenced ...

CHAPTER ONE

ON REMAND
1968–1969

On remand with us in Brixton prison were our brother Charlie Kray, Freddie Foreman, Joe Kaufman (a New York American) and one traitor . . . namely Richard 'Moggy' Morgan from Mile End. We were in a special unit which had been specially built for us a year prior. Ron and I had heard of this 'special wing' during the time the police were going around accumulating statements in the hope that they would finally be able to arrest us.

The unit was on the second floor of the building and was very secure. It consisted of about twelve cells. We had our own television, which reminded me of the feast before the slaughter. Even after just a few days the toll of captivity was starting to tell on Dickie Morgan and Joe Kaufman. I wondered how they would have reacted had they been in the hands of the Gestapo during the Second World War. As it was all they faced was some time in prison. If it had been the days of war they might have faced having their teeth removed with pliers. They seemed bad enough now . . . what would they have been like then? But that's getting away from the story, so I'll go back to the beginning.

In between trips to court I settled down reasonably well. Dressed in a pair of shorts, I would, for an hour each day, kick a football around the compound. This area was surrounded by wire mesh and barbed wire. My aim, which helped me to keep fit and made me sweat considerably, was to kick the ball against the wire mesh and catch it with either foot on the rebound. I would play this game and then go back to the wing for a shower.

Frankie Fraser was on the ground floor in one of the cells and sometimes I would stop for a chat. He was doing fifteen years for his alleged part in the case known as the Richardson Torture Trials. He was later to get another five years for participating in the Parkhurst mutiny and riots. I can remember it like yesterday. Frank said to me out of the window, 'Look at that pigeon on top of the wire, Reg. He's doing stoppo!' Which in prison slang meant he was having it on his toes! I could see the funny side; it was typical of Frank's sense of humour. Some time later at the Old Bailey, on the same day that Frank had an appearance (for a separate case), we were all waiting in the corridor to go up before the judge to be remanded. Frank was sitting at the bottom of some steps, pretending to play a trumpet. It brought another smile to my face.

Also in Brixton, in the special unit above ours, was Dennis Stafford, known as the Playboy. He had just been sentenced to life imprisonment for the killing of a fruit-machine rival in Newcastle. He was convicted along with one other man called Luvaglo. They had shot and killed a rival in what became known as the One Armed Bandit Killing. Luvaglo was also sentenced to life.

Stafford's real name was Dennis Seigenburg. Both Ron and I, for personal reasons, knew this. At the age of sixteen we'd been on a charge of causing grievous bodily harm during a rival teenage gang fight. We were charged, along with Pat Aucott and Thomas Organ, of causing GBH to two adversaries, namely Ronald Harvey and Dennis Seigenburg. They were both also sixteen.

Even at such a young age there was a code of honour among the criminal element – one didn't make statements against another. Both Harvey and Seigenburg broke the code. They claimed we had committed GBH on them during a gang war fight outside Barry's Dance Hall, the Narrow Way, Mare Street, Hackney, London.

So we found ourselves before Judge McClure in the No.1 court at the Old Bailey at the age of sixteen. The case had considerable national and local newspaper coverage, and we were eventually acquitted.

But all these years later Ron and I had not forgotten this slight by Dennis Stafford. I immediately marked Frankie Fraser's card that Stafford was not to be trusted. That's how it is in criminal circles. We give each other references and this is called 'giving the strength' or the SP on someone.

There was also someone else we knew in the Brixton security block. His name was Allan Gold and he was on a £4,000 robbery charge. It was a small world – Allan used to be one of our best customers in our billiard hall at the back of Mile End tube station. He was a pretty good snooker player too!

In one of the other wings was Billy Howard, a South London villain, whom I always had a lot of respect and admiration for. Billy was one of the 'old school' and could really have a fight . . . he was afraid of no one. He was also a smart dresser. He always wore a blue serge suit and looked immaculate. He was on a charge of demanding money with menaces and was in his latter years. As Ron and I passed him one day he greeted us with a hello. It was comforting to find there were people we knew, people who shared our adversity; it made for a kind of camaraderie. In better times we had shared a drink or two.

Both Ron and I, like Billy Howard, accepted that time in custody was all part and parcel of our precarious and hazardous occupation. I'm sad to say that Billy passed away some years ago. He will remain in my thoughts. He was a good man.

When I think of the year of 1968 an accolade should go to my mother for outstanding loyalty and devotion. For a solid thirteen months during our remand, our mother (God bless her) did not miss a single day's visit. She made sure that Ron and I were supplied with food and drink and clean washing. She also organized the visits for anyone else we needed to see.

Already, as I've mentioned, the toll had begun to tell on the traitor Morgan. I didn't detect this at first. He pestered Ron and me to get him bail sureties, and told us what wonderful feats he'd perform to get us free if we got him bail. So I in turn pestered my old man to try to get this organized. Morgan was on a charge of conspiracy to murder along with ourselves. In fact this is one of the charges I forgot to mention earlier – there were so many charges slung at us it was hard to remember them all. They threw the book at us!

Anyway, the devoted Morgan finally got his bail and was also very quickly acquitted of the charge. It wasn't difficult to see why; he was on the list of police informers. We never saw him again. My old man hadn't ever liked him – he always was a good judge of character.

It was one of the best tennis years at Wimbledon. We watched it on the small TV. There was an epic match between Charlie Pasarell and Pancho Gonzales; they were both brilliant. While we were watching play, one of the screws in the unit by the name of Jock Hughes came to tell us of the suicide of one of those charged with us in connection with the bonds. I cannot recall his name all these years later. I hardly knew him. One of our defence lawyers then showed Ron and me a statement written by the American, Joe Kaufman. He was really cracking up and putting all the blame on us for his involvement in the bonds charges. A couple of days later I noticed Kaufman sitting on the edge of a table-tennis table reading one of the daily newspapers. I took a couple of steps towards him and smashed a left hook through the newspaper and on to the point of his chin. He seemed to fly through the air before landing in a heap on the floor. He was out cold with blood pouring from his mouth and nose. I knew I had broken his jaw, which was my intention. I figure he would have ended up with a broken jaw regardless of whether he'd been reading the newspaper or not . . . the newspaper just added a little more surprise.

The screw Jock Hughes helped another screw to carry Kaufman down the stairs to the treatment room. He was then taken to hospital to have an operation – his jaw had been broken in three places. He had to have additional surgery, as part of his jawbone had gone up into his forehead.

I wasn't charged with this assault, though it was in the newspapers. I suppose the authorities reasoned I was on enough charges to keep me inside for a long time to come.

Sometime during the same week big Albert Donoghue, our friend from Bow, came to tell us that Mizle (a notorious police informer and receiver of stolen goods in the East End) had been saying that Ron and I were going to get a life sentence with a thirty-year minimum recommendation. Ron and I took it in our stride but it had a profound effect on Albert Donoghue. The next time we saw him was at Bow Street Court as a prosecution witness giving evidence against us.

Those in charge of our defence at the daily court appearances were putting up a hard fight on our behalf. My defence counsel consisted of the barrister Paul Wrightson, the best I'd ever seen in action or listened to. Ron was defended by John Platts-Mills. Our junior counsel were Mr Sherbourne and Ivor Laurence (who was later to become an MP). Others involved in the defence were QCs Mr Vouden, Sir Lionel Thompson and Peter Crowder. During one of the hearings I called the Prosecutor, Mr Jones, a fat slob – but I can honestly say it was nothing personal. He was actually quite a likeable fellow.

At one stage the judge, Melford Stevenson, suggested that we had tags placed around our necks like the war criminals at the Nuremberg trials. Melford Stevenson had been a young advocate at these trials. I had to say something about this suggestion of 'number tags' so, in an outburst from the dock, I said, 'Do you think this is a cattle market?'

There were various celebrities among the spectators during our trial at the Old Bailey. I saw the charming profile of John Profumo in the well of the court and, on another day, the dignified figure of Charlton Heston. Mickey Duff, the boxing matchmaker, was also there. He had never been popular with Ron and me; he'd barred us from one of his boxing clubs. We weren't alone. No one in the boxing circles of the East End liked Mr Duff. When Ron and I had our first professional fights he stopped us 2s 6d out of our £5 fee at the Mile End Arena. I guess there was no love lost on the part of Mickey Duff either. He came to gloat at us in court. He told people that we had sent a dead rat, neatly wrapped in a box, to his address. Mr Duff came to see what would happen to the gladiators in the arena.

Just before my entry into Brixton prison I had been living with a girlfriend by the name of Carol. Romance was still in the air (so to speak) and she would visit me periodically bringing food and clean washing. On one occasion, after a visit, I became aware that my underwear had got mixed up with someone else's – which led me to believe that Carol wasn't being quite as faithful as she claimed. Being a realist made my acceptance of the deceit that much easier. I knew it would be a long time before we shared sex again, if at all. Just prior to the last time I saw her I gave her £1,700 out of £5,000 I received for a newspaper article. In return I received a little peck on the cheek. In the thirty years since I've received only one letter from her . . . it went straight in the chamber-pot.

During a visit with my mother, after I had been sentenced, I asked if there was any news of Carol. My mother told me that she'd taken the ring I'd bought her but had left behind all the soft toys I had made for her at Brixton. I laughed to myself . . . Carol always knew what to place value on.

Other visitors at Brixton included the photographer David Bailey and the actor James Fox who came up with our friend Francis Wyndham.

There was an interesting prisoner also domiciled at Brixton during our stay. He was called John Silver. He was over seven feet tall and built to match. His was a sad case. One day he had had a brainstorm and killed his wife and children, believing that God had asked him to do it. An escort of eight screws took him everywhere he had to go, including solicitors' visits which are normally unsupervised for privacy. He was eventually certified insane and sent to Broadmoor Hospital for an indefinite period of time. He is still there today.

Also at this time Judy Garland made an appearance at the London Palladium. My mother went backstage to see her. Judy told her she was sorry that we could not be there and wished us luck. Sadly Judy died while I was at Parkhurst.

During our stay at Brixton we would make sure that the less fortunates in other parts of the building would get some of our food and cigarettes. We were able to smuggle the goods through the prison.

Each night after our court appearance the large Black Maria

would journey back to Brixton from the Old Bailey along with a cavalcade of cars, sirens blaring. We would pass by the Embankment and I would watch the beauty of London through blackened windows. Through these same windows we would see our names flashed across the placards at newspaper stands. Such headlines as:

KRAYS FOUND GUILTY ON CHARGES

On our last visit to the Old Bailey, 5 March 1969, we were found guilty of murder and sentenced to life imprisonment with a thirty-year minimum recommendation. We climbed down the stairs to the cells below to start our sentence. To ease the tension Ron and I shadow-boxed. Cornelius Whitehead was in one of the other cells; he broke down and wept after receiving a nine-year sentence. Whitehead, like Morgan and Kaufman, signed a statement incriminating Ron and me. We left it at that – it didn't do him much good at the end of the day.

We were kept in Brixton prison for four more weeks and then, early one morning, we were woken and told to get dressed, split up, and escorted to different cars. The Governor and Assistant Governor of the prison came to say goodbye. Ron's car headed towards Durham, Charlie Kray's to Chelmsford, and Freddie Foreman's to Leicester. The car I was in, along with my escort, sped off along a road that was to take me to the place where I would spend most of the next eighteen years – Parkhurst prison.

CHAPTER TWO

PARKHURST
1969–1970

One of the escort said to me, 'Why don't you cover your head with a blanket, stop you from being recognized?' I replied, 'Why should I? I've nothing to be ashamed of – you wrap a blanket around your face.'

A cine-camera was trained on the back of my head from the escort car following us. I suppose it was for their private use. The car I was in was speeding, well over 90, sometimes 100 m.p.h. The escort kept looking at me to see if I was worried about the speed we were doing. It was farcical. Only a year before I had lost my wife and now I was starting a life sentence. I was in a frame of mind where I couldn't care less if the car crashed or not.

We eventually reached the ferry that was to take us to the Isle of Wight. The car was driven into the hold and, before I knew it, we were on the other side of the water. It wasn't long before we reached the formidable gates of Parkhurst prison.

Still in handcuffs, I walked what seemed to be the length of the prison until arriving at another gate which was the entry to the security block. This was to be my home for the next six years. We entered a small alcove surrounded by bullet-proof glass. We then proceeded to a little office where one of the Parkhurst screws tried some amateur psychology on me. While he was looking through my record he said aloud (for my benefit), 'Is Richardson having any tea?' I kept poker-faced at this. The screw was obviously looking for a reaction. There had been a lot of publicity of late about gang warfare between the Richardsons and the Krays. My days in the East End had taught me not to fall for such tricks.

The office door was then opened and I was given the number of a cell on the second floor. The screw said, 'I'll leave you to find your own way upstairs.' I picked up one of the cardboard boxes holding my belongings and then spotted, just a few feet away, Tommy Wisbey, one of the Great Train Robbers. The last time I'd seen him was in the Kentucky Club, which I'd owned in 1963. Since then he had lost some of his hair. He greeted me with, 'Hello Reg, we've been expecting you.' I said hello back and added, 'Sorry you got so much bird.' About three yards away from him was a fellow about six feet three tall and broad-shouldered. He looked as nutty as a fruitcake and was staring at me intently. My instinct told me I would have trouble with this man, and it wasn't too far off. I made a mental note for future reference. His name was Mick Copeland.

Then Wally Probin introduced himself. He was doing fourteen years for robbery and firearms. He was later to be portrayed by Adam Faith in the film *McVicar*. It was Probin who planned the escape, not McVicar.

Dennis Stafford was the next to shake hands. He'd left Brixton before me. I spotted someone else I knew, Billy Cooper from Hoxton. He was also doing fourteen years. During my trial at the Old Bailey Billy had been in touch to mark our card. The police had been to see him while he was in custody. They offered him parole if he was prepared to make a statement saying I had shot him in the leg in the Senate Rooms Club in

Highbury. I appreciated this gesture of loyalty; it proved he was a sound person. Later on I taught Billy to do sit-ups in the gym, and he became known as 'Sit-ups'.

By the hot-plate I met Harry Roberts. In 1965 or thereabouts he had gunned down and killed three plain-clothes CID men in the area of White City. He had received a life sentence with a thirty-year recommendation. Harry introduced himself and we shook hands.

Another fellow was there by the name of Bernie Beattie. He was also doing fourteen years. He said we had a mutual friend, Joe Martin, whom he had been convicted with. Joe had received a life sentence. Bernie showed me to the yard outside. It was a little courtyard with flowers in parts, and a primitive glasshouse with vegetables in. I saw Eddie Richardson lying on the grass sunbathing. Peter Kroger, the spy given a long sentence for supplying atomic papers to the Russians, was sitting on a chair. He was an elderly looking man with white hair and a deep American accent. Beattie introduced me. I didn't like him on sight. He was a traitor who'd put millions of lives in jeopardy. Eddie Richardson then joined me. We shook hands and I thanked him for the fact that his brother Charlie had offered to give evidence for us at our trial.

I met three others when I got back to the wing. One was John Straffen, the baby-killer. He had a completely bald head and the mentality of a five-year-old. I couldn't help but feel pity for him. He was not responsible for his actions and would never be released.

I also met Charlie Wilson and Gordon Goody, another two of the Train Robbers. I had met them previously in a drinking club over in south London.

I had a look around the building. It consisted of about fourteen cells over an area of the ground floor and the two floors above. There were primitive showers and baths, a side room with a TV in, and a gymnasium with weightlifting equipment, a punch-bag and a punch-ball. By the time I had strolled around it was time for a measly tea. It was then time to bang up in my cell for an hour.

I made another quick cup of tea and started putting my possessions in some semblance of order. I put a photograph of my late wife on a shelf and got my record player ready for the evening. I'd be playing Timi Yuro records; she was a soul singer and one of the best. I used to take her records to all the parties we went to on the outside – the night wouldn't be the same without her voice.

When we unlocked I thought I'd take a walk to the gym, even though I wasn't dressed for gym work. When I arrived Harry Roberts was already there. I told him I'd never done any weightlifting in the past but I'd like to try. 'Perhaps you could show me.' In a way it was strange I'd never done any weights, especially as I'd had my own gym above the Double R Club in Bow Road. Harry said, 'Try lifting this above your head,' which I did and Harry told me I'd done well – it was 100 lb in weight. I decided I was going to take up weightlifting to help occupy my time.

Three weeks later I got a green grading certificate for power lifting, which consisted of a squat, a bench and deadlift. Over the years I was to win three medals and thirty-six certificates. Along with two others I represented Parkhurst and we won a shield for the Southern Area, beating all other prisons. We all got medals for it.

Sometimes I played football in a small yard along with Eddie Richardson, Tommy Wisbey, Charlie Wilson and Roy James. Bobby Welch, another of the Great Train Robbers, couldn't play because he'd had an operation on his knee which was unsuccessful. I also did bench presses with Gordon Goody.

During exercise one day, soon after my arrival, I was on the yard walking and Mick Copeland joined me. I got bad vibes from him straight away. All my instincts warned me against him. I didn't feel comfortable being close; it was like there was a danger barrier between us. I didn't like his conversation either. He said to me, 'I read that book by John Pearson about you, *The Profession of Violence*. I didn't think I'd like you but you're not as bad as the book says.' Outside I would have taken it as a slight but I had to contain myself. Seeing as Mick Copeland had stabbed two courting couples to death for no apparent reason, it was like the pot calling the kettle black. I let it slide but I was glad when the exercise period was over. I knew I couldn't take too much of his tongue.

We were all Category A prisoners on the block and a new ruling was introduced that concerned us. The ruling was that anyone wishing to come and see us would have to have their photograph taken and three copies submitted to the Home Office for their approval of the visit. Inmates all over the country fought and rebelled against this. Our whole block went on hunger strike, as they also did in Durham where Ron was imprisoned.

(Ron was in Durham with Joe Martin, an old friend, and Bruce Reynolds, another of the Great Train Robbers. Ron told me that on the landing above him was the slag Brady, the child-killer. Ron saw him from a distance and said he was an arrogant bastard. I could never understand Lord Longford having anything to do with Brady or Hindley.)

Charlie was also on hunger strike along with other inmates at Chelmsford. We lasted eleven days on hunger strike in Parkhurst. Ron and his crowd lasted thirteen.

I had been off the strike for only a day, and still felt nowhere near as strong as usual, when I walked downstairs to get my breakfast. I saw Copeland nearby. I thought he spoke but I was a little unsure. We were near the shower-room, which had a small entrance and Copeland said loudly and aggressively, 'Oi you! I said good morning to you!' I told him I hadn't heard him. Copeland then said to me, 'Get in here you,' beckoning towards the entrance to the shower-room. I knew he wanted a row and let him walk a couple of yards in front. I slung a right punch but it didn't connect properly due to his height. I grabbed him in a headlock from behind, got a good grip on him and pulled him towards the wall. He struggled as I butted him across the right eyebrow and split his eye open. I was pleased that I'd drawn first blood.

Before I knew it the screws were in and had my arms up my back. They pulled us apart. While holding me against the wall they ordered Copeland upstairs. We were then both locked in our cells. Our cells were close to each other, although on different landings, and I applied a little psychology to get Copeland wound up. I knew he would be listening so I put a Timi Yuro LP on and turned my record player up as loud as possible to freak him out.

The screws came to my cell, they'd been to his too, and wanted to know if we'd both forget it. They knew we'd use tools on each other. I told them I wouldn't forget it. They said, 'That's what he says too.' So it was going to be war.

The following day Copeland was shifted to the block and I was taken before the Governor charged with fighting. I got a £3 fine out of my canteen money and was told the fight was my fault. The Governor's name was Miller. I couldn't see how he reasoned the fight was down to me.

Copeland was then shifted to Durham prison. Ron had heard about the row and waited at the bottom of the stairs for Copeland. When he came down Ron hit him straight on the chin with a right-handed punch that felled him like an ox. Copeland was then shifted to Chelmsford. I understand Charlie gave him a strong pull in the TV room. Copeland said he wanted no more trouble.

Life continued. I started to make soft toys to pass out to my visitors as gifts. And I became obsessed by weightlifting.

Joe Martin arrived from Durham prison. Joe and I greeted each other warmly and had a chat about old times. Joe had been at the Green Dragon Club when I broke Sonny the Yank's jaw. A fellow by the name of John Richard Jones from Birmingham also came into the block. He was doing fourteen years for armed robbery. I didn't particularly like Jones. He was about twenty-eight years of age, five feet eleven, with ginger hair. He was out to impress. I got bad vibes from him. Outside, such people would not have got within fifty yards of me.

I told Joe I didn't like Jones. He didn't like him either. A few days later Jones walked into my cell without knocking and sat down uninvited on the bed. Jones looked at the photo of my wife on the shelf and pointed, rudely and aggressively, saying, 'Who's that bird?' In those days I was a lot worse than now. I've got used to such scum. But at that moment I felt the blood drain from my face. He saw the look in my eyes and tried to get out of the door as fast as he possibly could. I followed him out and along the landing, slung a punch at him and knocked him to the floor. I was on top of him – and then the screws were on top of me. They pulled me off and led Jones downstairs. He wasn't very lucky. Joe Martin was waiting at the bottom of the stairs; he slung a flurry of punches that put Jones on the floor again.

I was fined again for fighting and Jones was shipped out of the prison. In fact I did him a favour. They wouldn't put him back in any special units because he was too immature; he returned to the 'normal' prison regime.

The discomfort of this 'false' environment, where one had to mix with total strangers, people it was impossible to like, was one of the worst hardships of prison life – and will remain so until the day I am out. If any young kids read this story they should remember that prison is not a glamorous place. Prison is not a happy vocation, so take a tip from me and look for a career other than crime. Don't follow in my footsteps.

Around this time the Parkhurst riots took place, with Frankie Fraser as the leader. Frank and his crowd had a terrible fight with the screws in another part of the prison which was cut off entirely from those of us in the block.

One day an escape plot was uncovered by the screws. Had it succeeded it would have been one of the greatest escapes of all time. In fact it was so clever the screws called in specialist photographers from the Home Office. It was a tunnel beneath Harry Roberts's cell. It had miniature arc-lights as well as the equipment, torches, chisels etc. It was a long tunnel that he'd dug like a ferret deep down in his cell and then almost as far as the outer wall. This was an almost impossible feat when one realizes there was a twenty-four-hour vigil on each category A cell. Harry also had to get rid of all the waste. This was achieved by him and his friend tucking bricks down their waistbands and dirt down their trousers with the bottoms tucked in. They took it out to the garden area, loosened the bottoms of their trousers and mixed the dirt and bricks with the soil. They did this every day. The escape plot was eventually tumbled when Harry's mother was discovered bringing a pair of small bolt-cutters in under her coat on a visit. She was arrested, charged and taken to court. She was given probation.

I was locked up in this block for more than six years. Once a week we would watch a film. Sometimes we played football. Take it from me, if you live in close proximity to people for so long you begin to see more and more of each other's faults and life becomes unbearable.

Just before I left I lost my appeal against conviction and sentence for murder. I got the needle – but not because I'd lost the appeal. On my last appeal visit at Parkhurst, Governor

Miller allowed me only a quarter of an hour. Taking away the time to greet and later say goodbye to my friend Jim Harris left me with a visit of only ten minutes. Miller could have been more liberal. Jim Harris had travelled all the way from London to see me.

During the early years of my sentence I had to face up to the fact that a number of people, including many so-called friends, had double-crossed Ron and me. They had given evidence against us in order to try to save their own skins. I gave this a lot of thought and finally came to a decision. I knew I needed to have a strong sense of direction if I was to get through this sentence intact . . . mentally and physically. I couldn't be preoccupied with thoughts of vengeance. I reached the conclusion that I just had to get on with it. I dismissed the traitors in my mind as insignificant. I erased them from my memory. I decided that from then on my thoughts would revolve on and around a more stimulating plane. Ron agreed with my new-found philosophy. Life was too short to be bogged down with vendettas.

Early one morning in March 1970 my cell door came open and four screws came in. They told me to get my gear together. I was on my way.

CHAPTER THREE

LEICESTER

1970–1971

I was escorted to a van and driven again to the ferry. When we disembarked at Portsmouth the van headed towards the Midlands. A screw told me our destination was Leicester prison. Eddie Richardson was in the van behind me, heading for the same place. I found out later that Ron had passed me on the road on his way to Parkhurst from Durham. It was a general shake-up.

Eddie and I arrived at reception at the same time. Eddie said, 'You won't like this pisshole, I've been here before.' They put us in two very small reception cells. The screw walked away. An inmate walked by and nodded his head. I nodded back. This was my first sight of a person who was to become one of my best friends. His name was Harry Johnson, alias Hate-'em-all Harry. He was short and thickset with small features, fierce eyes and an almost bald head. Harry came from Nottingham and was doing eighteen years for robbery with violence.

The security block consisted of a total area of nine cells, a small cell converted into a kitchen, a small TV room, a snooker table and a tiny shower area. It made Parkhurst look spacious.

There was also a concrete exercise yard. Every time we went out on the yard or on visits we would have metal detectors run over us and a strip search as they looked for weapons.

I made up my mind to get into weights again. We used to lift the weights beside the snooker table. I showed Freddie Foreman and Harry Johnson my British Amateur Weightlifting Association book; it told us what weights we had to lift. It wasn't long before I had the Leicester County record for the Straight Arm Pull Over . . . 95 lb. Freddie Foreman and Harry Johnson also got certificates.

In the security block along with Fred, Harry and me was John Duddy. He was an accomplice of Harry Roberts in the killing of three police officers. Also there was a fellow called Hosein. He was one of the brothers from Trinidad, living in London, who had kidnapped and killed Muriel McKay, the wife of the deputy chairman of the *News of the World*. Her body was never recovered. Hosein was a brilliant table-tennis player and claimed to be the champion of Trinidad.

My first trouble in Leicester prison came about over a doughnut. I wasn't very keen on cakes so on a couple of occasions at teatime I had foolishly given my doughnut to a man called Pete Hurley. He was twenty-eight years old and doing fourteen years for armed robbery. Hurley was about five feet eleven, with curly ginger hair, blue eyes and the body of a weightlifter. He was covered in tattoos. On the second night I gave him a doughnut he just grunted his acceptance. Hurley was a very ignorant type; he had the manners of a pig. On the third night I didn't pass the doughnut over. I decided I wasn't there to feed him. He said, 'Where's my doughnut?' and gave me a menacing glare. I told him I was keeping it. The terrible look he gave me could only mean we were enemies. I suppose one could say he had just bit the hand that fed him.

When we were locked up at 9 p.m. I brooded over this

insolent bastard. I had noticed other traits that I also disliked. I decided that the area we lived in was too small for both of us. One of us had to go. The next morning I got up early in readiness. As my cell door opened I knew he'd be in the kitchen as usual making tea. The kitchen cell was opposite my own. I was out like a bullet. Hurley was washing a cup at the sink. I walked right up to him and smashed him in the mouth with a right-hand punch. Blood spurted from his mouth but he was a strong fellow. As he fell against the wall he reached for a knife in the sink. Hurley and I slung a few punches at each other and then the screws came in to break us up. I had made my move and now I would have to wait and see how it developed. It worked out OK. Hurley realized I wouldn't tolerate his demanding ways but I still always kept an eye on him in case he pulled a tool. It wasn't good for two people who'd had a row to live in the same area but I learnt to live with it.

One night there was another argument that came to blows. Harry Johnson was playing snooker with Arthur Hosein, and Harry lost. This was too much for the explosive Harry. After a violent outburst he hit Arthur on the chin with a left hook. It knocked Arthur out cold. I could tell that little Harry was proud of this feat.

During my year in Leicester prison, I had more than my fair share of trouble. My second problem arrived in the shape of John Duddy, the cop-killer. John was thickset with blue eyes and grey wavy hair. He was from Scotland and an ex-army man. He had a very coarse aggressive voice. One day in the kitchen area I found him talking in a loud tone to Eddie Richardson. He was going on about gays, and did so knowing that Ron was bisexual. I could read between the lines and knew that Duddy was inciting Eddie to run down gays too. He was hoping it would cause friction between the two of us.

I went to my cell where I found Harry Johnson sitting. I

said, 'Wait there, I'm going to put it on Duddy.' I walked out to the small area where we ate. I walked up and hit Duddy in the eye with a right-hand punch. He crashed to the floor and I scruffed him by the shirt collar, hauling him up to a seat. I tightened my grip on his throat and said, 'Any more out of you, I'll kill you, you bastard.' He had a massive black eye.

The screws locked us all up for an hour. There was a senior screw in the prison who weighed about eighteen stone. He was a black belt in judo with Dans to go with it. We all got on well with him because he was a sportsman. My cell door was unlocked and a screw told me that the judo man wanted to see me in his office. He was waiting for me when I arrived. He said, 'I've just spoken to Duddy and I'm going to have you both meet in the centre, where I'll be present, to shake hands. I want you both to forget your row.' He added, 'But always keep your eye on Duddy, he's got nothing to lose.' I replied, 'Neither have I. I'm doing a thirty-year recommended as well.' Although I did realize that Duddy had even less chance of getting out than I did.

I was locked up again. A quarter of an hour later the door was opened and I was told the judo man was waiting in the centre of the hall with Duddy. 'This reminds me of the gunfight at the OK Corral,' I mused to myself. I walked to the centre and they were both there. The judo man said, 'I'd like to see you both shake hands now.' We both extended our hands, not without hesitation, and shook. I believe I said the words, 'No hard feelings,' knowing full well there were . . . on both sides. But life was normal again.

Eddie Richardson hated it at Leicester and went on hunger strike. He was locked up for a short period of time in a separate part of the prison. We used the same toilet though. I figured the ploy of leaving hard-boiled eggs and other delicacies in the middle of the toilet roll so Eddie wouldn't go entirely hungry.

As long as it was written in the book that Eddie was still on hunger strike he continued to make his point. There was no reason for him to starve to death!

I went on hunger strike myself in protest at a national newspaper item which said I was involved in a plot to kidnap Lord Linley in April 1970. I wrote to Lord Snowdon, his father, to declare my loyalty to the Royal Family.

My stay at Leicester was mercifully short. I didn't like it there. It was too confined. I was pleased when early one morning three screws came to my cell and said, 'Pack your gear, you're on your way.' I hastily packed my Murphy radio (which was a dear friend), a record player, toiletries, clothing and a pile of letters. While making out I was going to the toilet I quickly slipped across to Harry Johnson's cell, pulled back the latch of the spyhole and shouted to him, 'I'll be in touch, Harry. See you later.' I also managed to leave half an ounce of tobacco outside his door.

I was escorted to the van. I asked one of the five-strong escort where I was going. He told me, 'Parkhurst – the security block.' I was pleased. I could look forward to seeing Ron.

CHAPTER FOUR

PARKHURST II
1971–1981

After a long journey we finally arrived. A couple of the Train Robbers were there to greet me but there was no sign of Ron. I was looking forward to seeing him again and I was really disappointed. At the same time I could feel a certain tension in the air. Tommy Wisbey told me that Ron was in the prison hospital because he had hit Bernie Beattie over the head with a bottle. There was an expectation of trouble between me and Beattie but I had always got on well with him. I was pretty good at evaluating situations like this; I had come across them before. I went to Bernie's cell to ask him what had happened. He was nursing a black eye and a cut on his skull. Bernie told me that he and Ron had fallen out, hence the whack to his head. I told Beattie I was sorry about their argument but hoped we would still be friends. He put out his hand and said, 'Let's shake,' which we did.

I then went to the main office to ask if I'd be able to see Ron. They told me they'd arrange it. I went to see him in the hospital, where he was in the care of Dr Cooper, a psychiatrist. I said to Ron, 'Get back on the wing and we'll do some weightlifting together.' Ron agreed and within a few days he was back in the security block with me. We did the weightlifting and Ron won some certificates.

Shortly after I was convicted I was given a scroll with the poem 'Desiderata' on it. It has helped me out both with my sentence and with life in general. Part of the passage reads: 'Avoid loud and aggressive persons for they are a vexation to the spirit.'

I found this passage to be particularly true of some of the inmates I had already met, especially Mick Copeland, John Richard Jones, Peter Hurley and John Duddy. There were undoubtedly more. The thought didn't fill me with joy.

Mick Copeland was an extremely weird person. He would go very peculiar when there was a full moon. He used to bang up alone in his cell. He kept a knife in there and I knew he wouldn't hesitate to use it.

The favourite dialogue of John Richard Jones was about how he would beat up his girlfriend with a chain, making her cower on the floor. This kind of talk was alien to me. I couldn't relate to it. In fact I couldn't stand it. This is why I was so antagonistic to the slag.

Peter Hurley was just bad-mannered and immature.

John Duddy's favourite story concerned some time spent in the army in Malaya. He would repeatedly tell the story of how he had knocked a Malay girl into the river after she upset him. He hit her on the chin. To me this was cowardly, bully talk.

All these people were without doubt 'a vexation to the spirit'.

Early one morning Joe Martin came down from Durham prison to join us. We were pleased to see him and to talk about old times. The three of us started training together in the gym. A few days later Harry Johnson arrived from Leicester, and Mick Green (one of the Wembley bank robbers) came into the block too. Harry joined us in our training. As well as using weights we sometimes used sixteen-ounce boxing gloves to spar with. We also used the swivel punch-ball and heavy punch-bag.

Another who joined us on the wing was a man by the name of Bill Skingle. He had killed a copper by shooting him nine times. The copper had only pulled him to take his car number. I always thought Skingle went too far. He was sentenced to natural life imprisonment when he was only in his early twenties. None of us liked him; he had no principles. He was to die from a heart attack at the early age of forty-one.

One day when we were all in the small yard, Harry Johnson and Skingle had an argument. Blows were exchanged. Harry lost his footing and slipped to the floor and Skingle jumped on top of him. Ron got Skingle round the neck and pulled him off. When we were all back in the block at the end of the exercise period, Skingle was strutting around as if he had won a victory. I knew this wouldn't last. Harry said to Ron, Joe and I, 'I'll do the slag first chance I get. I'll do him cunning.'

A couple of days later, sitting in my cell on the 2s, Harry walked in and said, 'Get rid of this weight, Reg. I've just done Skingle.' He passed me a 4 lb dumb-bell weight. I immediately got rid of it. Harry had hit Skingle on the cheekbone while he was washing up. They had to take Skingle over to the hospital, where he was kept until he had an operation on his broken jawbone. When he eventually got back on the wing he had lost his cockiness and wasn't so flash. Hate-'Em-All had taught him a lesson.

For a while trouble was rife in the block. Ron hit Mick Green on the chin during an argument, but it cooled over.

Although the security block was separated from the main wings news still filtered back to us. One day we heard that Frank Fraser had some trouble with another inmate called Mark Owens. Owens was serving a fairly long sentence and had just arrived at Parkhurst. He came from west London and was a loner with a reputation for being a good fairground and knuckle fighter. The story was that at an earlier time Mark Owens had upset Frank Fraser and Charlie Richardson. There had been a disagreement and a fight and Owens had been hurt. On his arrival at Parkhurst, Owens saw Frank Fraser on the exercise yard walking in. Owens walked across and hit Frank Fraser on the chin, knocking him to the ground.

Some time afterwards the two of them were involved in the Parkhurst mutiny. They were both charged and ended up in the dock together and so became allies in the face of adversity.

A former girlfriend came to see me with my mother and at my request brought me a pale blue budgerigar. He was OK for a while. I used to leave him unlocked to keep me company. But after a while he started to get on my nerves. He would dive-bomb my plate every time I had a meal. Also, every time I rolled a cigarette the bird would swoop down and claim the Rizla paper in his beak, tearing the roll-up in half. I decided to give the budgie to my cousin; she loved him and showered affection on him.

There were mice in the block so Ron decided to get a cat, much to the annoyance of Hate-'Em-All Harry. Ron got one of the screws to get him a black kitten, which he kept in a box in his cell. It used to snarl like a tiger and bare its teeth. Ron would have kept it longer, it kept the mice away, but he grew tired of Harry's incessant grumbling about the mess it made. Ron gave it back to the screw and asked him to find a home for it. The screw then had the job of smuggling the cat out again.

I was in hospital and absent from the wing when the following event took place, but this is how I heard it from Joe Martin. Ron had gone up to a screw and asked him for his medication but the screw had refused. Ron left and went to Joe Martin's cell and said, 'Joe, you're my friend so I don't want to see you in any trouble. Don't come on the landing, stay in your cell. I'm going to put it on a screw.' Joe tried to argue that he should be involved but Ron told him it wasn't necessary. Ron then left and went back to the screw. He hit him in the face with a right-hand punch and floored him. The alarm bell went off and lots of other screws arrived. Ron had already started walking towards the punishment block.

On adjudication the following day, he was given fifty-six days solitary confinement. That meant fifty-six days without contact with anyone, no furniture in the cell, no radio or tobacco. It was later on discovered that the screw, like Skingle, had a broken cheekbone. If it had been known at the time Ron would have got much longer. His sentence was broadcast on the radio.

One day there was a turn-up for the book. The placid John Straffen had a brainstorm and attacked Mick Green. For one of the 'faces' to be attacked by Straffen was a real surprise. It took a while for Mick to live down the embarrassment and Straffen was shifted, for his own safety, to Long Lartin.

Gossip was going around the prison at this time about one of the padres. It was said that he'd been questioned about the theft of women's underwear from clothes lines in the Isle of Wight area. We didn't, for some time, get the pleasure of meeting this gentleman because as residents of the security block we were not allowed to go to church.

The new arrivals at Parkhurst usually came at around 4 p.m. On this particular day I can recall a new arrival walking up the stairs to our landing with a couple of cardboard boxes under his arm. His name was Roy Grantham. He was about twenty-eight years of age, six feet tall, weighing fourteen stone, with dark hair and blue eyes. He had come from Gartree prison where there had been a riot and break-out. Grantham was doing eleven years and had just been found guilty of assault on eleven screws during the riot. He had come to Parkhurst to finish off his punishment, which was supposed to be some time locked behind his door, on his own. As he walked up the stairs Harry Johnson, who was a good judge of character, said to me, 'I'll lay you money you have a row with this flash cunt, he's trouble.' I felt there was some truth in Harry's words but said, 'I'll keep an open mind.'

So Ron, Joe and I and the others on the block made Grantham welcome. We laid meals on for him. Although in reality he should have been locked up until his time on punishment was finished, the screws had different ideas. Perhaps they were hoping that there would be a clash.

Grantham was one flash bastard. He was continually shadow-boxing and getting on people's nerves. When out on exercise for a walk or a run he would wear bandages on his hands and a mask, made out of a towel, around his face. He would shadow-box as if he was Sonny Liston. He had the bad habit of walking into cells without knocking, picking up photographs and passing comments – usually rude – about the women in them. He would also pick up pieces of food from your dinner plate and scoff them.

His worst habit of all was tracking me down to the toilet, where I'd be trying to get some peace and quiet. Grantham would stand by the half-length door, look over it, and give me a running commentary on various things while I was completing my ablutions. In short he was really trying my patience, and of the others too. Because he was on punishment we felt a moral obligation to look after him. He was mistaking kindness for weakness.

Early one evening he came into my cell while I was talking to Ron and just butted in on the conversation. Ron said, 'Do you mind leaving us, we're talking.' I watched Grantham's face go white; he was angry at being dismissed. Still, he left the cell.

The following morning I was still in bed when Ron came in to give me a cup of tea. The previous night I had made sure that a glass container of apple juice was on the table close to my bed. I knew I was going to use it as a weapon. Ron had just poured the cup of tea from a jug into my cup when the cell door was slung open with some force and in walked Grantham. He said aggressively, 'What was all that about last night, telling me to fuck off?' I was ready for him. Fully naked I leapt out of the bed, picked up the apple juice bottle, took two strides and brought it down on Grantham's head as hard as I could. The bottle splintered and blood shot up into the air. As Grantham raised his hands to defend himself I hit him with a left uppercut under the chin and he collapsed like a ton of bricks.

The screws had heard the breaking glass and came running in. They pulled Grantham out of the cell, put him on a stretcher and took him to the prison hospital. Dr Cooper gave him forty-five stitches to his face, set a broken little finger in plaster and tended to his fractured skull. Needless to say, Grantham was shifted from Parkhurst and we never saw him again.

After the attack Ron and I were taken to the punishment block and charged with malicious wounding. They brought in photographers to take pictures of the walls, which were covered in blood. The episode was broadcast on the radio and the Home Secretary began talking of splitting us up.

I wrote a letter to a woman magistrate called Mrs Hamilton. I told her in the letter, knowing it would be read by the censor, that if Ron and I were taken to an outside court over this I would call every category A prisoner in the security block as witnesses. The security bill would be enormous.

When the police came to question us we refused to see them. The authorities decided to take action internally instead. We were taken before a visiting magistrate called Mr Hadley. We called Harry Johnson and Joe Martin as witnesses to prove provocation by Grantham. We put up such a good defence that Mr Hadley said, 'I'm beginning to wonder if Grantham is the accused rather than you.' He gave us both fifty-six days solitary. Over the years I became quite friendly with Mr Hadley, who visited Parkhurst periodically.

You had to be in the company of Grantham to know what type of person he really was. He once said to me that he would hold a child for ransom and that he would cut off the child's finger if necessary and send it through the post. He was typical of a certain sort in prison – a slag.

I heard that the special psychiatric wing was opening and suggested to Ron that we should try to get moved there to get out of the security block. He agreed with me. I made the appointment to see Dr Cooper over at the hospital. When I was taken over I had an escort of two screws and a dog-handler. While I was in the waiting-room a man called Graham Young joined the queue. He was housed over the hospital and was doing a life sentence for poisoning his family and three of his workmates. During the conversation we had he said he was applying for a job in the kitchen. I found this slightly disturbing . . . the food was bad enough as it was!

I spoke to Dr Cooper and he said he'd give consideration to our request to join the psychiatric wing when it opened. Eventually it was agreed, and Ron and I left the security block. We put our boxes of personal belongings on a trolley and wheeled them over.

Just after we left a different batch of inmates went into the security block. One of them was known as Big H. His real name was Mackenzie. He had received a life sentence for killing three people and chopping up their bodies. He also shot in the head the only witness to his crimes, a six-year-old boy who was still holding a teddy bear in his hand. For these crimes he received a twenty-five-year recommendation. In comparison, Ron and I received a thirty-year recommendation.

The psychiatric wing housed some of the worst psychopaths in the country; many were sex cases. The building consisted of three tiered landings, not a bad building as such. They had professional medical staff there for all the inmates on some form of medication or other. They were all nutty, including me a bit! I didn't really consider myself a nutter but my attack on Grantham was sufficient certificate for entry on to the wing.

Ron and I settled in reasonably well. There was one likeable fellow there whose name I forget. He was doing a life sentence for a series of burglaries up and down the country. He couldn't comprehend why he was doing a life sentence, and neither could I. He was doing time the hard way and was heavily drugged up. Early one morning I was there when the screws went into his cell and lifted him, unconscious, on to a stretcher. He had taken an overdose. He never recovered consciousness and died in the hospital.

The psycho wing had its own punishment block beneath the wings. It was an area of about eight cells and if any of us got in trouble we would be put down there for a few days.

Ron became friends with a man called Ken Jones. Ken had been in and out of institutions all his life. He used to get dejected every day at the thought of making his bed. He was a continuous worrier. He would say he couldn't stand the thought of making his bed any more; he'd been doing it for so long in so many different institutions. Sometimes Ron and I would feel sorry for him and make the bed ourselves. All these years later I too hate making my bed!

I met a fellow from Durham by the name of Wally Lee. Wally was a keep-fit fanatic but had an anxiety complex. He would also worry about everything, including how I should keep fit. Bill Lovall from Birmingham became a friend of ours too.

Nobby Clark from Liverpool, who was about forty-five, was also doing life in the wing. He had a habit of raising his fists in the air in a victory sign, like the Black Panthers. He and Bill Lovall had an argument one day. Nobby thought it was finished with and went downstairs to fill his flasks with hot water. As he was walking back upstairs Bill Lovall was walking down with his own flask. As they got close to each other Bill smashed Nobby in the face with the flask and Nobby went flying down the stairs. He landed at the bottom with a thud. We found out later he had concussion.

Six-foot-two Mickey O'Rourke started to bully the placid Ken Jones and Ron got to hear of this. At 5.45 p.m., unlock time, Ron went tearing out of his cell, like a fire brigade wagon, and straight towards O'Rourke. He was standing talking to a screw on the landing. Ron let fly with a right overhand punch that connected with the point of O'Rourke's chin. His legs collapsed beneath him and he landed heavily on his knees. The screw talking to O'Rourke looked momentarily confused; after the shock wore off he rang the alarm bell.

We hadn't been on the wing long before there was a hostage-taking. Three cons, Big George Wilkins, Taffy Beecham and Alan Poutney conspired with others to take a screw hostage. I'll tell it as it happened. I was on the exercise yard and noticed that Big George Wilkins was in the corner of the yard whispering in the ear of Taffy Beecham. I knew they were both unsettled on the wing and sensed there would be some trouble. I marked Ron's card and then we went and had a cup of tea. A con, Eddie Wilkinson, came into my cell and said, 'Big George Wilkins and Taffy Beecham have taken a screw hostage in one of the corner cells.' They had tied the screw up and were holding a pair of scissors to his throat, demanding their immediate release. No sooner had we learnt this then a herd of screws came on to the landing and started locking us away.

We were banged up all day, without food or drink, in our cells. I fancied a cup of tea and guessed that the other cons did as well. I rang my bell and said to the screw who came to my door, 'Why don't you let me take tea round to all the cells . . . I give you my word, I won't get involved with the hostage-takers.' The screw told me to hang on a minute. He came back with the Assistant Governor, Thompson. The AG said he'd let me take the tea round . . . and asked if I had any ideas on how to solve the crisis. I told him I didn't. I delivered the tea to each cell and then walked by the one where Beecham and Wilkins were with the hostage. There were lots of screws milling around outside the cell door. As I passed it I shouted out, 'George, do you, Taffy or the screw want a cup of tea?'

George shouted back, 'No thanks Reg, we're OK.'

I continued giving the tea out then went back to my cell, satisfied. Assistant Governor Thompson came to my cell and thanked me for creating a bit of good feeling on a difficult day.

The local CID were called in to negotiate and I could hear all the activity. Apparently AG Thompson had approached Alan Poutney to help in the negotiations, and he had agreed to do so. Poutney and his father had been convicted of murder and both were serving life sentences.

About eight o'clock that evening I heard a mass of running footsteps. It was the screws. They were running and screaming loud obscenities at the same time. I had never heard the simultaneous rush of so many screws' feet. I found out after-wards that they had charged in to Wilkins and Beecham, who had negotiated to change hostages – the screw for a CID man. The CID man was supposed to be handcuffed to the landing. Both the screw and the CID man broke loose and the screws jumped all over Wilkins and Beecham, kicking them down the stairs to the punishment block. From my cell I could hear thuds, kicks and screams coming from the two men . . . it sounded terrible and lasted for some time. I found out later that the screw taken hostage, who was called Slater, had been cut on his neck with the scissors.

Taffy Beecham was sent to Long Lartin, Alan Poutney to Park Lane Hospital, and George Wilkins to Hull, where he later died.

Assistant Governor Thompson put in a report that 'Kray had used presence of mind in a difficult situation.' But I wasn't looking for medals . . . just a decent cup of tea!

There were all sorts in the psychiatric wing. One con used to sleep with a soft toy, a furry teddy bear, in his bed. Another, by the name of Bleatman, had a string of convictions for kidnapping young boys. He would dress them up, buy them gifts and sexually abuse them. During his time on the wing he made beautiful miniatures and sold them for tobacco. I was outside his cell one night when Bill Lovall smashed him on the chin and knocked him into the air.

Ron and I stayed in the psychiatric wing for about three years before we left to join the hospital part of the prison. In the second year the wing had its first murder. Doug Wakefield was serving a life sentence for strangling his uncle and crushing his skull. He came from the north and was powerfully built. Although I would sometimes buy tobacco from him he gave me a bad feeling. I sensed something like an evil aura around him.

Wakefield became friendly with another lifer on the wing called Terry Peake. Peake was the best portrait drawer I've ever seen. He did a brilliant caricature of Ron on a Daler board and gave it to him. Just before lock-up at teatime one afternoon the screws found Terry Peake sitting in his chair, dead. He had been garrotted and his head was smashed in. They linked Doug Wakefield with the killing, which was a carbon copy of the murder of his uncle. He was taken to Winchester Crown Court and given another life sentence. Wakefield was then shifted back to the hospital section of Parkhurst.

A few years later Wakefield witnessed the attack by Jimmy Costello on Peter Sutcliffe, the Yorkshire Ripper. Wakefield ended up breaking the prison code by giving evidence against Costello.

Two pieces of news came to us from different areas of the prison. One was that Lord Longford had persuaded the staff in the hospital section to build a special yard, screened off by a wooden fence, especially for the use of Ian Brady, the filthy child-killer. All the other cons had the right needle over this. We couldn't see why the slag should have preferential treatment.

Although I am jumping the story a bit, there came a time when Ron and I would spend each morning in this yard. We were allowed to use it because Ron had been certified and was waiting to go to Broadmoor. All our meetings had to be arranged. Needless to say, Brady was always absent . . . much to our regret.

I would also like to add that in the time Ron and I were separated, Lord Longford did help in a campaign during our sentence to get us back together again.

The other bit of news we received was that Harry Roberts, in the security block, along with Bill Skingle and Cyril Burkett, had made an escape attempt. The only one to get out of the block, through the wire fence and into the woods nearby was Skingle. He did well to evade capture for a couple of days but was eventually spotted by a helicopter. Skingle was seen high in the treetops and was surrounded and captured.

Parkhurst was a pretty heavy place to be in. A killing happened in the main wing. A football match between inmates had just ended and they were returning to the wing when an argument started between Burt Coster and another con. Roy

Shaw was also present. Blows were exchanged and the con, whose name I forget, crashed to the floor with a fractured skull. He never regained consciousness.

Burt Coster and Roy Shaw were taken to Winchester Crown Court. The end result was that Coster received eighteen months for manslaughter. Burt Coster had been a very good amateur fighter, representing his country in boxing.

Yet another hostage-taking was to happen in Parkhurst. This time it occurred in the chokey block area. One of the cons in the block was a fellow by the name of Albert Baker. He was a member of the UDA and was doing life for some killings. Baker was not in an enviable position. According to newspaper reports he was now on the hit list of both the UDA and the IRA. He had nowhere to go . . .

So, on this particular day, Baker tried to escape. He managed to get hold of a large pair of scissors, grabbed a screw round the neck, held the blades to his throat, and demanded that a helicopter be sent to pick him up. From the psycho block we could see the helicopter hovering. To us it was a little excitement on an otherwise dull day. Baker was known to be a professional ex-soldier and quite capable of carrying out his threats. He had been an expert marksman and a firearms expert so the authorities were taking no chances; they had to take him seriously.

Negotiations went on for the best part of the day. In the meantime the authorities bargained with some cons to jump Baker in the block. This plan eventually worked and Baker was disarmed. His escape attempt was over.

We found out afterwards that the army had been called in and special marksmen, both in the helicopter and the surrounding buildings, were told to shoot Baker at the first opportunity. I believe this to be true but have no way of knowing for sure.

Nearly all the cons on the psycho block were heavily

medicated. The medical room was in the area of an old cell and there was a hatch in the cell door for dispensing purposes. The medicines Largactil, Stelazine, Modecate and many others were given out in tots three times a day. Some cons would buy another's medication so they could get a buzz or crash out depending on what they were looking for. They would often barter tobacco in exchange for medicine. I saw, on many occasions, cons pretend to swallow medicine from the tot, walk away, and then spit it into another tot kept in their pocket. They would then exchange it for tobacco with another con. The con who bought the medicine observed the ritual of the spitting-out but did not bat an eyelid.

I can remember one particular day which shows how strong the influence of medicine was on the cons. Ron and I were sitting in a cell close by the medicine hatch when the cell door opened and in rushed a con by the name of Jacabussi. He said, 'Hello, Ron. Have you got any tobacco? I can't stop, I'm in a hurry.' He was on the chokey block on punishment and an escort had brought him upstairs to collect his medicine. He had broken away, dashed in to Ron to ask for tobacco and then forced his way into the medical room brandishing a home-made knife. He grabbed the young screw by the hair and demanded medicine. We heard all the commotion and went to see what was going on. The screws, once more, locked us all away and about an hour later unlocked us again. Jacabussi had been overpowered in a struggle and things returned to normal.

One day a fat Scotsman, a twenty-eight-year-old by the name of Pete Murray, came on to the wing. He was of broad build with an old scar down his face. I didn't like him and I liked him even less when he tried to force his way into the company of Ron and me. I used to give him a half-ounce of tobacco every week to scrub my cell out. He was always on about violence. In a way I was taking the piss out of him. One day Ron told me he was suspicious of Murray. Ron was sure he had caught him speaking about one of our letters to a screw in the censor's office. Lots of funny things went on when Murray was around.

One day I had an interview with Dr Cooper, the resident psychiatrist in the hospital. I put it to him that Murray was an informer and was working in collusion with a screw by the name of Bishop. I had found all this out when Ron and I questioned Murray in his cell. Murray told us that the local police, along with Bishop, had offered him parole if he would seek to obtain information about us. Murray broke down and cried, giving us a card with the name of the copper in question on it. Dr Cooper didn't deny that any of this was true.

The fat slag Murray did get parole. He went out and, with three other young men who he had influenced, sexually abused and strangled two young teenagers. He made them commit indecent acts with him before they died. For these two murders he received a life sentence with a long recommendation.

Later, while I was working in the machine-shop, the screw Bishop came in. I was so enraged that he had helped a slag like Murray get parole that I told him exactly what I thought of him. I challenged him to a fight there and then. I wanted him to remember for ever more that Murray had got parole for insignificant information and, but for that, those two teenagers might not have been subjected to such a terrible death. Bishop told me he wasn't in a position to fight – due to his job.

Another con serving a life sentence at Parkhurst was Johnny Patten, who came from Kent. The last time I saw Johnny was in the hospital area. About a week later he stabbed to death a con by the name of Magee. The story goes that Patten and Magee were friends who had met on the wing. The night before Magee's death they had an argument. The following morning Magee was lining up at the hot-plate for his breakfast

when Patten stealthily crept up behind him and plunged a six–
inch knife into his back. Magee fell to the floor mortally
wounded. Patten just walked away and went to his cell. They
told me that a hushed silence followed the assault but the cons
lining up for their breakfast continued to collect their cereals and
baked beans as though the stabbing had never even happened.

The screws went in number to Patten's cell, talked him into
giving up the blade and took him to the block. He was given
another life sentence. The last time I heard of him he was in the
cage at Wakefield.

A number of people with serious personality problems and
defects ended up at Parkhurst. Among these was a con called
Colin Robinson. He was doing life for murder. He had smashed
an old woman over the head with a brick. During his sentence
Robinson had been certified insane and sent to Broadmoor; he
then came back to continue his sentence in the hospital at
Parkhurst.

I was in the hospital at this time for an operation. A con
was sitting in the garden on a chair when Robinson and another
inmate walked across to him. They pulled out quarter bricks
from their pockets and repeatedly crashed them down on the
innocent party's head until the lawn was saturated in blood.
The alarm bell rang and the screws overpowered them.

Robinson was sent to Broadmoor again for an indefinite
period of time. Before leaving he was on remand on F2 (observation) wing in the hospital. I was there at the same time and
opposite me was Robinson's luckless victim, who was recover-
ing from a brain operation. The doors of the cells had slits in
them which could be lowered down. One day Robinson's victim
shouted across to me a greeting, hello or some such words, and
did the same across to his attacker. He did not know either of
us. He was virtually a mental cabbage. I recall Robinson saying
he was sorry for the fellow and wished it had never happened.

Round about this time Ron and I were given seven days down the chokey block for each bringing in a tin of tobacco from the visiting-room. We'd been doing it for a couple of years so we couldn't really grumble! We were really fed up with the psycho wing so we agreed the best way to get out of there was to try to get into the hospital block. I suggested to Ron that we refuse to leave unless they put us in the hospital. We told the screw in charge that we wanted to see Dr Cooper. The following day he came to see us and agreed to let us go to the hospital block. He said we would have to stay on the F2 (observation) landing and we agreed to this. For various reasons many of the cons feared being housed on F2 wing, yet Ron and I were there for thirteen months. I spent a total of five years in the hospital there. For these five years I was locked up virtually twenty-two hours a day and had no access to any food or drink other than the bare prison diet.

Parkhurst prison was heavy with paranoia. Having spent eighteen years there, and many more in other prisons, I think even I could do with some respite. To put it bluntly . . . I could do with a holiday! The last holiday I had was in 1966 for two weeks in Tangier, Morocco.

The Isle of Wight has three prisons on it, Parkhurst, Albany and Camp Hill. All three are safeguarded by a vast expanse of sea. I did meet one fellow in Parkhurst who later escaped and swam across to the mainland. He was from Bethnal Green. His name evades me but he was a likeable character.

The violence continued in Parkhurst. Jim McCabe on the main wing was refused permission by the Assistant Governor to make a phone-call to one of his relations. McCabe pulled out a knife, grabbed the AG by the throat, and took him hostage while he used the phone. It turned out to be quite an expensive call. The police were called in and canvas sheeting was put up around the office while negotiations took place.

Forty-eight hours later McCabe released his hostage. He was sent to Broadmoor but later returned to Parkhurst.

I remember a con by the name of Powell. He had started off with a six-year sentence in Chelmsford. He was attacked by another inmate and in turn hit this fellow over the head with an iron bar and killed him. For this he received a life sentence. I knew he wouldn't last long; he couldn't see the end of it. His world was getting smaller and smaller. He refused to come out of his cell and sometimes I'd speak to him up at the window to try to comfort him. Eventually he hanged himself.

Ron did not settle as well as I did in the hospital. He stayed on F2 longer than I did, remaining there until he went to Broadmoor. He made one great change while he was there. One day Ron asked Dr Cooper, 'Can I have a record player?' We always got on well with Dr Cooper but on this occasion he said, 'No you can't. They would be too noisy.' Ron responded logically, 'What's the difference between a radio and a record player in volume?' Dr Cooper smiled . . . and finally conceded. After that they were allowed.

One day the alarm bell rang on three different occasions when Ron had fights with other cons in the hospital. To put it mildly this was a bit of a strain on my nerves. I used to watch Ron like a hawk wherever he moved. Another day I was upstairs, above Ron, when he slung a chamber-pot and its contents over a six-foot screw called Bill.

The reason for this was that the screw kept walking up and down outside the cells whistling and it was getting on the patients' nerves. The screw should have known better; he was listed as one of the medical staff and used to go on TV talking about treatment. Anyway, the screws leapt on Ron and pinned him to the floor. While this was happening Dr Cooper came along; he prevented the screws from getting out of control.

Once, when Ron and I were walking round the garden part

of the hospital, a big black fellow had a fight with Ron Easterbrook. Ron pulled the black fellow off and stopped the fight. Easterbrook was in the hospital for seven years and as a protest never spoke to one person during that time. He used to write everything down, which took great willpower. Ron Easterbrook was later given a life sentence for shooting at the police.

Again, while strolling round the garden, I noticed one of the patients walking in circles and swinging his arms. He walked up to a screw and smacked him on the chin, knocking him to the floor. The alarm bell went off and they came and took him away. When asked later why he had done it, he replied, 'I don't like midgets!'

Another time I was sitting in the TV room and a patient walked over, picked up the set, and smashed it on the ground. I also saw a fellow throw himself in the pond. On yet another day a tall con called Noel Palmer climbed a tree and stayed up there among the branches for an hour before they coaxed him down.

Once, when I was walking with Mick Petersen, a friend of mine, I noticed him go all white in the face. He just walked away from me, went to the toilet windows and butted them in. He sat down. Then he was taken away. In later years I was to meet Mick again; he had changed his name by deed poll to Charles Bronson.

I used to watch another con called Ronnie Abrams walking up and down the garden. He would keep to about a twenty-yard area, never walking out of it, and march up and down furiously. If anyone went near his patch he would go berserk. They used to call him the screaming skull because he wore his head shaven and weighed about seven stone. He was serving a life sentence for killing his mother. At one time in the main wing I was there when he got kicked down three flights of stairs by another con and ended up with concussion. I met him again in later years at Long Lartin.

Also in the hospital was George Davies. (Not to be confused with the George Davies who had the freedom campaign going for him.) An elderly man, he was built like a barrel, and had served forty-three years in prison. He had been convicted of some field offence during the war and was still in prison.

While he was at Parkhurst Ron had electric shock treatment administered by the doctor and medical staff. Ron told me it gave him spasms around the spine which would practically jerk him out of the chair. I am of the opinion that shock treatment should not be allowed, as no one really seems to understand the side-effects or consequences of it.

It was a sad day when Ron had to leave me, in 1980, to go to Broadmoor. We shook hands before we parted company. It would be the first time in our lives we had been split up for any length of time. I knew Ron would be better off at Broadmoor because he couldn't settle into prison life.

For an hour at night I would go into the TV room, a big dull green room, very austere apart from some chairs, a table and the lone television. I would sit on my own over to the left by the table while the others sat to the right. I wrote my letters in this hour, in between talking to the patients who came to my table. Some of them were nutters, in a raw state before being assessed for where they would go – their medication still hadn't been sorted out.

There used to be a tea urn which was our only luxury. Underneath it a bucket had been placed to catch all the drips. I recall seeing one of the patients scoop up a cup and drink it. Some of the things that took place in the hospital reminded me of scenes from the film *Midnight Express*.

There used to be a Chinese fellow who came up to my table every night. He would say in broken English, 'You know Soho, me fitted up, CID, bad man, me fitted up . . .' I would just nod my head. He used to go through the same dialogue for about half an hour.

I tried to be tolerant towards the patients there; I knew they were sick.

At Christmas time I went to the toilet window and looked out. I could just make out the sea in the distance. I spent two Christmases up at the window. It's not an ideal way to spend Christmas, but that's how it was.

Colin Robinson returned from Broadmoor to Parkhurst, so I was in his company for a short period of time. Robinson could be very forceful in his manner and attitude. Once, when I walking round the garden area, he joined me and said aggressively, 'Why are you blanking me?' I was fed up with his bad moods, so I threw a left hook at him. He fell on the lawn and I jumped on top of him; the screws came and pulled us apart.

On the funnier side, during Robinson's stay in hospital he deliberately swallowed bedsprings, a tobacco tin and razor blades. This resulted in him having three operations on his stomach and also got him in the magazine *Titbits*. Robinson said that the doctor had told him he couldn't operate again if he swallowed any more bedsprings. I said to him, jokingly, 'You should do some sit-ups – they're good for your stomach muscles!' Even with his bad record the Home Office still released Robinson before me from 'high risk' prisons, and put him in a Category B.

Peter Sutcliffe, the Yorkshire Ripper, used to be on the same landing as me. I spoke to him occasionally. He had very strange eyes; looking into them gave me the impression that he was tortured from within by very complex thoughts. He was a good painter, although he used to depict some very strange scenes.

Each Sunday I would visit the church, not especially to pray but to see my friends from the main prison area. It was here I met Steve Tully, who was to become a close friend of mine. I later joined him over on the main wing. One of my observations about the churches in prisons is that they were often used by the 'born-again' cons to try to get parole. Many of the padres in charge are so gullible that they are duped by these people. The worst offenders were often the sex cases.

One of the last times I was at church in Parkhurst I spoke to Nicky Gerard. I knew Nick's father, Alf, and Nicky was just going home. He had been arrested and then released for the killing of Italian Tony, the fellow who had stabbed to death Ronnie Knight's brother. I shook hands and wished Nicky luck, although I did not know him that well. Some months later I picked up a Sunday newspaper and read that two people had blown away Nicky Gerard with a shotgun.

The visiting-room in Parkhurst was fairly comfortable. During one visit I was sitting close to Tony Balderesso. He was serving twelve years and was due for release. He too was to have a short life. After release I heard that Tony had barricaded himself in when police raided his house in Surrey. He was wanted for a number of bank raids. He blew his own brains out. Rather than let the police take the money, he burnt it all before killing himself. They found the embers in the fire.

During this period I was only allowed to see Ron once a year. I petitioned to try to get more visits – but it was a waste of time. Some years later, when I was at Gartree, I was allowed to visit three times a year.

John Cheeseman was another I met in the hospital block. He was a lifer, in for murder, and had also killed again in Broadmoor. He was very dangerous and yet professed to be a born-again Christian. That did not stop him from taking two young cons hostage, on separate occasions, at Wormwood Scrubs and trying to rape them. I didn't know Cheeseman's history when I first met him and at the time I was very ill with paranoia. I said to him, 'If you watch my back I'll not forget it. I'm expecting some trouble.' He agreed. It turned out to be unnecessary as I had no trouble with anyone – but I didn't forget the favour. A year or so later in the main wing Charlie McGee tried to scald him with boiling fat from a frying-pan. I prevented this. Rightly or wrongly I was keeping my word. I felt morally obligated to return the favour he had granted me.

I would often see Cheeseman go into the toilet area and pick up beetles and spiders and place them in a matchbox. He said he collected them to examine their behaviour patterns. I found this quite amusing, as it wasn't their behaviour patterns that were in question . . .

From the hospital I went to the main gym three times a week, which kept me fit. One day the instructor said to me, 'Why do you use such a small space to train in?' I was used to using a small, confined space in the hospital and had forgotten what it was like to have a wider open area. Being banged up in the hospital cells for twenty-two hours a day was making my own world a very small place.

After four years I asked Dr Cooper if I could get a shift out of the prison. He told me he was thinking of sending me to Long Lartin. Later that day, when I was taking a walk round the exercise yard with a friend of mine called Martin Long, I told him what Dr Cooper had said. Martin responded that I would 'find it very strange in a "normal" prison after being locked up here for all these years'. I was to remember those words. I was not to be told when I was leaving as I was still Category A, a high security risk. However, one evening in January 1981 I just got the feeling I'd be going the next day. When my cell door opened at 5 a.m. and the security screws came in to tell me I'd be leaving, I was ready and packed. They couldn't believe it – they thought someone must have tipped me off.

CHAPTER FIVE

LONG LARTIN

1981–1982

Long Lartin prison lies in a valley at Evesham in Worcester-shire. I arrived there just before lunch. While I was sitting in a cubicle in reception I was given a meal of ham, egg and chips, which, after Parkhurst food, I considered to be quite good. By the time I'd unpacked my gear and settled down it was time for tea and, to my surprise, I walked straight into a situation. Lots of cons were refusing the food, saying it was rubbish. Some were taking food and others not. On that particular day I decided to take mine.

One of the cons told me that inter-wing visits were allowed and sure enough at 6 p.m. my name was called on the intercom. I went down to the ground floor were I was greeted by an old friend of mine from Hoxton called Jimmy Briggs. He was serving fifteen years for armed robbery. With him was Bunny Harris, another old friend from Bow, doing five years for robbery. Jimmy and Bunny used to use the Double R Club. Jimmy had been convicted with George Davies, who became notorious through his 'George Davies is innocent' campaign. They told me that word had gone around that I'd reached Long Lartin and that Johnny Woodruff, among others, would be over to see me later. Johnny was doing eighteen years and during my trial the police tried to persuade him to give evidence against us. He was sound and refused to do it. Jimmy and Bunny had a parcel of gear for me, sheets, pillowcases, etc. They also gave me about £20 in 50p pieces. We were allowed to spend our own money there, but only coins up to the value of 50p were allowed. It felt strange to have money in my pocket again. I was pleased with the welcome they gave me.

Jim and Bunny brought me up to date on who was in the place. I sat at a table with them for half an hour with a cup of tea and then left to go upstairs to my own wing. A couple of cons came to say hello to me: Neil Adamson, who was doing a thirty-year recommended for shooting a copper, and Paddy Hill, the Irishman convicted with others for the Birmingham bombings.

The next day I was called to the office to see the Chief and Principal Officers of the wing. The conversation went something like this:

'Hope you settle down here. As you probably know, Mc-Vicar was here and he helped to keep the peace. So we gave him a job on the gardens. He eventually got parole . . .'

The PO added, 'If you help to keep the place orderly and quiet we'll consider giving you a job on the gardens.'

To this I replied, 'I've got enough problems looking after myself without helping to "keep the peace". I may as well tell you now I intend to sort out my own problems and no one else's. I'm a loner and I'll remain that way . . . I'm not looking for favours of any kind.' I then left the office. A couple of days later I was given the job of wing cleaner, cleaning sinks and toilets!

I was soon buying money off one of the prison dealers. This enabled me to buy more out of the canteen. It cost a fiver for every three pounds of change but I was able to live reasonably well in comparison to the bare, spartan times at Parkhurst.

Not long after I arrived a young con from Birmingham came on to the wing. He was called Ray Wilson. He was twenty-two years of age and doing nine years for strangling his wife. I felt sorry for him. He wasn't a nonce case, just a young kid who'd been unfortunate enough to lose his temper. I befriended him and made him welcome and after a time he made friends with someone of his own age-group, a fellow from Wales.

I began to notice that the kid was getting withdrawn. I'd had a lot of experience with prisoners and their moods at Parkhurst. I told a screw what was happening in the hope that he could help him. I said Ray should talk to a doctor. Ray had been in a cell upstairs but moved down to one opposite mine. One night he came to my cell and asked if I had any tobacco I could give him; I told him I hadn't and he looked very disappointed and upset. I could tell he was looking for some kind of comfort and made a mental note to talk to him the next morning. When I banged up for the night I couldn't stop thinking about him; he seemed so sad.

The following morning we were late unlocking by a couple of hours. I knew something was wrong on the wing. When we were finally unlocked Neil Adamson, who was in a nearby cell, came to tell me that Ray had killed himself. I can still see his eyes . . . they weren't the eyes of a villain, just a sad young kid. This was one of my worst times at Long Lartin.

When walking the compound each morning I noticed there was sometimes a gathering of Londoners in the middle of the field, deep in discussion. The following day – on some pretext or another – a strike would be called. People were not asked if they would like to join the strike, rather they were told it was simply in progress. I also noticed that those who incited the strikes were the ones with all the mouth, full of what good people they were, and how 'staunch' they were. Yet it was these same people who never participated fully in the strikes, and also seemed to have a 'calming' effect on the strikers. It was obvious to me, watching from a distance, that the instigators were then deflating the strikes for the authorities. I made a mental note of these 'staunch' cons, and how they eventually got parole through using others. They didn't care at all how the lifers suffered as a consequence. Some of these people professed to be friends of mine but I could see right through them and their selfish motives.

One day when a strike was called by the unknowns, I said to Neil Adamson, 'Surely you don't stand for all this shit; you're doing a recommended thirty years yet you have no say in what goes on!' Neil replied, 'It's always been that way here.' I told him, 'I want to at least be asked, so I won't take part in this strike today.' And I didn't.

One of the things that got on my nerves at Long Lartin was the single daily topic of conversation – parole. I could hardly believe how grown men, clutching at straws, would grovel for parole. Most of them were a really sickening lot. I found the topic pretty boring so I started to take walks on my own to avoid all the incessant whining. I had a bad confrontation with the authorities over a girlfriend of mine. They wouldn't let me see her as I was still a Category A prisoner. I threatened them with how I would bring to light how corrupt the system was, the way they catered to parole grovellers. This didn't do me any good in their eyes. But eventually I was allowed to see Beverley.

I went through a bad patch. One day I was walking the long distance from the wing to the visiting-room and my legs began to feel unsteady. When I stood up after the visit, it was like standing on feathers rather than legs; they didn't seem able to support me. With difficulty I started walking back to the wing. Half-way along the passage I had to stop. My legs just wouldn't carry me. A friend of mine, Jimmy Turrant, stopped and asked if I was all right. I asked him to stay and talk with me for a while as I couldn't walk. Jimmy was very helpful and assisted me back to the wing.

It was one of my friends and visitors, a magistrate by the name of Dora Hamilton, who suggested what was wrong. She told me I had all the symptoms of agoraphobia, a fear of open spaces. This had probably come about for two reasons: one was stress, the other that I had been locked up in isolation at Parkhurst for too many years. It would have amounted to about five years solitary confinement. Prior to going to Long Lartin those in authority should have eased me into circulation more slowly.

Round about this time, in the early hours of the mornings, I thought I could hear a clicking sound in my cell. I mentioned this to a couple of cons, saying I thought my cell had been bugged. One of them suggested I could be paranoid, but I thought otherwise.

A friend of mine from 1958, Patsy Manning, came to the prison while this was occurring. Patsy was five years my junior. He told me a fellow had ripped him off for some money, they'd got in a fight and Patsy had hit him over the head with a hammer. I arranged for Patsy to come on to my wing. He arrived after three weeks and we had some good laughs together. Micky Ishmael from Bow Road used to send us over lokshen soup twice a week so, for a while, we were enjoying ourselves. Patsy and I used to like relating the story of how we first met. I had just walked out of a tobacconists in Burdett Road, off Mile End, when Patsy approached me and said, ''Ere mate, d'ya know where there's a barber round 'ere so I can get an 'aircut?' I told him, 'Three hundred yards down on the left, Chris the Greek. Tell him I sent you . . . the name's Reg Kray.' I also told Patsy that when he was finished he could come and have a cup of tea in the snooker hall I owned in Eric Street. Patsy said OK and went on his way. He joined me later for a cup of tea and a chat and we've been friends ever since. Patsy has good principles and is one of the 'old school'.

Inevitably, though, we began to get on each other's nerves. Prison life was getting on top of us and the fact I was getting paranoid didn't help. The story I am about to tell is terrible. For the sake of the young whom I'd like to deter from going to prison, I promised myself I'd write *all* the truth in this book, the good experiences and the bad. I know that Patsy, who sees life as just a stage 'and all the men and women merely players', will prefer me to tell the story as it actually happened. I had been rowing with Patsy. I was withdrawn and began to believe that people were out to poison me. I still thought my cell was being bugged. On two particular days I was convinced that Patsy and a number of others were plotting to kill me. Just before 6 p.m., open-up time, on the second day I calmly had a shave, put on my best clothes, and decided I would go out in style . . . taking one of the plotters with me. Sad to say I decided Patsy was the main conspirator.

I had a smoked glass cup which I smashed on the concrete. As soon as the door opened I bounded up the stairs to the third floor and met Patsy on his way down. I had the broken cup in my hand and as Patsy got close I plunged it into his face. The blood spurted and the screws came running. The screws circled round and a couple, along with some cons, tried to get near me to take the cup away. I refused to talk to the cons at first, thinking that they too were plotters. I finally gave the cup to a screw. I was escorted to the block and placed in a cell. Later they brought my radio down and charged me with being in a fight.

I was in a terrible state. I had reached the climax of despair. I had my glasses with me. I took them out of the case, trod on the lenses, picked up a piece of glass and sawed at my wrists. Blood from the wounds cascaded over the radio. The next thing I knew alarm bells were going off. They took me to the hospital where my wrists were stitched. They applied some ice-cold stuff that seemed to freeze them but was very painful at the same time.

I was at the hospital for a couple of days then taken back to the block. I went up before the board, the charge was read out and I received a 50p fine for fighting. I couldn't understand why it was so low. They sent me back on the wing. It seemed a strange thing to do. Under normal circumstances we should have been separated and segregated. I decided they wanted me back on the wing so we'd have another row. I made up my mind that I was going to get the confrontation over and done with as fast as possible. I knew they wanted me to get hurt.

I walked back to the wing under escort, placed my gear in my cell and then went straight to Patsy's cell upstairs. Patsy was sitting on his bed and I could see a long pair of scissors so I said, 'Can we talk downstairs?' He followed me down to my cell and when we got there he passed me a perspex cup and said, 'You can use this if you want.' I took it the wrong way, grabbed the cup, and again hit him over the head. The screws who were waiting nearby heard the commotion and rushed into the cell. They twisted my arm up my back and frog-marched me back to the block. I was put on another charge for fighting and this time fined about £1. I thought this was ridiculous but they also kept me down the block this time.

I liked it down the block. It was nice and quiet, so I decided to do everything I could to ensure that I stayed there. I got my mattress into a heap, set light to it and waited. The alarm bell went off and I was pulled out of the smoky cell. This kind of situation is very dangerous as one could well suffocate. I was charged with setting light to the cell.

It got worse. Eventually, I took a disposable razor, broke it open, and climbed into bed in the hope I would not be seen. I hid beneath the covers, thick coarse blankets, while I sawed at the flesh below the bicep of my arm. There were thick steel bars on the windows and I felt like a caged animal. I felt like an animal caught in a vicious snare.

As I cut deeper the pain became more terrible. I could feel the tissue and the muscle. I was sweating profusely. I was intent on the job – that my life should end there and then. There was a part of me that seemed to be enjoying the 'hide-and-seek' secrecy of it all, as though I was getting away with something I shouldn't. The wound was getting very deep. I could smell the blood, the strange, sickening, almost metallic scent mixing with the smell of my own sweat and of the coarse blanket that covered me. Eventually I passed out.

I awoke to a sea of faces and to find my arm bandaged up. I was slung into the 'strongbox' in the hospital, on to a canvas sheet, where I lay totally naked. The bandage on my arm was tied so tight that my arm went numb. I was told later that it had been tied dangerously tight, and that gangrene could have set in. I had the presence of mind to rip off the bandage completely and felt a sense of relief as the blood rushed back into my arm.

I was in the strongbox three days when I got a visit from my brother Charlie and Laurie O'Leary, a friend. I told them everything that had happened but they really weren't in a position to help. When you are within the walls no one can be of much help.

I was in a small cell in the hospital a couple of days later when I had a surprise visitor. It was none other than Patsy Manning. It was quite an emotional meeting. Patsy said, 'If it had been anyone else attacked me the way you did, I'd kill them – but we're old friends.' I believed him. I knew he was telling the truth. The friendship between Patsy and me is like a bond of steel. We have seen good and bad times. I hope the bad are over . . . and that more of the good are yet to come.

I have seen more than my fair share of blood and gore. I have tried to write it all down factually, as it happened. I didn't enjoy the violence and often, during the writing of this book, I've been tempted to play it down. But my philosophy is that no truth is ever a lie . . . and so I have told the truth. I suppose one could say that in my time I have sunk to the depths but thankfully I have risen again.

During this particular time at Long Lartin I alternated between the chokey block and the hospital wing, depending on where they wanted me to be. One of the most sickening memories I have is of when I was in the strongbox after cutting my wrists. A screw had brought me a bowl of soup with a plastic spoon stuck in it. The bowl was blue plastic. This bowl was in one corner of the cell, on the right-hand side, and on the left was a chamber-pot full of excreta. As I glanced from one to the other I felt physically sick. Even today the thought of that sight, the bowl and the chamber-pot, with me sitting on the floor in the middle, nauseates me.

When I wanted to get back to the chokey block, I started a second fire in my hospital cell. I gathered all my stuff on the bed, just as I had done before, and put a match to it. The lot went up in flames, including some of my treasured address books. The alarm bell went, the screws came running, and I was back in the strongbox.

On another occasion, the screws released me from my cell

to try me out watching television. I walked over to the TV, picked it up with both hands and hurled it to the floor, smashing it to pieces. I don't know why I did it. I was still paranoid and ill. Again, I was rushed off to the strongbox.

After coming out and going on the wing I was taken back to the chokey block. One day, just before lunch, the Principal Officer (PO) came to my cell, unlocked the door and sat himself at the foot of my bed. I was sitting in my chair at the time. (It was made of compressed cardboard, as was the table, so that neither could be used as weapons.) The PO looked at me intently. He said, 'Look, Kray, we've spent enough time on you and your problems. We don't intend to spend any more. You have a choice: either go back on the wing and start another fire in your cell or you can finish it down here by having a row at the hot-plate with the staff. It's for you to decide which way you want it. The choice is yours.' He didn't mince his words and I knew exactly what he meant. I said to the PO without hesitation, 'I'll finish it down here.'

The PO left. I could hear the cell doors of the cons being locked. My door had been left open to enable me to walk to the hot-plate area, where lunch was normally served. There were about twelve screws waiting in a circle. I walked with a plastic cup in my hand. I crossed to the tea urn and filled the cup. I looked up at a fat pig of a PO who was in charge of the block. As our eyes met I threw the tea in his face. The next thing I knew there was a rush of arms and legs; the fat pig grabbed me by the throat with thumb and forefingers and I was involved in a struggle. I tried not to mark any of their faces. It would only be evidence that I had been unnecessarily violent. I was overpowered and carried to the strongbox where I was thrown on the floor. The screws sat on my shoulders, hands and feet. Each time I tried to take in gulps of air one of them twisted my toes until I shouted out in pain. I don't know how long this went on for. Eventually they went. I was left alone with my thoughts.

Being in the strongbox didn't bother me. I felt I had made the right choice. If there was to have been an ending, I preferred the choice I had made. I didn't want to die by fire. At this time I'm sure that God walked close by me in order to let me live.

Some time afterwards I was shifted back on to the hospital block and another series of violent episodes erupted. The first of these was when I had an argument with a PO I didn't like. I grabbed him by the lapels and swung him round like a cat in the small area we were in. Two other screws nearby grabbed my arms and between the three of them they got me back in my cell. After this episode they wouldn't unlock me unless there were eight to ten screws standing outside my door. This didn't deter me from slinging punches at them on occasion.

I remember once a tall ginger-haired screw unlocked me. As soon as he did I hit him in the stomach with a left hook and as he fell to the floor I leapt on top of him. He tried to knee me from his prone position, which seemed rather peculiar. Then the screws were on me again. They forced my feet under the bottom rail of the bed and sat on top of me for a while.

A couple of other times, while slopping out, I chucked the urine contents of my chamber-pot over the screws. On some of these occasions I was the only person in the hospital block; I was lucky they didn't kill me.

The doctor in charge put me down to see the head man of Rampton Mental Institution. I was in the strongbox, for slinging punches at the screws, on the day the doctor arrived. His name was Dr Pickering. I was anxious about the meeting. I was worried that he might decide I should be detained indefinitely at Rampton. I didn't fancy going there at all. To make matters worse I met the doctor only ten minutes after one of the chamber-pot incidents. I was terribly scruffy and dirty, wearing an old blue prison singlet. I hadn't bathed or shaved properly for some time. I was paranoid to such an extent that I believed the screws might try to drown me, or that I might be deliberately electrocuted by the light-bulb that hung above the bath.

To my great relief I found Dr Pickering to be a charming and amicable man who was also sympathetic to my plight. He asked me a few questions. I told him that I had the urge to write. I felt that writing was my new-born vocation and a blessing from above. I was to use my eyes as a camera, and my memory, and put it all down on paper. It was, as I explained to Dr Pickering, most peculiar because although I had no formal education, words would come to me out of the blue and even before I checked them in the dictionary I knew exactly what they meant.

At the end of the interview Dr Pickering told me to relax as he had no intention of certifying me. He told me I was quite sane. He advised me to continue my writing and suggested that, if things went well, and the current political climate changed, then I might be released in the future. I shook hands with him. He had just given my opinion of mankind an enormous boost. He came across as very humane and at the time of our meeting, when I was in the depths of despair, he was the first ray of sunshine after the dark wintry days of my adversity.

Another person who helped me greatly at this time was Mrs Dora Hamilton, my friend and a magistrate. Mrs Hamilton visited me regularly along with my mother during these turbulent times. On more than one occasion she spoke to the doctor in charge on my behalf. All along she had said that I would not be certified. She gave me the encouragement I needed.

My mother was also in great despair but never showed it. She was always cheerful in my company. In these latter years I wish that she and my father were still with me, because these are better years and my mother had such hard times.

I had spent a lot of my time at Long Lartin in solitary. I went through a very bad time. I didn't sleep well and woke up drenched in sweat. While I was there I remembered a film I'd seen as a kid. I don't recall the name but the actor was Robert Young. In the film he was being tortured, and to beat the pain and to strengthen his resolve he would re-live his past, running through all his memories from when he was a child. I would lie flat out on the mattress, face down, and try to do the same. The person in my memory who seemed to help the most was Billy Hill, my late friend. I would recapture all the times Ron and I had sat drinking and talking with him in his flat in Bayswater, and the happy times we had in Tangier. Reliving the past in this way seemed to help – it helped to shut out the reality of my situation.

I had many disturbing experiences at Long Lartin. It would be impossible to relate all of them. The reader will have to imagine the full extent of my ordeal. One final example happened at night. As a screw was going past he pulled down the flap on my door and said, 'Don't forget the matches and your pyjama cord, Kray. I'll see you in the morning.'

I was in Long Lartin in this state for about six months before it was decided that I should be sent back to Parkhurst. My mother told me on a visit that I was going home – Parkhurst felt like home to me then. My mother also looked upon the place with friendly eyes and she was happy, even though it meant longer journeys for her.

Going back to Parkhurst was considered a backward step for me, one that would lessen my chances of early freedom in the future. Before I left, the screws would taunt me by saying, 'Parkhurst is considered the end of the road.' I knew this to be true but I was still looking forward to a fresh start in those familiar surroundings.

I had partly lost my identity at Long Lartin. This is the

worst thing that can happen during a prison sentence, but the risk is always there – on a long sentence it is almost unavoidable. It has to do with anxiety, followed by a loss of confidence. Perhaps the main factor is simply being in a strange and abnormal environment. Being shifted from prison to prison also causes disorientation.

CHAPTER SIX

PARKHURST III
1982–1986

The day eventually arrived when I was taken back to Parkhurst. In March 1982 I made the now familiar journey across the sea by ferry to the Isle of Wight. On my arrival I was placed in the hospital block on the F2 landing. This was the observation landing, where one was watched for twenty-four hours a day. Dr Cooper, the psychiatrist, was in charge of it. Ron had once spent twenty months here; this was considered a very long time. He had hit a screw on the chin during his time in residence and was given fifty-six days solitary confinement.

On my second day I was escorted to Dr Cooper's office. During our discussion he told me that during my time at Long Lartin I had suffered a breakdown and that I also suffered from paranoia. He prescribed Stelazine medication, twice daily, to help prevent the paranoia. I told him I was glad to be back at Parkhurst.

My mother came to visit shortly after. The Governor of the prison, Mr Sandies, came to see me in my mother's presence. He said, 'Pleased to see you home.'

I quickly got back into the old and familiar habits of the hospital. One of these was to walk very quickly in a circle around the garden. I would walk so fast that many of the other patients couldn't keep pace with me. They would drop out and leave me in peace with my thoughts.

I had only been there for a while when I had a mental relapse. One night I cut my wrists again. I was overwhelmed by paranoid thoughts; I believed the authorities were trying to harm my family and myself. I lay quietly under the blankets, using a piece of glass to saw at the skin, just as I had done on the previous occasion. I must have fainted or fallen asleep and I awoke at around 7.30 a.m. to the clang of the lock springing open. I climbed out of bed covered in blood and sweat. I walked out of my cell to go to the toilet. I saw other inmates look aghast at the sight of me; one of them must have called the screws because they came running to escort me to the doctor's office. A doctor called Stewart stitched me up. While he was doing it I noticed a cup of tea on the table. I don't know why I did it; I picked the cup of tea up and threw it over him. A big screw who was standing behind got me in a headlock. The alarm bell was rung and other screws came running into the office. They escorted me to the strongbox and left me there. This strongbox had a glass ceiling so the screws could observe you.

I was only there for a few hours before I was escorted back to my cell. I can honestly say that during my stay at Parkhurst hospital I was always treated fairly, under the supervision of Dr Cooper, and no liberties were ever taken. In my opinion Dr Cooper and his aide, the Chief, Reginald Bunker, OBE, did a good job in the hospital under very difficult circumstances and with sparse amenities. Ron and I got on well with them both.

After this initial bad patch I began to respond to treatment and to regain my confidence. The idea occurred to me that I should write a book on Cockney slang. I hesitated at first but, being an advocate of positive thinking, decided to put aside the word 'maybe' and replace it with the words 'I will'. It was a challenge and gave me a target. In my mind I started to collect all the slang words my father had taught me and all the ones I had picked up in the East End. I also sent away for words from friends in other prisons. I finally began what was to be my first book. It was called simply *Slang*.

Shortly after I had cut my wrists for the third time a friend by the name of Fred Bone came to visit me. He left me a book. It was an autobiography by the Mafia boss and financial wizard Meyer Lansky. I glanced at the book in my cell and, still being a little paranoid, wondered why Fred had left it. When I did pick up the book I found I couldn't put it down – it seemed to give me inspiration. The theme was that one should *never* give up. I read the words, in my paranoid state, as a direct message to myself. After I had finished reading it, I proceeded to have a wash and a shave; I had several days of hair growth. In the corner of the cell was a pillowcase overflowing with unanswered letters. There were also letters strewn all over the floor. I began to tidy them up, got them in a semblance of order and then began to answer them. From the day I read that book I never looked back. If Meyer Lansky can pick up messages from his spiritual world, I'd like to say, 'Thanks for the message!'

One day I was leaning over the rail of the landing when the medical screws brought someone in. He appeared to be a very old man with completely white hair. He was in a wheelchair and it was obvious he had just had a stroke. He didn't look like he had long to live. I didn't recognize him. Someone else told me that this was the lifer John Duddy, who I'd rowed with at Leicester. I couldn't help but feel sorry for him. It was terrible to see how old he looked; his eyes seemed haunted by fear. I think he knew he would die in prison. This happened a few months later.

Nobby Clark was also in the hospital block at this time. He desperately wanted to get to court, under any pretext, so he could try to reopen his case. One day he made a wooden spear out of a broom handle, sharpening the point at the end. He chose a victim at random. Creeping stealthily into the bathroom, he came up behind the bather, lifted the spear and with all his might threw it into his back. Nobby's victim let out a tremendous scream which brought the screws running. Nobby stood there staring at the spear sticking out of the other con's back. When the screws arrived he told them he was responsible. His ploy was simply to get charged and taken back to court. He succeeded in his mission.

During the court case Nobby argued convincingly that if he had wanted to kill the bather he could have done so. As strange as it may seem, he was acquitted of attempted murder. The jury accepted that he only became a part-time Red Indian because he needed to speak of his previous murder charge in court. But he had no success in reopening the case. In fact he was certified insane and sent to Broadmoor.

About two years later he was returned to Parkhurst. I was still in the hospital. He looked much older and was ill with a weak heart. A few months later I heard the alarm bell go off and a group of screws came running by me on the landing. One of them was carrying an oxygen cylinder. Twenty minutes later we heard that Nobby had died of a heart attack.

I wrote and told his nephew in Liverpool. Nobby had given me his address some time before. All cons have a habit of collecting addresses, so they might meet again under better circumstances. Nine out of ten times this never comes about. It's a kind of wishful thinking, a pastime of all cons. With a few exceptions, most who get out immediately forget all those they have left behind.

During my walks in the garden I noticed with interest the

little goldfish pond which the fish would lazily circle. It was mentioned to me that the pond had been built by Frank Mitchell. It seemed strange that I should now be relaxing by this very pond. During my trials of 1969 I had been charged, along with Ron, Charlie and Freddie Foreman, of his murder. We were acquitted on this charge, but I was found guilty of helping Mitchell to escape from Dartmoor and also of harbouring him. Five years was added on to my sentence for the escape. As I went to leave the dock the judge, Melford Stevenson, said aloud to the warders, 'Bring that man back, I've not finished with him yet.' He gave me another nine months for harbouring Mitchell. It seemed a rather unnecessary journey back to the dock – I'd already got a thirty-year recommended minimum.

Frank Mitchell spent many years at Dartmoor, and some at Parkhurst. Most of the screws were afraid of him. He was physically very strong. In 1959, when I was in Wandsworth with Frank, he used to carry a knife, even in sight of the screws. He used to like getting the screws in his favourite grip, a playful bear hug, and would joyfully crack a couple of ribs!

Each day we patients would trudge off to work in the little shop that was designed for us. We would sit and paint toy soldiers. As we ambled along we looked pretty ragamuffin. The cons on the main wing named us 'Cooper's Troopers'.

Each morning the click of the bolt being pulled across the door would awaken me, like an alarm clock, to another day. It was also like an alert, a reason to get up in case someone with the needle wanted to jump you in bed. Some cons used an illegal 'wedge' to block the door for 'security' reasons. I have even known inmates who use their chamber-pots regularly as they're afraid to go out to the toilet in case they are caught off guard.

Early one morning at 3 a.m., I was surprised to be disturbed in my sleep by the cell door opening. Four screws came in and stood hovering over my bed. I asked what they wanted and they said, 'We want you to stand on the landing. This is a spin.' They were going to search me bodily and also search my cell. I pulled on my trousers, put on my shoes and stood outside the door. They rubbed me down and proceeded to search the cell. They didn't find anything. A day or two later I was told that someone had phoned in to say that I was in possession of a gun. I had some strong suspicions as to who this might have been. An inmate I knew had gone out on home leave. Ron had given him a valuable watch and I found out that he had sold it as soon as he hit the street. This particular con wouldn't have wanted me at Parkhurst when he returned. I was even more convinced when he didn't come back from his home leave. He was eventually found and arrested. He was taken to Winchester prison instead of coming back to Parkhurst, which was his allocated destination. I also found out that he had agreed to see the police regarding Ron and me.

Sometimes screws mark a con's card. They'll tell you who you probably will and won't get on with – and most times they're right. It was a screw who marked my card about this con. He told me about the police interview. I knew it was genuine by the details he gave me. Of course, it's also important to watch out for screws trying to mix it. I was aware on more than one occasion of screws placing someone they didn't like in the cell next to mine in the hope that we would clash. I saw through these moves and the con usually ended up on my side because I'd mark his card as to what they were up to.

One such case was when they put Neville Winn next door to me. Neville had a glass eye, a broken nose, and a reputation for fighting with screws and cons. But I'd had a lot of experience with cons over the years and knew how to handle him . . . we got on like a house on fire. He was doing nine years for a stabbing and came from Paddington. He later died of a stroke outside. When I was with him I told him one day I'd write a book on prison life. He said, 'Don't forget to tell them about me, Reg.' Neville had a ruddy complexion, fair hair and looked quite Germanic. He was a bit of a character and I enjoyed some good parties in his company. He liked to put a mattress up against the wall of his cell and have a work-out by punching it. He shaped up like a real pro-fighter. One time I saw him hit another con on the chin with an uppercut and knock him out. Another time, on the main wing, he was attacked by six cons wielding broken bottles and broom handles with glass on the end. Even though they cut his eye open, Neville still had plenty of fight left when the screws jumped in and halted the trouble. Neville loved a drink and life in general. His wife Joy used to come and visit him regularly. I could tell a lot more but suffice to say Neville was a throwback to the villains of yesteryear.

Vincent Hickey was in the hospital with me. He was on hunger strike in protest at his conviction and life sentence for the murder of the newspaper boy Carl Bridgewater. His conviction was later found to be unsafe and he was released.

Around this time a friend of mine by the name of 'Joe the Greek' was charged with stabbing a con on the main wing. He was placed on F2, where I met him again. He'd been put there for observation. Joe was doing a life sentence. Later, our paths would cross again.

There was a lifer on the block who'd been given his sentence for stabbing a copper to death during a robbery on a chemist shop. He'd stolen five pounds' worth of drugs. I didn't like this con; he had a very aggressive attitude. One day we were both filling our flasks with hot water and although I offered to let him fill his flask first he became very abusive towards me. I waited for him to return to his cell and then I followed him. I walked up and knocked him over with a right-hand punch. He crashed to the ground. No screw saw this but Dr Cooper got to hear about it. He called me up and said it must never happen again.

Lord Longford came to see me. Although deep down I believe him to be a good man, he is eccentric in his ways and liable to go to extremes in his opinions. I couldn't agree with him on the subject of Brady and Hindley. Once he asked if there was anything he could get for me. I answered, 'You could get me a book if you wish, but not a heavy one.' Lord Longford replied, 'Do you mean heavy in weight?' I found him to be quite humorous.

During this time I would see Ron once a year and the visits would take place in a closed room. There were always four screws, two from Parkhurst and two from Broadmoor, sitting almost on top us. We were inhibited from free speech of any kind, which was very aggravating. In later years I instructed my then solicitor Stephen Gold to endeavour to get us better visiting conditions. He was successful in doing this. After that our visits took place in the main visiting-room at Broadmoor. This was in privacy and away from the screws. The visiting-room was a large, circular-shaped area. It was somewhat ironic that in 1963 Ron and I had taken the well-known pianist Winifred Atwell to play there at a concert; Winifred had since passed away but Ron and I continued to sit there together, once every six months, in the same circular room.

Ron and I used to write to each other every day. Ron always retained his sense of humour. I remember one letter in particular when he related a story of a scene he had recently witnessed at Broadmoor. Two of the patients were arguing furiously, and one said to the other, 'How dare you speak to me like that! Don't you know I'm the Prime Minister?' The other patient turned to Ron and said angrily, 'Take no notice of what he's saying. He's mad! He's a fucking liar. He's not the Prime Minister – I should know, I'm the King of England!'

One of the things I really tried to do in prison was to abstain from sexual thoughts. I felt they were self-tormenting and so no good for me. I analysed the situation and reasoned that there can be just as much pleasure from abstention as indulgence. Sometimes, for example when you're trying to get very fit, there are some things you have to stop doing in order to achieve it. There can be as much pleasure in giving up drink to get in perfect shape for one person, as there is in getting extremely drunk for another. It's all a matter of attitude. It was a torment to indulge in sexual fantasies and so I ceased to think at all about the sexual act.

There were many bad cases hospitalized at Parkhurst. I remember one young fellow, in his early twenties, who was a convicted arsonist. Early one evening while I was sitting in my cell I heard the sound of running feet along the landing. This was followed by a loud banging on a door intermingled with the noise from the alarm bell. There was also a slight smell of burning. When I was unlocked later I learnt that the young arsonist had set fire to his cell. The screws had got him out safely and he'd been placed in a strip cell for observation. About three evenings later I was in the TV room upstairs and the kid was sitting there as if nothing had happened. We got into conversation and out of concern for him I said, 'I want you to give me your word that you won't set light to any more cells. You could endanger your life, and you still have everything to live for.' He seemed quite cheerful and readily gave me his word. That evening I went back to my cell feeling pleased that I might have helped the kid.

Early the following evening there was again the sound of running feet, the bang on a cell door and the ringing of the alarm bell. When I slopped out I learnt that, yet again, the kid had set fire to his cell. Some days later when I saw him, I tried to find out what made him tick. He told me that starting fires gave him a buzz and he also liked the attention it brought him. I felt truly sorry for the kid. Some weeks later he was certified and sent to Rampton for an indefinite period. He was one of life's many losers and the type of case one rarely reads about in books.

Places such as Broadmoor, Rampton and Park Lane house many people who have uncontrollable urges to commit acts abnormal to society. In the five years I was in Parkhurst hospital I talked to many such cases. I suppose, by many, they'd be considered the dregs of society . . . but perhaps we should try to understand that some are born with abnormalities and should also be pitied.

One lifer I met was the 'resident' barber . . . he was quite mad and had been convicted of cutting his new-born baby's throat. At first I was reluctant to have my hair cut by this specimen; it was against my principles to associate with anyone who had killed a child. But then I took into consideration that he'd been certified insane and was really to be pitied. I did allow him to cut my hair on a few occasions, not only out of necessity but also curiosity. I sometimes felt that I was walking a dangerous tightrope while he stood above me holding a large pair of scissors. Knowing he wasn't the full shilling I asked him gently, because I genuinely wanted to know, what had motivated his murder. I wanted to understand him a little better. He told me he considered the world to be so evil that he couldn't bear the baby to grow up in such an environment.

It was apparent the fellow was going through mental torment; I had seen him watching TV, when he would scream and shout abuse at the women on the screen. There was one time when he proved he could be dangerous. When he was working in the tailors' shop, after being discharged from the hospital, someone upset him. He went and filled up a large tea-jug at the urn, came back, and poured the contents down his tormentor's neck. The victim was severely burnt, and the lifer was hauled off to the chokey block, where he remained on Rule 43, protected for his own safety.

There was another case I remember of a fellow who came from Rampton to be placed on F2. He was also a lifer. For the first few days he seemed quite jolly but this was not to last. I believe he was only going through what is termed the 'honeymoon' period, a time when one is simply happy to be in a new environment. His behaviour changed drastically one lunchtime. We were all banged up when I heard loud kicking and banging noises from the cell belonging to the Rampton man. I heard the screws go to the door to try to calm him down, but it was to no avail. About an hour later Chief Bunker arrived and tried to quieten him, but also without success. The smashing of the door continued throughout the day and into the evening. I was used to all this and could switch off and go to sleep. The poor fellow was suffering from some claustrophobic disorder and couldn't bear to be locked up. He became very ill and some months later he died on F2. He had been shifted before his death to the very end cell on the landing. This was the cell everyone knew was allocated to those who didn't have long to live. Whenever I walked past that cell I tried not to look in. When the patients died they were wrapped in a plastic container and taken to the morgue. Many went without a proper funeral service.

When I think about the kid who was an arsonist and about this poor fellow, I realize that some people do not even get a glimpse of happiness in their lifetimes. I saw many of them at Parkhurst.

I only came across one blatant gay in the hospital. He was known as Mary. He/she was serving a life sentence and worked in the tailors' shop. One of the cons, mistakenly, thought Mary was weak; he bullied continuously. Mary was slightly built with shoulder-length hair and was a likeable person. One day the con split Mary's lip open and in the ensuing fight Mary picked up a pair of scissors and plunged them into the attacker, killing him instantly. Mary was charged with murder and the case was heard at Winchester Crown Court. The judge and jury were sympathetic. The sentence was reduced to manslaughter and Mary received seven years to run concurrently with the life sentence. Word soon spread through the prison . . . and no one tried to take liberties again.

One doesn't always have to be directly in conflict with someone to end up getting hurt or even killed in prison. In some cases, as I've mentioned before, it is simply a means to an end for a con who wishes to get moved to somewhere like Broadmoor. The weakest inmates are easy targets. One time a lifer, doing a recommended twenty-year minimum, asked me if I could get him a knife. He wanted to stab a black fellow so he could get certified and sent to Broadmoor. I resented this request for more than one reason: the proposed victim had done me (or anyone else) no harm; I didn't wish to become an accessory before and after the fact to a possible murder; and finally, it was against my principles to be involved in anything so fundamentally immoral. I told this fellow lifer my thoughts. I told him not to mention it to me again. The situation made me feel pretty helpless. I didn't wish to go to the authorities and I just hoped that the whole episode would peter out. This happened, but not before I received a call-up from Dr Cooper. He asked me if anyone had requested my help in getting hold of a knife. I replied, 'As you know, I'm a loner. I don't get mixed up in other people's business – it has nothing to do with me.' Before I left the office he said to me, 'If you hear anything perhaps you'll let me know.' In the event, thankfully, nothing came of the con's plans.

Billy Gentry was an old friend of mine from North London.

He didn't like it in Parkhurst so he created trouble in any way he could. Eventually he was placed on F2. His complaint was that he wished to be in a London prison so he could see his daughters on a more regular basis. This request was refused so Bill turned to dirtier tactics. He refused to wash and left excreta all over the floor. The situation got so bad they had to hose the cell down. After six months of this behaviour Bill finally realized his wish to be moved and was sent to Wormwood Scrubs. I have known many cons who, when down the block, covered themselves in excreta to prevent a beating by the screws. The screws didn't like going near them in this state.

One day I was kept waiting for my visit when my mother had come to see me. I went downstairs to the office and complained loudly. I threatened to make regular visits to the office to complain if it happened again. They took me so seriously that the following week the work screws built a cage at the top of the stairs; this would prohibit anyone going downstairs until the cage was unlocked for them. The cage is still there today.

My mother continued to visit me regularly. One day she was very upset due to the illness of my father. She was very concerned for him and couldn't help breaking down on the visit. I used to joke with her (although I seriously believed it) that she'd live as long as her parents, who were ninety-seven and ninety-five years old when they died. My father's bad health, however, led me to think that he wouldn't survive much longer.

My mother tried to remain cheerful but on the next visit she said she felt very tired and would have to have a rest from visiting Ron and me for a while. On the same day the mother of a friend of mine, Micky Ishmael, was also up to see him. We exchanged greetings and our mothers said they'd try to get down together one time to see us. At the end of the visit I kissed my mother goodbye. As she left I had a terrible feeling of emptiness, along with a premonition that I would never see my mother again.

This feeling wouldn't leave me. I wrote to my brother Charlie and told him he must bring my mother to see me again. Over the following weeks I repeated the request but he did not heed it. Then I received a phone message telling me that my mother was in Bart's Hospital. I received a letter from her and I wrote straight back. I couldn't put aside the premonition I'd had; I spoke to Welfare and asked if they could arrange for a phone call between us. Even though I explained everything to him the bastard refused my request. In August 1982, a couple of weeks later, I was called to Dr Cooper's office one morning. He said to me quietly, 'I'm sorry to have to tell you that your mother died peacefully in her sleep last night.' I went numb with shock. I didn't know what to say in response. I thanked him for telling me and left the office. I went back to my cell and broke down.

To hear about a death at any time is difficult but in prison it is even worse. You can't share your grief with those who are closest to you. Feelings have a hollowness about them. It's a very lonely experience. It is hard to express true emotions in the presence of strangers.

The next day I was sitting in the garden, deep in my own thoughts. Guy Armstrong, the resident padre at Parkhurst, had the audacity to come and stand by the garden bench and start to preach about how I should express my feelings in this hour of sorrow. In my anger I more or less told him to fuck off .

I was allowed to go to my mother's funeral but it turned out to be an undignified farce. Parkhurst sorted out three screws to accompany me in the van, one of them very tall. I was to be handcuffed to this particular screw for the day. For the journey I was cuffed to two screws, through the ride on the ferry and then in the van all the way to Chingford in London. I felt claustrophobic, packed like a sardine between them. There was also a police escort and while we were speeding through London the sirens were screaming. With the speeding van, the police escort and sirens, I felt a growing resentment that I was being deprived of any peaceful thoughts on this sad and special day.

When the van arrived at Chingford police station there were three van-loads of police waiting in the courtyard. They were there to receive both myself and Ron. He too was handcuffed to the tallest male nurse they could find. It seemed to me they wished to create a particular impression – they were more concerned with spectacle than with grief.

At the church I was taken to the back of the vestry. Ron was there with his escort. To add insult to injury, we were kept apart in this large room and not allowed to talk to each other. Ron and I let this pass, treating it with the contempt it deserved. We were shown separately to the front of the church where we sat down with our escorts. Our father was sitting behind and there were other close people all around but, handcuffed to the screws, I felt no warmth. All through the service, through the hymns and the prayers, I couldn't get it out of my mind that I was handcuffed to strangers and separated from those I loved.

I saw Diana Dors and Alan Lake sitting to the left of me. My eyes searched the crowd to try to find my old friend Billy Hill; I wanted to shake his hand, knowing that I'd probably never see him again. Billy Hill was the gang boss of London in the 1950s and was a good friend to Ron and me. He was getting on in years. When I heard he was going to attend my mother's funeral, I wrote and asked Charlie to organize the seating so Billy would be close to me. He wasn't.

When the service finished Ron and I went to the row of seats behind us and shook hands with our father, Charlie and a few others. I also managed to shake hands with another old friend, Georgie Woods, from Upton Park. Then Ron and I left the church. The TV cameras were on us and the photographers were taking pictures. I noticed someone nodding to me who wasn't wearing a tie . . . it was John McVicar. He never did know how to dress.

I had mixed thoughts on the way back to Parkhurst: extreme sorrow at the loss of my mother; indignation at the spectacle that had been created; disgust at not being allowed to spend a little time with Ron; and anger towards my brother Charlie – I wanted to say my goodbyes to Billy Hill. I was filled with sadness that I would never see my mother or Billy again. I didn't know it at the time, but it was also the last occasion I was to see my father.

In the van one of the screws said, 'I'll put it in my report that you behaved with dignity at the funeral.' I replied, 'How did you think I was going to behave?' His reports meant nothing to me at this particular time.

That evening I got back to Parkhurst in time to go to the sparse, familiar TV room and watch the events unfold on screen. It was strange watching again what I had already witnessed a few hours earlier. I was lonelier than ever that night.

In the ensuing weeks I received over 200 letters of sympathy. I replied to each one personally. It seemed that through her death my mother had left a legacy of goodwill. Thereafter, the press seemed less vindictive and they ceased referring to us as 'evil'. I felt as if my mother was helping us from beyond the grave. Life was never to be the same again but Ron and I both knew we had to carry on.

Seven months later I was to have another premonition. This time I knew, without being told, that my father had died. I received a phone message that my friend Fred Bone would be coming on a visit that day. On entering the visiting-room Fred shook my hand and said very quickly, 'I'm sorry. Your father died last night.' I told him that I already knew. He could tell by my lack of surprise that this was the case. I broke down and lasted the visit as well as I could. It was another night of loneliness. Neither Ron nor I went to the funeral.

I had seen the many sides of Parkhurst and I decided it was time to join the main wing, C wing, of the prison. It was my intention to enjoy myself as much as possible. On one of the last visits with my mother she said to me, 'You never know what will happen in life, so always enjoy yourself as much as possible.' I remembered those wise words and took heed. They were to become part of my everyday philosophy, and still are to this day.

So I moved on to C wing. One of the people who came to greet me that first night was my friend Steve Tully. He stood in the centre of the cell and said, 'Reg, I've got a request to make.' I told him to go ahead and he replied, 'I want you to teach me all that you know about business and about life in general.' I had never been asked to do anything like that before but I replied, 'If that's what you want I'll do my best.' From that day on and for a period of almost three years, until he had his freedom again, I taught him all I knew. He was a good pupil and learnt very quickly. In later years, when he was arrested on suspicion of a quarter-million-pound fraud, the *East London Advertiser* put in a write-up that he was a protégé of Reg Kray! I had to laugh at this. But in fact, on a more serious note, I always advocated that he should stick to straight business.

Steve and I worked hard on finishing my book *Slang*. When it was finally completed we stood up and shook hands! A short while later I had another brief attack of paranoia and much to my regret I had to return to the hospital. We kept in touch through stiffs (illegal letters), which were passed through various channels in the prison. In this way I continued to share my experiences and my thoughts – past, present and future.

Steve and I used to go to the gym together and sometimes when we returned we'd have our own kind of parties. Patsy and Joe Lee were among the others who'd join us. Just before I was returned to the wing, Steve was called to reception on the pretext that a parcel was waiting for him. When he arrived he was met by a dozen screws who said they were taking him to Albany prison. Steve protested but he didn't have any choice but to go. Once there he immediately went on hunger strike and also managed to seal off the wing so that, for a while, the screws couldn't get up the stairs. He proceeded to smash the wing up . . . windows, toilets, sinks, everything he could lay his hands on. This took a lot of guts, as it laid him open to a good kicking. He was eventually taken to the chokey block, where he continued his protest.

Back in Parkhurst I heard of Steve's troubles and plagued the doctor, the Governor, the Assistant Governor and anyone else I could get to listen, to see reason and allow him to return. The Governor was a reasonable man and listened to my argument. After about a week of negotiation by me and plenty of noise from Steve he was finally brought back to Parkhurst.

I know, on my record, that I am down as a manipulator. I don't deny this. To survive in prison one has to manipulate to some extent. I don't consider it morally wrong. Most business people could be termed manipulators in a certain sense.

Steve had a visit around this time from the actor Alan Lake, husband to Diana Dors. Even though Alan had troubled to come all the way from London, he was turned away at the door because Steve had forgotten to put him down on his visitors' list. This is how petty some of the prison regulations are.

Many years ago, before my conviction, I was friendly with the Levy family and their brother-in-law Freddy Bird who came from Hackney. The Levys were Jewish and all of them had done time inside, as had Freddy. Whenever we went to their house in Mile End they made Ron and me very welcome. Freddy had a couple of kids aged about eight and ten. We would buy them chocolates and sweets and give them a few quid. One day, at Parkhurst, who should come along and introduce himself but one of Freddy's kids. He was in his early twenties, serving four or six years. I invited him into my cell and made him welcome. It was a long way from the old house in Mile End. It felt strange to be sitting in a cell in that prison environment with the same kid all those years later. Unfortunately, for some, it is part of their school of life.

Steve and I had a bit of trouble with a con by the name of Tommy Kerr. Kerr found fault with our cleaning of the landing. On hearing he had a problem we went to find him; he was in the TV room sweeping up. I walked straight up to him and said, 'I hear you've got the needle with us.' He took off his jacket and said, 'I'll take both you cunts on now.'

In reply to that Steve kicked him where it hurts and I hit him on the chin with a right-hand punch. Just as the action started two screws came into the room and we had to stop. The screws didn't see anything but they were suspicious. Steve and I left the room, Kerr following us, until we reached our cells – Kerr had the one opposite mine. As he stood facing me he shouted, 'You're an old bastard.' I walked across and hit him with a punch that sent him sprawling half-way down the landing. Steve made the mistake of going towards him and at this very moment a screw arrived and thought it was Steve that had sent Kerr sprawling. He nicked Steve for assault and he got three days down the block.

Steve and I were shifted to B wing. There was a lot of racial tension on this wing but I got on well with people of all races. I often acted as peacemaker between the cons. I knew a black fellow called Henry who was very paranoid. He accused me of being racially prejudiced. I invited Henry into my cell and sat him down and talked to him. I told him about my black friends, Joe Louis, Henry Armstrong and Sonny Liston . . . three of the greatest black fighters the world has known. I reasoned with him and eventually he realized he was wrong.

Steve and I got very involved in a charity for a little girl who had kidney trouble, Julie McGuire. We worked hard to raise money for kidney machines for the hospital where she was being treated. We organized joint charity events with other prisons and helped raise thousands of pounds. It was very satisfying. Our efforts reached the newspapers and we received letters of thanks from Julie's parents.

A new Assistant Governor came into the prison. It was obvious that he wanted to change the whole place in a matter of days. His philosophy was 'a new broom sweeps clean . . .' and I knew he'd want to start with me. I was correct in this assumption. He called me to his office and said, 'Look, Kray, you're writing far too many letters and it has to stop. When you go to a Cat B prison you will find the rules are even more stringent – they will prohibit you from writing so much. You'll have to adhere to the rules if you want to get out.' I had had an idea this was what he'd want to speak to me about and so I was prepared. I used a lesson I had learnt from a book; the lesson was to take the object of the argument away from one's adversary and thus eliminate the cause of the argument. I did this by saying to the AG, 'I agree. I'll concede to your wishes. And I realize you're only telling me for my own good.' He looked at me in amazement and with obvious relief. I knew he was expecting to have a struggle with me over the issue. So in his relief he forgot the object of the argument. I said, 'I'll go along with what you want but I'm sure you'll be reasonable in return and let me write to all my correspondents to inform them of the situation.' The AG replied, 'Certainly, Kray. I realize you'll have to do this.' Off I went to continue writing to my heart's content. I had over 1,000 correspondents in my address books – his agreement would allow me to keep on writing for some time! I have used this method many times, both with staff and inmates. It hardly ever fails.

On 24 October 1983, close to my fiftieth birthday, I was sitting one night in Steve's cell with Steve, Paul Edmunds from Canning Town and Harry Grace from Chester, when a con who had just come on to the wing called me out of the cell. This con was very aggressive and very disturbed. We had been in the hospital together so I knew him from old. The day he came on to the wing I said to Harry Grace, 'It's odds on that I'll have a row with this fellow, it's a cert he'll make a beeline for me.' I thought that Dr Cooper was wrong in releasing him from the hospital, that he wasn't yet ready to be on the wing.

As I walked to my own cell I waved him into it before me. I noticed he was sweating profusely and had a very violent look. He was standing with his chin jutting out as he spoke. He started to make a lot of personal insults about me. I knew my capabilities as compared to his and didn't really want to resort to violence. I said to him, 'Look, I've got to go back next door, would you leave.' He took this as a sign of weakness and even more obscenities spewed out of his mouth. He was adamant that he wouldn't leave. I was trying to be patient but it was getting me nowhere. I wanted him out of my cell and in the end I had to hit him with a right hook on the chin. The blow lifted him off the floor and slammed him against the wall. As he hit the wall his head hit a picture of the actor Richard Harris and all three, the frame, the photograph and the con hit the deck with a thud so loud that my friends in the cell next door heard it. This brought them out in a hurry. The con was spark out on the floor, where he remained until I told Steve to drag him out.

No screws saw the blow but a senior screw saw Steve drag him from the cell and knew that I was involved.

I was told to go to my cell, where I would have to wait, locked up, until they could take me to the block at nine o'clock. During my wait Steve, Harry and Paul talked to me through the door. I was kept in the block until eleven o'clock the next morning and then they let me go as there was no evidence against me. The con was shifted to another nick.

Shortly after this Steve was released.

While I was at Parkhurst I received a letter from an inmate at Wandsworth. It was obvious that he was mentally ill and paranoid. Although I didn't know him and had never even met him, his letter indicated that he had a fixation that I was out to do him harm. He had all the classic symptoms of schizophrenia. His letter claimed that he had heard voices through the radio and TV saying I wanted to injure him.

Some time later who should arrive at Parkhurst but this same inmate. I had made a mental note of the name and I spoke to him when he arrived to try to put him at his ease. Shortly after I was in the gym at the same time as him and he kept staring at me. There were plenty of weights about and so I was wary and on my toes but fortunately nothing happened.

This type of thing does happen in prison and especially so in my case, my name often being in the newspapers. From experience I know that schizophrenics can get fixations on people mentioned by the media and can look upon these people with either good or bad eyes. I should mention that at this time the authorities censored all mail, so they must have known about this particular inmate's fixation.

Another lifer by the name of Ronnie Gibson was convinced that he was the son of Jack McVitie. Just to make sure there was no animosity when he arrived at Parkhurst, I sat down and had a cup of tea with him to explore his thoughts. We had an amicable conversation. Ronnie came from Paddington. He was a likeable and sound person. The reason I say he was sound was because one time he fell out with a group of about six inmates. He had threatened one of them with a knife he kept in his cell, usually placed in a bucket of excrement to make it more lethal. This group attacked Ronnie in his cell with heavy batteries wrapped in socks. He suffered quite severe head injuries but when the screws found him bleeding he would not name any of his attackers. Afterwards he was always known as a sound man – but it was not the easiest way to be given such a reference.

Another situation cropped up that nearly caused a confrontation. A young fellow arrived at Parkhurst. He was the lover of the late George Cornell's wife, and was serving about six years. This eased over however and at a later date the fellow was certified and sent to Broadmoor. I marked Ron's card that he might have a possible enemy in his company but I'm glad to say Ron ended up looking after the kid. The fellow, whose name I can't recall, received a battering from the nurses after he had some trouble there. Ron was very generous to him.

My fiftieth birthday was approaching and I planned for it to be the best night Parkhurst had ever seen! I got the use of three extra cells, whose tenants were friends of mine, to use as a base for the party. I passed the word by mouth to over eighty cons in B wing inviting them to join in the celebrations. They were of all colours and creeds, black and white, Turkish, Indian, German, Greek, Maltese, Pakistani and many other nationalities. The only ones not invited were the sex cases and baby-killers.

The eighty cons went to and fro, from one cell to another, through the evening. My cell was packed out like a sardine tin! It was a colourful scene. Everyone wore different attire, bright tops and vests. The music blared out and food was eaten. Many of my guests brought me gifts and cards to show their respect. As I looked at this sea of faces each one told me a different story and yet all were a part of mine. I had learnt from each of them and they may have learnt from me too. One day we would take our separate paths but this was *our* night, a night to remember. I went from cell to cell to make sure everyone was OK and that there weren't any problems. I was in my element. The night reminded me of others I had spent earlier, at the Double R Club, the Kentucky, and Esmerelda's Barn. I was a good club man and I enjoyed playing the host. At a quarter to nine on this special evening I had just left one of the cells and was standing in the middle of the landing looking down on the floors below, when all of my guests suddenly came out, encircled me and sang 'Happy Birthday, Reg'. It was a complete surprise and I was taken aback by the nice gesture. I couldn't help but feel very emotional.

At five-to-nine Bollard, the senior screw, came to see me on the landing. He said, 'If you go back to your cell now they'll all leave. You've had your fun. Let's call it a night.' Bollard, who sported a beard, was a decent fellow, so I said to him, 'Let me make sure they're all locked away safely, then you can lock me up.' He saw the sense in this, so I quickly spoke to my guests and they were happy to end the evening without any problems. They went peacefully to their cells and I went to mine. As the door shut behind me I looked at the remnants of the party, the record that had stopped turning on the player, the left-over sandwiches, the gifts I'd received. I had a head full of memories . . . I went over them for the rest of the night. It had been a very special evening.

The following day I went to work in the little shop. The screw in charge, Stan Turner, made me a cup of coffee and told me the whole prison, from the block to the officers' mess, had heard the party in progress and it was the talk of the day. I was

The twins' boxer's licences, issued 1951.
(Unless otherwise indicated, all images are from the author's personal collection)

Reg (right) and Charlie, with his son, Gary.

Reg in the mid-1950s, outside the Regal Billiard Hall, Mile End, with among others Charlie (right) and Ron (below).

Above: (Left to right) Charlie, 'Big Pat' Connolly, Tommy Flat and Reg outside Regal Motors.

Below left: Reg at Vallance Road.

Below right: (Left to right) Reg, Curly King and Ron.

Above left: Gold-bullion robber Georgie Woods, in his early twenties.

Above right: (Left to right) Billy Donovan, Johnny Squibb and Reg at the Double R Club in Bow Road.

Below: (left to right) Charlie, Reg and ex-boxer Pat Connolly.

Reg's father, Charles Kray, relaxing on holiday.

Violet Kray with Reg's dog, Mitzi.

On holiday with friends in France.

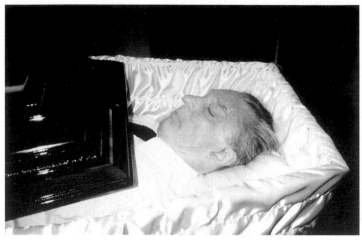

Above: Ron at rest, W. English & Son, Bethnal Green, 1995.

Below left: Reg at Ron's funeral, St Matthew's, Bethnal Green, with Frankie Fraser behind him. *(Dave Hogan)*

Below right: Shaking hands at Ron's funeral.

Above: Reg leaving Ron's funeral.

Right: The cortège for Ron, processing over the Bow flyover to Chingford Mount Cemetery.

Reg's final farewell to Ron, Chingford. *(Dave Hogan)*

quite proud of this . . . walls do not a prison make. Stan Turner was a decent screw; he always treated me like a human being. He was a gentleman.

In Parkhurst, as in all prisons, we used to get periodic spins. A spin is a search and we could suffer one any time of day or night. The screws would search for contraband or anything illegal. When coming off visits we would normally get a strip search. This would normally be embarrassing, but after suffering them for years they simply became a formality.

A screw I didn't like at Parkhurst, by the name of Bishop, one day asked me to sweep a landing. I didn't like the attitude he had but I left it a day while I thought about what to do. I eventually told my mates what I'd decided and they said they'd help me. I walked up to Bishop and said to him, 'Are you OK? You don't look so good.' I kept staring intently at his mouth, which seemed to make him uncomfortable. One by one the others in the group did the same thing to him, expressing their concern in different ways. It had the desired effect. He became so anxious that he went on sick leave and was absent for a month! It was all down to the powers of auto-suggestion!

I remember two brothers at Parkhurst by the name of Nolan. They were from Kentish Town. I was on friendly terms with them and knew that one of them always kept a cache of weapons beneath his floorboards which the screws never found.

I had a friend by the name of Murphy in prison. He's my Murphy radio. My mother brought me this in 1968 when I was on remand in Brixton and it's been with me ever since. Murphy has been my constant companion and has rarely left my side. This radio has seen it all, been covered in blood, been knocked over, crashed to the ground, but has continued to entertain me throughout all the years. I hope, one day, to take Murphy out of the gate with me.

I reached the stage in Parkhurst where I was wandering

constantly from cell to cell each evening, looking for fulfilment in company and conversation. I found it had all been said before. Then one day in December 1985 something was to happen that resolved the problem for me. This happening was in the shape of a young con that I passed on the landing just before I was due out on a visit. His name was Pete Gillett and, because of some trouble, he'd just come from Coldingley to Parkhurst on a transfer. As he passed me on the other side of the landing I just noticed there was a newcomer on the wing. I didn't think a lot of it. I went to see a friend, Ray Johnson, and found him talking to the new young con. I said to the newcomer, 'Do I know you from somewhere?' I thought he looked familiar. He answered, 'No, you don't know me, but I know all about you.' I told him I was going on a visit but if he wanted to share a cup of tea later he could come down to the threes landing. I was in cell 17. He said he would and we shook hands and parted.

At six o'clock that evening Pete came to my cell and we had a chat. He told me he'd been busted in Coldingley and had lost six months remission. Although there were others in the cell, Pete and I got on so well with each other that we were completely oblivious to them. Pete had a great personality and a good sense of humour. He told me that as he and the escort entered the gates of Parkhurst he had hung his head back and his arms out, and said aloud in James Cagney style, 'I made it, ma!' This was typical of Pete. He also told me it was strange we should meet because in his previous prison days at Albany and Coldingley he would tell a Reg Kray story. Pete had a scar on his shoulder, about an inch long, and whenever he was sunbathing people would comment and ask how he got it. He would say, 'Reg Kray did it, when I had some trouble with him!'

Pete and I teamed up and I helped him out, as a personal

manager, when he left jail. He made a record, went on a TV documentary about a desert island with Annabel Croft, and did a lot of club work. He had numerous articles and write-ups. He also made his acting début in the film *The Krays*. Once, when Pete had a home leave, Wilf Pine and I arranged that a boat would go across from Portsmouth to the Isle of Wight to pick him up. When he arrived at Portsmouth there was a white Rolls-Royce waiting to pick him up. He then went on to a restaurant and to see Fred Dinenage at the TV studio, where he was filmed for *Coast to Coast* viewers.

A nutter came on the wing. He was a right weird bastard. He had come from the hospital and had somehow managed to get hold of his medical papers, which he was showing to everyone. The psychiatrists claimed that he would definitely kill again. They also said that when he looked at people he had the urge to kill, it would make him go to the toilet and open his bowels. This appeared to be connected to some kind of orgasmic response. Someone showed me these papers in his absence. Then one day he came along and asked me if I wanted to read what the psychiatrists said about him. It was my theory that you should never show fear to a nutter. I said, 'I don't want to read your fucking papers, they don't impress me.' I walked away. Some time later I did a deal with him, that he clean out my cell each week in return for a half-ounce of tobacco. I did this partly to freak him out and partly because I liked playing with danger. I noticed that whenever he was in my cell and I watched him working he would end up going to the toilet.

I had some strange experiences at Parkhurst. As well as the healing powers I discovered, there were other odd occurrences. Once, just after tea, I was in my cell locked up. A stiff (a note) came under the door. It was posted by Bernie Glennon, who was working in the kitchens at the time and so remained unlocked. The note was about a friend called Eddie; he'd been taken over to the hospital, unconscious, on a stretcher. I knew Eddie had been recently upset because his wife was receiving painful treatment for cancer. I wondered what had made him unconscious. My first thoughts were emotional ones on his behalf and then I said a short prayer for him. Then I decided I would try and psych him out of the state he was in. I willed myself to visualize his exact whereabouts and I paced my cell, repeatedly saying in an indignant tone of voice, 'Wake up Eddie, wake up, you must wake up!' I did this for some time until, gradually, my concern began to lessen. I knew I had raised him from his sleep. I looked at my watch and it was a quarter to six. I made a mental note of the time. Five minutes later the door was unlocked. I went down to the office and asked the screw in charge to phone the hospital to see how Eddie was. He did this and told me that Eddie was now awake. He had woken up at a quarter to six.

Another unusual experience also concerned Eddie and his wife, Carol. Due to Carol's illness I was very concerned for them both and for the future of their little son. I was so worried about it all that on one particular night I said what was quite a strange prayer. I offered myself to God and Jesus Christ as a born-again Christian, if in turn Carol could be cured. After a certain amount of treatment Carol responded and eventually recovered. So I guess, in my own way, I am a born-again Christian because I vowed to be so. Perhaps my interpretation of what that means won't always be the same as others but, as they say, God works in mysterious ways.

One time I received a letter from a woman in America. She was English but had moved to live in Texas. On her flight to the States she had read an article about me and decided to write. A couple of days previously I'd received a pamphlet. It was a request from someone in Liverpool for help in financing operations for a badly burned child. Plastic surgery and major rebuilding of the child's face were needed and this could only be done in an American hospital. An idea came to me. In my response to the lady in Texas I enclosed the pamphlet on the child as well as various phone numbers in Liverpool where she could link up with people. I suggested that she go to a local newspaper and create some publicity about the child. I said to only use my name if she felt it would help. I received a second letter from the lady in Texas and she told me that everything had gone according to plan; the locals had decided to take the child under their wing and had arranged for a flight and for treatment at the hospital. My prayers, faith, hope and efforts were answered by the kind people of Texas.

My friend Micky Fenlon was on his way to Exeter prison, on accumulated visits. On the journey he pulled out a blade and hijacked the coach and all the occupants, cons and screws. He drove the vehicle for about fifty miles, until he was close to London, and then had it on his toes. He was only out a short time before he was recaptured and received six years on top of his previous sentence of thirteen. Mick was returned to Parkhurst. Another friend, Dave McAllister, had a similar adventure on his way to a different prison. He also hijacked the van he was in but he too was eventually recaptured. They were a lively lot at Parkhurst.

While I was at Parkhurst I started to analyse my own behaviour. I had grown up in the tough environment of the East End and had learnt to be aggressive. I slighted easily and often responded, as others did, with violence. It continued in prison. I felt I was in a position where I had to stand up for myself or I'd be trodden underfoot. I met aggression with more aggression. Gradually I came to the conclusion that there must be another way. I needed to express myself verbally, to talk, rather than holding my tongue and letting all the pressure build up inside me. I decided that in future I'd do my best to reason with any adversary. One of the people who helped me most, without knowing it, was David Jacobs with his radio programme *Any Questions*. This was broadcast on Wednesday evenings. I had listened to it for a number of years and taken a liking to it. The people who participated threw topics around until they reached a conclusion, and even if they continued to disagree about a subject they did so in a civilized manner, without coming to blows. I began to understand the power of speech.

One evening at Parkhurst some bad trouble started between different groups of inmates who were fighting each other on the 3s landing. Involved in the row was a Turkish fellow by the name of Yilmaz, two Israelis, and a number of Londoners. The Israelis had been convicted of kidnapping and attempting to smuggle a Nigerian out of this country for political purposes. They had knocked him unconscious with an injection. I knew all the people involved well. I stayed out of this row. It lasted for some considerable time and there were many injuries.

Yilmaz used to invite me to his cell on the top landing and after I had climbed the metal staircase he would welcome me with a glass of orange juice and ask me to sit down. He would offer me dried fruit and nuts and other healthy delicacies. He would also do his best to influence me to join him in the business of heroin dealing. He had a lot of contacts both here and in Turkey. But I was as adamant as he was persuasive that I wouldn't get involved. We would discuss this subject amicably while we ate and drank. He was a very charming man and well-mannered. He told me that if I ever visited his country I would be a welcome guest at his house. Once, when we were discussing the film *Midnight Express*, produced by Sir David Puttnam, Yilmaz said that it was not a true picture of his countrymen.

As a matter of interest, I knew David Puttnam many years

back when he first started out in an office off Park Lane. This was before he made the brilliant film *Bugsy Malone*. David Puttnam was a very charming and likeable man.

But I digress. Yilmaz told me that his brother had been shot in Holland. I did not say it with the intention of upsetting him but pointed out that I viewed the selling of heroin as a curse. At the time I was not to know that the curse would also befall this friend of mine. I regret to say that when Yilmaz was released a short while later he was shot dead in North London.

I knew a black fellow by the name of Bike Campbell. One day he was agitated and refusing to lock up. This was on the 3s landing. Bike had previously shown me a lot of respect. One day some cons had been going round blocking the locks so the screws couldn't lock us up. Bike was one of those taking part but when they reached my cell door he came in quietly and said, 'Reg, I respect you, so I've told the others not to touch your door lock.' I respected Bike for this. So on this night when he was agitated and all the screws were hovering around him and getting closer, I went up to the 3s landing and calmed him down. I did this for his benefit not for the screws. Eventually, Bike calmed down and allowed the screws to bang him up. My friend Bike was released from prison but sad to say he is now in Park Lane mental institution. Shortly after his release he shot and killed someone outside the old Regency Club in Hackney.

A Buddhist monk called Bhante used to visit Parkhurst regularly. He always wore just a long fawn robe and sandals on his bare feet despite the cold, which was often bad on the Isle of Wight. He had blue eyes and a red ruddy face beneath his shaven head. Once he entered a cell where several inmates were enjoying themselves with a bucket of hooch. When he was inside they wedged the door behind him and as Bhante sat on the bed they merrily kept on drinking. It was funny to witness because Bhante was obviously very uncomfortable, and couldn't get out of the cell quick enough! He was a nice fellow though and many, including myself, gained from his wisdom and knowledge.

Early one morning my door opened before all the other cells were unlocked. In came four screws who said I had to go to the block. It was 1986. As I left the wing I managed to stop outside Pete's cell and tell him, through his spyhole, what was happening. Once down the block I was taken before the Assistant Governor, Trufay, who said I was going to Wandsworth on an F72, known by us as a laydown. This meant I would be locked up for twenty-three hours a day for a period of one month. Trufay claimed I had been strong-arming cons. I said this was ridiculous; I gave away more tobacco to cons than anyone else in the jail.

I was taken by escort in a van to the ferry – from there we would proceed to Wandsworth prison. I had just stopped smoking, after thirty-three years, and I could have done with a roll-up. But seeing as I'd promised Pete I wouldn't start again, I kept my word and went without.

CHAPTER SEVEN

WANDSWORTH, WORMWOOD SCRUBS AND BACK TO PARKHURST
1986–1987

As the van arrived in London I was pleased to be in old surroundings. The prison gates of Wandsworth, dark and foreboding, reminded me of another time. In 1959 I had done an eighteen-month sentence. It seemed I had come in a complete circle. When I was shown to the block nothing much had changed. In the cell, five screws surrounded me. One said, 'It's up to you which way you want it, easy or hard.' I knew that, apart from these five, if anything started another 100 could come running. I just said, 'The quicker I get out of here the better.' It occurred to me that they wouldn't win any medals for valour in the face of the enemy.

It was very dull to be banged-up in Wandsworth. The cell was completely bare, apart from my bed and a cardboard table and chair. I was allowed one hour of exercise each day, alone in a cage. Those in the block were also searched each time they left or entered the cell. I was permitted one shower a week. I had been in this same block for three days in 1959 and so the routine was known to me.

I knew I was back in London. I could tell by the dark clouds looming in the sky. I could tell by the pigeons, which weren't afraid to walk close by my feet, and by the cockney sparrows flying around and settling in different parts of the yard. Though I wasn't happy to be in Wandsworth, these signs of London gave me a warm feeling and brought back many memories. For too long I had seen nothing but seagulls on the Isle of Wight.

My stay was during a winter month. Icicles were frozen to the pipes which lay behind the old broken toilet doors. It seemed that nothing much had changed in twenty-five years. Yet since I was there last I'd lost my wife, my parents and been separated from my brothers. A lot of water had passed under the bridge.

One day while exercising I was pleased to see my old friend Neville Winn, wrapped in a heavy raincoat, in a nearby cage. The snow was falling heavily. We exchanged greetings. I told him I was glad to hear he'd soon be out. Neville said he thought they'd taken a liberty putting me on a laydown after all the bird I'd done. When I looked at Neville I thought to myself, 'We are brothers in arms.' It was good to see a friendly face.

On my second day at Wandsworth I received a legal visit. I was glad to get out of my cell for a while but I wasn't so pleased when the solicitor's clerk passed me the *Sun* newspaper and pointed out a short article. It was about an ex-con by the name of Bill Bailey. He claimed that Pete Gillett and I were having a gay affair at Parkhurst. I had the right needle at this and knew Pete would as well. Bill Bailey was a real slag. Although he claimed to be a friend of Ron's, he had not sent him even a Christmas card in seventeen years. I reminded him of this when he first arrived in Parkhurst. I put him on the blacklist, hence his spiteful write-up. He wanted to get his own back on me. Pete wrote and said he was in bed when another inmate brought him the write-up to read. He then did the unexpected. Instead of bowing down to the stick from other cons, he turned the tables and humorously assumed the mock-role of a gay, speaking with a pronounced lisp and acting out all the mannerisms. This was typical of Pete and I admired him for it.

One day I heard loud screams and thuds coming from another part of the block. It sounded as if a good kicking was taking place. I rang my bell in the hope that if the screws were assaulting someone at least they would know I was listening. I thought it might deter them a little. A screw came to my spyhole and said in a gruff voice, 'What do you want?' I said, 'Nothing, just forget it.' Then I went and lay down on my bed.

About a week later, as I came back from the showers a screw over six feet tall stopped me in the passage. He introduced himself; he was an ex-ABA boxing champion from Portsmouth. He knew my friend Tony Burns, the coach at the Repton Boxing Club. The screw was a decent fellow, as most real fighters are. It showed me once again that once you had been a fighter it opened doors to others in the boxing world, wherever or whoever you might be. The screw came to see me three or four times during my stay. We spoke about boxing, which was a break from the dullness of the day.

One morning, while I was having my usual cold water shave, the door opened and a screw said, 'You're wanted by the reception officer down at the hot-plate.' I left my face all lathered with soap, thinking the screw would only keep me a minute and then I could finish my shave. The screw was waiting there with a pen and paper. I didn't like him on sight. The look on his face made it quite clear that he didn't like me either. He started to go through a long list of what I had brought with me in the way of possessions, and to tick them off. This was despite the fact I'd obviously come to Wandsworth with very little. It was clear the screw was trying to provoke me by keeping me waiting in the cold with my face covered in lather and the soap beginning to dry. But I decided to use some psychology and turn the moment against him. I gave the impression I was really enjoying my stay in the open area away from the cell. The screw seemed very perplexed. He was caught in a dilemma and couldn't decide which was better – to keep me there or to send me away. He had reached the stage of asking, 'Have you any false teeth?' when suddenly I saw him falter. His brain, though not working overtime, had finally reached a conclusion. He said abruptly, 'That's all. You can go now.' I went happily back to my cell.

At the end of the month I was pleased to gather up my papers and letters in preparation for the journey back to Parkhurst. But something just didn't feel right. The door opened and three screws, strangers, stepped into my cell. 'Come on, you're on your way.' I said, 'Hold on, you're not Parkhurst screws.' They replied, 'No, we're taking you to the Scrubs.' I asked for an explanation but they wouldn't give me one. I was escorted to a small Black Maria van and put in a cubicle which was then locked.

On arrival at the Scrubs I was taken to the block and met with the reception committee again. 'Which way is it going to be?' This time I said, 'What am I doing here?' The PO in charge replied, 'You're here on another month's laydown.' I was sick at this. I was shown to a cell which overlooked the exercise yard where the remands walked. This pleased me, as I knew I could at least get up to the window and have a chat with some of them. I lay on my bed and thought about things. Another month's solitary; I knew I had to get on with it. As I lay there it reminded me of being on a slab in a morgue. There was just about the same amount of life going on.

While I was at the Scrubs I had a visit from my brother Charlie, Roger Daltrey and Geraldine Charles. Roger wanted to inform the press that I was locked up for twenty-three hours a day – he saw it as a liberty. I thanked him but declined the offer.

One day on exercise I was pleased to see my old friend Joe the Greek brought into the cage to join me for a walk. He too was on a laydown. He had just cut a screw and was waiting to go to court for it. He told me the screws had already given him a good kicking. Joe was doing a life sentence and received another five years for the offence.

I heard there was a strike on at Parkhurst which had erupted into violence. The security screws, known to us as the 'burglars', were searching cells. I was concerned for Pete when he wrote and told me that just after tea, to his surprise, they had found a highly flammable bomb in his cell. It seemed that the burglars had been tipped off. They took Pete to the block and showed him how the bomb would have worked, igniting it with a match. The effect was devastating. If it had gone off in his cell he would have been burnt alive. I was very anxious and worried when I read the letter. He never found out who had placed the bomb there – but we all have enemies in prison. Just before leaving the Scrubs I read in a newspaper that Rocky Hart had been stabbed to death by an inmate at Parkhurst. Rocky was a friend of mine and a good barber; he had often cut my hair. The inmate was the same person who some time back had wanted to show me his medical papers saying he would kill again. If the reader recalls, it was him who would use the toilet whenever he was going to resort to violence.

I found out the full details later when I went back to Parkhurst. The night before the murder Pete Gillett had gone to Rogers's cell to borrow a guitar and had found Rogers standing staring at the wall. Pete said he had felt an evil presence in the cell and left immediately. The following day, for no reason,

Rogers plunged a kitchen knife into the stomach of Rocky Hart and killed him. Why Rogers was ever allowed on the main wing when psychiatrists knew he would kill again is beyond reasoning.

I was also told that the cons at Parkhurst were going to lynch Rogers if they got their hands on him but he remained in solitary after the murder. Much later Rogers was given a life sentence at Winchester Crown Court for the murder of Rocky Hart and I believe he was ordered to be detained in a mental institution such as Rampton or Park Lane.

I also found out that the strike at Parkhurst was the reason for my second laydown at the Scrubs. The authorities did not want me to go back while the strike was in progress.

I was glad when the day finally arrived for my return to Parkhurst. I enjoyed the journey back through London. I was pleased to be travelling again towards old friends.

One afternoon, after my return to Parkhurst, Pete and I got involved in a fight on the football pitch. Pete was playing and I was watching from the side. Pete had promised me he wouldn't get into any fights during the game. But one of the cons had a go at him and I saw it happen. I stepped on to the pitch and knocked the fellow over with a left hook. Some of the others then joined in and Pete kicked one of them with a karate kick to the nose; it split wide open. Though we were outnumbered four to two we finally came out in front. Just afterwards another fight started on the pitch between a different group of cons. These two fights happened in front of many cons and screws and were a talking point for years to come.

On another occasion the gym screw asked Pete and I to go to the gym, as an outside football team were coming in to play and had asked if they could meet me. The team were a young group of fellows from Sussex. They greeted us warmly and some asked for autographs. We all had a good day.

While I was at Parkhurst I was visited by John Conteh, the former light-heavyweight world champion, John H. Stracey, ex-welterweight world champion, along with the boxing legend Jack Kid Berg, ex-junior lightweight world champion, and Alex Stein, the entrepreneur.

One of the funniest sights I saw at Parkhurst happened one morning just after breakfast. A six-foot-four con by the name of John, who had a history of crack-ups, had overflowed the bath on the ground floor. This was near the hot-plate area. He was doing his best to clear up the water with a mop. He was a giant of a fellow, in height and width, with long straggly hair down the back of his neck and a shaggy beard. He looked every part a mountain man. Because all the cons knew him to be unpredictable they were skirting round him on their way to breakfast. John, though busy with his mopping, looked up occasionally. The cons did their best to offer their usual 'Good morning, John,' and also tried to be completely nonchalant, as if the overflow and mopping-up procedure were normal daily events.

Whenever John cracked up the screws would get on the phone to the hospital and send for Mr Brooks. Mr Brooks would take John for a quiet rest in the hospital. Pete and I always got on well with John. Like Pete he was a good guitar player and would often join us for music sessions. John was also into black magic. I put a lot of his problems down to this and advised against its practice, but he was adamant that it was OK for him.

One day a tall burly-built Scottish-born Londoner named Josh came to Parkhurst. He was bald-headed. His reputation had preceded him and we all refused to have him on the wings. It was known that he had held other inmates hostage and forced them to commit indecent sex acts with him. The staff were told in no uncertain terms that if he came on the wings he would be severely hurt, so he was put in the chokey block, where he stayed for his own protection. This did not stop him from whistling and calling out to other inmates from the yard where he paced up and down during his exercise period. He would call up to the windows and try to strike up conversation. He was one cheeky bastard.

Shortly after his arrival he left the confines of the chokey block to go to Albany prison, where he worked in the tailors' shop. Also in the tailors' was a young Arab terrorist by the name of Albana. Josh approached Albana for sex but Albana refused. As a consequence Josh plunged a pair of tailor's scissors into one of Albana's ears and seriously hurt him. Josh was taken to court for attempted murder but was acquitted. Before this attack took place I had known Albana from his stay at Parkhurst hospital. I had found him to be likeable and easy-going. But after the attack, when I met him again at Parkhurst, he was a different person altogether. He had become withdrawn and paranoid, which was understandable. Unfortunately, Albana was certified insane and sent to Broadmoor for treatment. He was on friendly terms with my brother Ron while he was there. I knew that Albana was highly respected in his circle and that one of his relatives was a top-ranking terrorist.

Years later, when I was at Lewes prison, I was approached one day by a tall burly inmate who I didn't recognize. It was Albana's attacker, Josh. He was leaving Lewes prison that day and he said he'd like to give me a gift out of respect, which I accepted. It was a set of CDs of classical music. I thanked him. I only realized later, when I made inquiries, that this giver of gifts was Josh. As far as I know this was not his real name but an alias. I thought he was a very strange person.

Josh was not long in free society. One day, while sitting on a park bench, a car passed by. Shots were fired, hitting Josh in the head and killing him.

I hope that Albana was eventually able to return happily to his own country and people.

I had been at Parkhurst for almost eighteen years, on and off, when in the winter of 1986 I was interviewed by Mr Gregory Smith from the Home Office about a shift. I also spoke to the Assistant Governor, Crosby. The people from Nottingham came to interview me but they painted such a bad picture of the place – probably because they didn't want me there – that I turned it down even before the end of the interview. Two people also came to see me from Maidstone and I found out later that they had turned me down. Smith and Crosby were in agreement that I shouldn't go back to the Midlands because of my bad experiences at Long Lartin. I was told by Crosby that a suitable prison would be found and, like all Category B prisoners who were given a shift, I'd be given three months prior warning so I could adjust my thoughts and prepare for the move.

However, I began to get those familiar feelings that something was amiss. I felt sure they'd move me quickly. I mentioned this to Pete and told him how my instincts had always been right. One morning we did our cleaning job and then both went on exercise on the compound. It was a beautiful day, very mild with a light breeze. We went to the dome and did some sit-ups. Then I went for a walk on my own. When I saw Pete later I told him again that I was certain a move was imminent. He didn't believe me. We went back to the wing. In the evening we went to the gym, then had supper and a chat. At five to nine, bang-up time, I said, 'Goodnight, God bless, see you in the morning,' then went next door to my own cell and banged up.

I still had that uneasy feeling. I had just started to do a pencil drawing, which I was donating to a children's charity, when the cell door opened and four screws walked in. The time was about 9.15. One of the screws said, 'You're wanted down the block.' I knew I was on the move so I said, 'I'll come with you quietly if you let me go next door and say goodbye to Pete.' They allowed me to do this and when they opened Pete's door he looked up in surprise. He couldn't figure out what was going on. I felt terribly sad to be leaving and also angry at the way I was being shifted without notice. I said to Pete, 'I've got to go. I think I'm being shifted. Take care of yourself. Give my love to Liam (Pete's son). God bless. I'll be in touch soon.' I left the cell and the door was locked.

I was taken down to the block. After asking they told me I was leaving in the morning although they wouldn't say where to. Even though I'd been taken off Category A and was now a Category B, this was a blatant Cat A shift. It seemed I was a Category B in theory but still a Category A in practice.

This was even more apparent the following morning when I was taken to a Cat A van with escort. I asked why this was. One of the screws said the Cat B van had broken down. I told them I thought that was bollocks and that they were still treating me as a Category A prisoner.

It was only when the van pulled away from Parkhurst that I was told we were going to Gartree prison. I thought, so much for Gregory Smith and Mr Crosby's contention that I shouldn't be returned to the Midlands. I could only reach the conclusion that this was a deliberate policy shift to freak me out.

My last memory of Parkhurst was of the night in the block. In the block the windows are frosted over so you can't see outside.

CHAPTER EIGHT

GARTREE

1987–1989

We reached Gartree at lunchtime. It looked very different to Parkhurst and was a massive new building. Before I got to D wing, where I had been allocated a cell, I passed through huge iron gates and a maze of passageways. This was to be my home for the next two years.

On my arrival one of the senior screws had the audacity to tell me I was in Gartree for the purpose of assessment. I was to hear this again and again. It seemed ridiculous after all the years of reports.

The first con to come to my cell was Harry Roberts. Though he looked older he hadn't, as a person, changed a bit. Paddy Hill, one of the Birmingham Six, was the next to arrive. The first new friend I met was a fellow called Mick Bartley. He was twenty-six years old and serving a twelve-year sentence for robbery. He came from Durham. Although I was only in his company for two years it is a lot to his credit that we never had a single argument in that time.

I'd only been in Gartree for a couple of weeks when I couldn't help but notice that on each Saturday, at around 10 a.m., two screws would come and stand in my cell while I was writing letters. With a paper and pen in their hands they would ask me to call out a list of everything I had in the cell – such as how many mattresses, which of course was one, and how many pillowcases, which of course was also one, and on it would go. I knew they were trying to wind me up. It was all part of the 'assessment' process. It was all such a waste of time. I said to them, 'Get the farce over and done with as soon as possible, and don't bother coming back.' I was so incensed at this behaviour I went to see the Assistant Governor and told him I was too old to be a part of such pathetic rituals and he should end them as soon as possible. When they next visited I continued writing and refused to answer their stupid questions. After that the rituals ceased.

At around the same time I was told that my case officer wished to see me for assessment for parole reports. A case officer is a screw assigned to an inmate on his arrival at jail. I prefer to call them screws because I've always been under the impression that an officer is someone of high rank but, alas, 'officer' is present-day prison terminology. I had been told that this particular officer was an arrogant type and one for the rule book; his father was a prison governor in another jail. I knew he would try to have a field-day with me because I was high-profile. I used my own brand of psychology and deliberately kept him waiting for the appointment. I made myself some tea and filled my flask and then, taking flask and cup with me, I arrived at the side office ten minutes late. I walked into the room and immediately moved the chair I was to sit in to another position. I poured myself a cup of tea, introduced myself, and said, 'I understand you wish to see me.' He said in reply that he was my new case officer and was there to assess me. I think he expected me to stand to attention.

He started off by asking if I ever got depressed or fed up and suggested that I tell him all my thoughts about the days I spent down the chokey block. I knew this officer had not been in the service for long. I thought his questions were an extreme audacity. I had already spent many years in prison and knew there were plenty still to come, yet here was this inexperienced person 'assessing' my future. I decided to reverse our roles and place him, so to speak, in the chair I was sitting in. I asked him, 'How long have you been in the prison service?' He replied, 'Eighteen months.' I followed this up. 'What were you doing before?' He told me he had been a welder. I asked him, 'Have you ever been down the chokey block?' He replied, 'No.' I continued to fire questions at him and he began to feel uncomfortable. A flush came to his cheeks and he got very hot under the collar. Although I was intense in my questioning and I was genuinely indignant, at the same time I was rather enjoying my new role as prosecutor and judge. Eventually I had had enough. I said, 'You have got the audacity to ask me about my feelings, my remorse and my regrets, and how I felt during my times down the block, yet you've only been in the service eighteen months and your previous occupation was as a welder. You are not qualified or experienced enough to either put these deep questions or to understand my answers – and my answers could affect parole one way or another. Don't ask to see me in future.' I terminated the meeting, picked up my cup and flask and left the office.

I went to the Assistant Governor on the ground floor, knocked on the door and went in. I said, 'Don't send that fucking screw to see me again while I'm in this prison because he's not qualified to ask me questions.'

As in all prisons, there was violence at Gartree. I remember an instance where one con got the needle with another and he ground down some glass into a fine powder and put it in the toothpaste tube of his enemy. Eventually, it would have ripped apart and poisoned his gums.

There were some really bad cases at Gartree, cons who had committed the most heinous of crimes. There was one who, on a robbery and rape, had ended up putting a shotgun between his female victim's legs and pulling the trigger, killing her. Also, I knew of a young inmate who was serving about six years for an awful robbery. He had been convicted, along with two others, for robbing a grocery store but while doing so they had sadistically poured petrol over the face and body of a young employee and set him alight. One of these three, who was a copper's son, got home leave and parole at his first request. Another con by the name of Blackhouse had killed his wife for the insurance money. He had deliberately slashed his own face after the murder so that he could say he had fought with his wife's attacker. His plot had come unstuck and he was convicted of murder.

As I've said before, prison life isn't glamorous. Of all the changes I have noticed over the years, the most profound is the calibre and principles of the cons. Almost gone are the days of the staunch and loyal inmate. As society's values and morals have changed, this has been reflected in the principles of the inmates. Prison has become an even more terrible place to live.

I came to the conclusion that Gartree was just a human cargo warehouse. There was no attempt at rehabilitation. It was run on the theory that the only thing the staff needed to know was how to turn a key in a lock. The inmates were simply to be contained . . . until they could be passed on to their next destination.

There were some real characters at Gartree. In particular there was a con who had such large ears he had an inferiority complex about them. One time he stuck them down with superglue! He had to go to the hospital to get them freed. There was also a top drugs and narcotics dealer who told me he was too lazy to go into any other kind of crime . . . so he chose the drugs racket. There were a lot of convicted terrorists at Gartree. I got on especially well with an Iranian, Kouroush Fouladi, who was serving seven years. In outside life he was a wrestler. Sometimes, when I was talking to him, he would just leap into the air, do a somersault and land on his feet!

Another character I met was sixty-year-old Bernie Clewitt, who I nicknamed Bernie the Bolt. He was a lifer who had been convicted of the first crossbow killing in this country. He was on appeal at the time and I saw the photographs of his victim which were being exhibited at his appeal. They were very gruesome and showed the bolt protruding from his victim's chest. Bernie was my neighbour and we got on well together. I gave him a plant which he tended with great care.

A likeable character I met there was a fellow called Frank Winston. He was later to have a love affair with a screwess and eventually marry her. He had been in prison since the age of fifteen and was serving a life sentence. He was always up to mischief; Frank and another con were suspected of taking the lock off the canteen door and emptying it of all the tobacco. Frank was a gypsy and had lived with his family. In later years I read that he had escaped from prison and to my knowledge he is still free. I hope this is the case. Perhaps with his gypsy blood he found it harder than most to be locked in by bricks and mortar.

I was in a cell one day talking to Frank when we heard a whirring noise coming from above. It was so loud we stopped talking and went to the end of the wing to look out of the window that overlooked the exercise yard. A helicopter landed suddenly in the middle of the field. Two cons called John Kendall and Sid Draper clambered aboard and within seconds the helicopter was airborne again. This was followed by a funny scene as some screws with their dogs came running on to the field; they continued to walk round in circles as though they weren't quite sure what to do. Gartree was abuzz at this escape. There's often a fair amount of humour in prison and this situation was exploited to the full. Shortly after, a few notices appeared on the board:

Helicopter trips,
to and fro:
Leicester to London.
All enquiries to: Chief Security Officer.

Another read:

Please check your luggage before helicopter flight.

And another:

Helicopter trips all full for the season.
Check for vacancies at a later date.

Of course security were furious at this escape. They brought in anti-escape devices, including orange-coloured balls stretched across the field. From a distance they looked quite pretty, especially when the arc-lights were flickering on them. I could look out of my window at night and see all the lights . . . and the screws patrolling with their dogs!

During my stay at Gartree the screws on one particular day brought sniffer dogs on to the wing when we were locked up. In fact it was a complete lock-down for the whole jail and the dogs, led by the screws, searched each individual cell while the occupant waited outside. They were searching for firearms, cannabis and powder (heroin). The search went on the for the best part of the day. I have witnessed search parties of this type at work in other jails.

Among the cons I met at Gartree was one by the name of

Steve Waterman, who was a likeable person and one of good principles. He was doing eighteen years for bank robbery and though he didn't make a big deal of it he told me part of his story which I found of interest. After he'd committed the robbery and was on his way from the bank there was a collision between two cars, and although he may have jeopardized his escape he stopped his own car and gave aid to an injured woman involved in the crash. This little story was one of the factors that made me aware of Steve's principles.

Another inmate I met and befriended was Raphael Rowe. He was a good-looking half-caste with dreadlocks who'd been convicted of the M25 murders along with some others. He showed me the papers regarding his case and also talked to me about it – I was convinced beyond any shadow of a doubt that he was innocent of the crime. It was blatantly clear that he was fitted up by the police. The witnesses in the case gave descriptions of white male perpetrators yet Raphael was still convicted. He was later freed on appeal.

I also met Mick Ahmed, who was resident in London before being convicted of murder. He originally came from Pakistan. One day a London fellow and Mick had an argument and the London fellow gashed Mick's chest open with a broken sauce bottle. I was close by his cell when the staff brought him out and I saw his chest bleeding profusely. I was to meet Mick again at Nottingham jail.

A familiar face was Dave McAllister, who was part Scots and had spent some time in Australia. We used to work out together in the gym for an hour each day. I'd previously met him at Parkhurst and so I knew his story. He was now serving twenty-three years in total because he had escaped twice and on one of these escapes he'd robbed, before leaving, the contents of the prison safe. On the other escape he had enticed a civvie teacher to work with him by pretending he had forced her to take him in her car. Dave hid in the back and the escape was successful. He was only out for a month before being recaptured. The teacher had fallen in love with Dave and this she would regret at a later date. On questioning she threw up her hands and admitted aiding and abetting Dave to escape. She said that Dave had told her to tell the story that he had claimed there was a bomb in the car and unless she drove him away he would detonate it. She was convicted of helping Dave to escape and was given a six-year sentence. I suppose it can be said that love works wonders or otherwise.

In the gym I met and became friends with Winston Silcott, who had been convicted of the murder of PC Blakelock. This conviction was overturned some time later although he remains in prison for another murder conviction; it was alleged he killed a professional fighter by the name of Tony Smith. Despite media portrayals of him as some kind of thug, I found him to be otherwise. In fact he was quite an amicable person by nature and one of very strict discipline by way of diet and non-drug participation. I was to meet him again later at Maidstone.

One of the most interesting people I have met in any jail was Paul Di. He had been convicted of a major drug offence and sentenced to a term of forty years imprisonment. Paul had allegedly set up a major drug network that stretched across the world, including the USA, Pakistan and India. Some of the stories he told me of his journeys were fascinating. He had appealed against his conviction and sentence and I learned at a later date that his sentence had been cut considerably. At the time of writing this he has been released.

Steve McFadden and his brother John were two who also used to eat with me. Steve was a lifer and he and his brother were from Scotland. Some years later Steve was taken on a journey from one prison to another. When the vehicle reached the area of King's Cross in London Steve pulled a blade and injured one of his four escorts and escaped. I read in the newspaper that he had been recaptured after a short period of freedom and the last I heard of him was when he sent me a letter from Belmarsh prison.

Charlie Bronson, whose real name was Mick Petersen, and whom I have mentioned in previous chapters, also came to Gartree for a short period of time. He remained segregated in the block. One day one of the senior staff approached me and said, 'Charlie Bronson wants to talk to you on the field. We've agreed to let him do so each weekend as long as he talks only to you and stays in your company.' So I said it would be my pleasure as he had been my friend for many years. We used to walk the field while we chatted about different times; sometimes we would sit on the grass verge and talk. Charlie at the time had a large handlebar moustache in the style of the actor Charles Bronson but much longer. He was very strong and powerfully built. Sometimes we'd have tests of handshake grips and show each other exercises to keep fit. Charlie had become part of prison folklore by reason of his strength, fighting ability and his habit of knocking screws out and taking them hostage. Some hostages were prison governors and on one occasion it was a doctor. When I had known him years previously he had asked if I could arrange for him to fight in an illegal boxing match in London. I arranged this with friends of mine who put him in a show in Canning Town, east London. The fight took place and Charlie Bronson was declared the winner in the second round. But some of the crowd were not happy. In fact some were almost on the point of lynching him because Mr Bronson had head-butted and kicked his opponent. This fight was videoed and to my knowledge remains one of Charlie's prized possessions. It has not always been a one-sided battle with Charlie, as he has been kicked and battered insensible in solitary by staff in retaliation. The story goes that one time he was beaten so badly parts of his hair were plastered on his record sheet and sent with him on transit to another jail. Over the years Charlie has become a writer and cartoonist of depth; he has had a book published on his experiences in prison. I believe the title of the book is *The Liquid Cosh*; this cosh is used on occasions by the staff to overpower and make someone submissive.

Charlie became very firm friends with my brother Ron for a number of years, first at Parkhurst and then later at Broadmoor. Charlie writes to me periodically from jail to jail. The last letter I received said he may be going back to Broadmoor because he had been charged with taking hostage three Iraqi terrorists. This was in Belmarsh prison. The letter had come from Wakefield, where he was being kept in solitary in what is known as the 'cage', a place where only very violent prisoners are held. He said that when he got to Broadmoor he would spend ten minutes in silence in my late brother Ron's old room, which has been left vacant since his death. He would do this out of respect for Ron, who had been his friend.

There is much more I could say about Mick Petersen, alias Charlie Bronson, but there is not enough time to write it all. His name will remain part of prison folklore, but as Charlie will tell kids who are tempted to follow his example, it has been a very costly and painful path.

I met Billy Clarke from south London at Gartree. He had been convicted of the murder of a well-known underworld figure, Henry Bottoms, who was killed on his doorstep by a shotgun blast. He was shot by a young friend of Clarke's and although Billy didn't pull the trigger he was convicted because it was claimed he put the contract out. I got on reasonably well with Billy Clarke. We worked together pushing the barrow round Gartree picking up the rubbish. I also met his wife, a nurse, a couple of times on visits and held their son Billy in my arms.

Others at Gartree included Jimmy Brown and Kevin Rusko. Jimmy later got home leave from another jail and didn't return. He went to live in Spain. I met him again in Maidstone jail. He was one of the old school. I was also to meet Kevin Rusko again, in Nottingham. He had ice-cold blue eyes which used to freak people out.

Someone else I met briefly at Gartree was Jeremy Bamber, who blasted his sister Bambi to death along with her two children and his adoptive parents at their farmhouse in Essex, for the £500,000 inheritance.

There was a well-known inmate at Gartree by the name of Stevens. He was involved, along with others, in an escape plot from C wing. They had sawed through the bars in a cell and then camouflaged them so they looked intact during searches. Eventually, the little group were ready to seek freedom. But on this day, for some unknown reason, Stevens went to the staff office and held up his hands to the would-be escape. Some claimed he also named the rest of the group but I don't know the full facts on this so I will make no comment. I did know, through various conversations, that his sentence had cracked him up mentally. Although it's not excusable that he declared all, prison can affect some more than others so I guess one could have pity for him. Before he went to that office he was known as a sound man.

Sometimes the past has a way of following a person. When I was in Shepton Mallet Army Prison at the age of eighteen I had an argument with another soldier-prisoner. He was about six feet three. We had a fight and I hit him on the chin. When he fell to the floor I got him by the hair and rammed his face into my knee. One day in Gartree, some thirty-odd years later,

I was walking down the staircase and who should be coming up but this bloke! We were both walking in the centre of the stairs. He said, 'I bet you don't remember my name.' But I did and I gave it to him in a split-second. Thereafter we became friends!

In the two years that I was there I would continually walk the wing corridor each evening looking for a reasonable screw who would let me use the office phone so I could contact friends. On the law of averages I did reasonably well. At this time public phones for inmates had not yet been introduced and as I didn't watch television I found using the phone was a better way to spend my time.

There were many grasses in Gartree among the cons. They didn't even bother to try to conceal the fact, talking blatantly to screws on the landings and in the office. That's how prisons are today. Some time ago a Governor put forward a proposal to the Home Office suggesting an integration programme be introduced in all prisons, to help prevent escapes and riots. Those who would normally be separated from other inmates due to the disgusting nature of their crimes (rapists, child-murderers, etc.) are sometimes placed on the main wings where they can provide the staff with information. In effect they are there to police the prison in much the same way as the staff, and undoubtedly gain themselves many privileges along the way. I believe this is morally wrong – but I found out years ago that prisons aren't run on morals.

In the early weeks of 1989 there was some good news. After twenty-one years in the dispersal system I was told I would be moving to a Category B prison. This was due to take place in February. My thoughts were a mixture of anxiety and joy. It was hard having to wait but the move was a first step towards eventual release. As February approached I packed all my possessions in preparation and sent them to the prison reception. Then I was told I would not be moving until March. March came and went and the proposed date changed to mid-April. It felt like mental cruelty. All lifers entering Category B are told well in advance when they'll be moving and the date of departure is rarely changed. I was the exception. While other lifers were being moved, without delay, I was left to wait. Finally, it was confirmed that I'd be leaving on 19 April. My new home was to be Lewes in Sussex.

CHAPTER NINE

LEWES

1989–1990

I arrived at Lewes at 3.45 p.m. Compared to Gartree, everything seemed very slow and sleepy. It didn't take me long to settle into a new routine. The day started when a bell was rung at ten to eight and I would go straight to the showers as soon as the door was open. Then I would slop out and tidy my cell. After that I'd fill my flask for a cup of tea and go to collect breakfast. My cell was quite large with big windows; it was painted in pale blue and white. I had photographs around the walls, of my mother and father, my beautiful late wife Frances and my brother Ron. I would work in the mornings, have lunch, and read my mail during the midday lock-up. In the afternoon I'd go to the gym for three-quarters of an hour, do light weights, go on the punch-bag and do sit-ups. I'd have another shower after this. Afternoon exercise was for forty-five minutes; we went out into the compound and walked around or lay in the sun if it was hot. Tea was served at 4.30 p.m. and we were locked up again from 5 p.m. until 6.10 p.m. In the evenings I would sometimes wander round the other cells and chat with friends. At 8 p.m. I'd bang up for the night and would usually be asleep by about nine o'clock. I'd wake again in the early hours of the morning, perhaps at 3 a.m. or 4 a.m. and start my letter-writing.

I met some people at Lewes whom I had known previously at Parkhurst. One of these was Bob Maynard, who had been convicted of the 'Torso' murder. This was the case where they had found a head in the toilet of a public house. Bob and his co-defendant Reg Dudley have always denied this murder. In fact each Christmas Bob Maynard would go to the block as a way of protesting his innocence. I first met Bob Maynard in my early twenties when I went to a party in Finsbury Park. I believe that, like Raphael Rowe, Bob Maynard and Reg Dudley are innocent and were wrongly convicted.

John Hilton was also at Lewes. A few months later he went to Kingston prison from where he escaped. He was recaptured and owned up to a murder he had committed in the 1960s. As he was already serving a life sentence for murder, he got another one and the judge said he was never to be released. I read in the newspaper that John Hilton said during his trial that he had met me once at Lewes and that I was afraid of him. I could not understand this because I'd only spoken to him twice, very briefly, about nothing in particular, and I have never been afraid of anyone. I inquired about this report when I spoke to Billy Gentry, who knew Hilton. Billy had just come to Lewes on accumulated visits and he told me that Hilton had said this to help a friend who was also charged with him in the same dock. This enlightened me somewhat and I understood the reason why. There is usually more behind headlines or articles in the newspapers than the reader knows about. This was the first time I'd seen Billy Gentry in years, since we were together at Parkhurst. Ron and I had sold him the El Morocco club in Gerrard Street in 1964.

John Williams was also at Lewes. He came from Nigeria and had been a legionnaire for some time until he became active in crime. We used to have parties together and he told me his father was a tribal chief. John Williams was a positive person who resided in Brighton on the outside. While he was in Lewes he wrote a book and this was broadcast on Radio 4's 'Book at Bedtime'. The book was titled *On Wings and Landings*. I remarked to John that he had a majestic profile which could help him in the future film career he was hoping for. This was not patronizing, because John did have a good profile. He was a likeable person and I received mail from him in later years.

During exercise periods I would walk the yard where there were two volleyball posts, one at each end of the yard. Between walking, on exercise periods, I would do sets of pull-ups from the posts which helped keep me fit. Frank Fraser's son David also did different exercises, press-ups, touching toes or whatever during this association time. David and I occasionally had a chat together.

I met a fellow called Dougie Lard, who was part Indian though he was born in the East End of London. One day he complained to me about a bad shoulder due to weightlifting. He hadn't been able to lift any weights since his injury. I told him to sit down, which he did, and I massaged his shoulder for about three minutes, directing the heat from my arms and hands to the injured area. I also said a short prayer for his benefit. Then I told him that his injury was better. He stood up and flexed his muscles and found to his amazement that the arm was OK and not impaired at all. Some time later he left Lewes to go to another prison and on his arrival the doctor said to him, 'I understand you had a shoulder injury and you have seen a specialist who can do nothing for you.' Dougie replied that his shoulder was now better and the doctor asked how this was possible. Dougie told him, 'Reg Kray cured my shoulder within three minutes.' The doctor said, in some anger, 'Don't be ridiculous, Lard.' But regardless of what the doctor said, the shoulder had been cured by means of faith healing. I have done this on five or six occasions with other inmates, working a cure on similar painful injuries. I can only believe that I've been blessed to a certain degree with the power of healing.

I used to freak Lard out because I could often tell him what he was going to say before he said it. One time I did a psychic on him and gave him a description of a woman who was causing problems between Dougie and his wife. It was his mother-in-law. This caused great humour because from this point on Dougie was always afraid of coming into my company, in case I foretold any future disasters. Many years later he wrote to me. He had been released but was once again back at the old resort of HMP Wandsworth.

One night as I was standing outside my cell in the passage-way near the office, I saw a new arrival enter the wing. It was about 6.30 p.m. The newcomer was around sixty-five years of age and his name was John Copley. I introduced myself to him and we shook hands. We struck up a friendship that remains in place even today. He was serving a life sentence for murder and had just come down from Wakefield jail. He was born in the north of England. John is one of the most knowledgeable men it has been my pleasure to meet. He has psychic powers which I had good reason to become very aware of. John had been to Canada, New York and other parts of the world; he had led a very diverse and interesting life. He is one of the most graphic writers of letters and writes in grand style. We had an occasional drink together, and he would sometimes bang-up early to escape to the peace and quiet of his cell. There he would write and meditate and recharge his batteries. John had also travelled the astral plane and I bore witness to this one time when he visited another inmate at Wormwood Scrubs. His name was Steven Gutteridge and he was about twenty-five years of age. When John told me he had visited I didn't put too much emphasis on it until, a few days later, I received a letter from Steven. He wrote, 'Reg, John Copley was with me last night. I actually saw him on the landing and so did one of my friends. Then he disappeared.' Steve went on to say, 'Do me a favour, Reg. Tell the old bastard not to visit me in such a manner!' When I read the letter I could see the humorous side of the story.

During my twenty-two-month stay in Lewes a number of inmates had the needle with John McVicar. They read in a newspaper article that he believed that those who took part in the riot at Strangeways should have been hosed down from the roof they were protesting on.

At lunch I used to stand at the hot-plate early before the other inmates arrived. Lewes prison was the most disrespectful type of environment I had been in and 90 per cent of the inmates jumped the queue in one mad mêlée. At this time of the morning young offenders who had been convicted or who were on remand used to file by the area and they would often seek me out to shake hands, ask for a signature or just make general conversation. One day a senior staff officer said to me, 'Stop shaking hands and talking to the inmates as they go by.' So I said in reply, 'That would be very difficult to do. If I did they would think it was very ignorant and also that I was snubbing them. It's not my wish to stop so I won't be doing so.' The next day a young inmate by the name of Jason Nicholls greeted me, shook my hand and conversed. He told me his name and I still remember it today. That same evening, just after being banged up at 8.30 p.m., my door was opened and one of the screws handed me a charge sheet and said something to the effect that I was being charged under Rule 47, that I did shake hands with and speak to another inmate when I had been told not to do so.

The following morning I went to the block where I was

placed in a cell to await the time of my adjudication, due to take place around 11 a.m. I appeared before one of the governors and after he had gone through the formalities of reading out the charge he asked me, as I had pleaded Not Guilty, what I had to say in my defence. I told him that I did not see it as legally or morally wrong to speak to another inmate and if any approached me in the passageway I'd do the same again. As far as I recall I was given a suspended sentence of seven days solitary confinement and had to pay a fine of £5 out of my canteen payments. I was paid about £7 a week for daily cleaning of the landing. I have been a professional cleaner, so to speak, all these years while in custody. I am looking forward to my retirement!

In the ensuing days I noticed that the young offenders were escorted past the hot-plate at a different time so they didn't come into contact with the older inmates. In the end this minor infringement was solved through compromise.

Somewhere among my many papers I still have the charge sheet of that day. Some years later I also received a letter from Jason Nicholls, who was by then free, and he seemed quite proud of the fact I had been nicked for shaking hands with him! This brought a smile to my face.

John Copley left Lewes to go to another jail. I received a letter from him which said, 'Your psychic aura is beginning to darken and you will soon be shifted without warning.' In prison terminology that meant I was going to be shanghaied. I went to see the Assistant Governor and told him of this psychic prophecy but the AG, who was a religious man, gave me his word that this would not happen. I was not reassured. I too am a little psychic at times; I felt I *was* going to be moved. A couple of days later I repeated my concerns to the AG and he said, in no uncertain terms, that it would not happen. Three days later, on a Friday morning, I noticed we were still locked up ten minutes after our usual time and so I was wary. I had good reason because, lo and behold, the door opened and standing there were about four screws and a senior member of staff, a Principal Officer (PO). The PO said, 'You're on the move.'

My instinct had already told me to pack a few personal possessions. I joined the escort out of Lewes prison although not before getting reassurance that the rest of my possessions would follow later. I was escorted to a waiting car which we cons call a 'taxi'. In the courtyard I spotted Dave Fraser in another taxi; he was also being shanghaied and we gave each other a wave. I knew that one day in the future I'd be able to relate this tale to Dave's old man Frank.

Before leaving my cell I had been handcuffed. Three screws and a driver were my company on the journey, which was to end, I was told, in Robin Hood's old territory – the city of Nottingham.

CHAPTER TEN

NOTTINGHAM
1990

We arrived in Nottingham later that day, in December 1990. I found out on my arrival that I'd been shipped out because of a gun scare. It was claimed that those in charge at Lewes had reason to believe I had smuggled a firearm into the prison and was planning an escape. These were totally ridiculous allegations. But I know from experience that the authorities are always more paranoid than the inmates and they are prone to shifting cons across the country on the flimsiest of evidence or reasoning. Probably it is sometimes done to remind the public of the wickedness of those held in custody – and such moves make good headlines and articles in the newspapers!

About teatime that first evening I became aware that both staff and inmates seemed to look at me with interest and curiosity. Periodically they requested signatures and asked me to sign photographs of their families. It was not until later that an inmate told me they had watched a film there the other night. It was called *The Krays*. It was only then that I realized why I was the centre of attraction, or otherwise, depending on who was looking at me.

I have often been asked about the film that was made about

Ron and me. So many different stories have circulated that I want to state the facts. We had *no* control over the script or cast. There were many inaccuracies – including the portrayal of my mother; she was a strong, quiet, dignified woman who *never* swore. Nothing is ever black and white. A film is only a personal interpretation of events.

The cell allocated to me on the ground floor was next door to a young inmate called Darren Horn, alias 'Basher'. The reason for this tag was his reputation as a fighter on the streets. He was short and thickset, in his early twenties. He told me he came from Northampton and we discovered we had some mutual friends from the area. I recall he gave me half a tub of Brylcreem when I ran out, and we had some good chats together. He was a likeable person and still writes from time to time. Unfortunately it's usually from different jails as he is always being convicted of assault. He and a London fellow had an argument beneath the showers and despite both being naked they battled away for some time. I was told it was a good fight although I personally didn't see it.

One of those who came to my cell to have photographs signed was a small, wiry kid who came from Nottingham. His name was Paul Marcus Morgan. He asked me to sign a photograph of his mother, Ann; in fact he came down twice more that evening with similar requests. I said to him jokingly, 'I don't mind signing them but you're making a bit of a career of it.' He said, 'I'll give you some privacy now. I don't like the way they all look at you from the landing above.' I said to take no notice as I was used to it. Then he said a polite thanks and off he went. But we were to meet again. In fact I now consider him as part of my close family – but I will get to that later on.

I also met a big pleasant fellow by the name of Aylen. He was serving a twelve-year sentence for firearms and I would sometimes go to his cell, which was on a side wing off the main spur, and have a chat. We became good friends. Sad to say, a few years later, when he had been released, he died of a brain haemorrhage.

One of the people who visited me at Nottingham was my friend Alan Mackay, the jockey. He would give me racing tips that I passed on to others because I'm not a gambler, although during the sixties Ron and I ran gambling clubs.

On reflection I believe that the authorities shifted me to Nottingham because I am from the south and they didn't think I'd like my stay there. But I came to enjoy it and struck up friendships with many people from the city of Nottingham.

I had only been there for a couple of weeks when one lunchtime I was in my cell getting ready to go to the gym for a work-out. I had just read a number of letters I'd received, but I'd not read them properly. There was one from John Copley and I read it again. It was a good job I did. He said, 'Pack your kit, Reg, you will be shanghaied in a hurry.' I thought about it and seeing as John's prophecy had come true at Lewes I felt I had to act. I rang the cell bell, as we were still locked up for lunch, and asked to see security. The screw said I couldn't see security but could see the Governor in his office. He left the door open so I went next door to Darren Horn's cell, which had just been opened. I told Darren there was a possibility I was going to be shifted and would he tell the people on the 2s landing whom I wanted to keep in touch with. Darren said he'd do this but he looked at me as if he thought I was being paranoid. I told Darren I'd keep in touch with him too if I was shifted.

I went to the Governor's office, which was in a separate corridor, and he welcomed me and asked me to sit down. He was a reasonable man and I told him of my concern over the letter. He said to me, 'That's strange. I've just had a call from Lifers Division at the Home Office. You're going to be shifted to Gartree in the next five minutes.' I asked if I could make a phone-call to my friend Pete Gillett to let him know I'd be leaving. The governor gave his consent and I made the call; Pete was upset to hear I was being moved in such a hurry.

After the phone-call permission was given for me to return to the wing and collect my belongings. Before going I asked the Governor, 'Can you tell me why I'm being shifted so quickly, after I've just arrived?' He replied, 'Someone phoned through to the Home Office and said you were involved in an escape plot.' Whether they had given the information any credence or not, it had been decided to move me to another area. I said to the Governor, 'It seems ridiculous that anyone can make a phone-call and get me shifted.' The Governor said he sympathized with my predicament but there was nothing he could do. He had to follow instructions from the Home Office. He said, 'It's nothing personal.' I accepted this, shook his hand and then departed from the office. I went back to my cell and packed my personal belongings, then I said goodbye to Darren Horn, who was waiting outside the door.

CHAPTER ELEVEN

GARTREE II

1990–1991

The escort accompanied me to the van. I was on my way back to Gartree, where I had already spent two years. On the journey I contemplated how I was being shifted back into the dispersal system; this is very rare for a con once he has left it.

When we arrived I was allocated a cell on the second floor. Almost opposite was my old friend Kevin Rusko. He told me that all the cons were on strike from work, protesting about the bad food, and would be refusing to go back to their cells at evening lock-up time. I thought about this and decided that I would compromise by keeping out of my cell for half an hour at lock-up – then I would bang-up. I felt this was showing my solidarity with the cons but at the same time I had to do my own thing. I hadn't had the chance to decide if the food was good, bad or indifferent, and I always like to make my own decisions and not be a sheep.

Paddy Hill, one of the Birmingham Six, was to the left of me on another spur. Charlie McGee was also in the prison, as was Dave McAllister. Charlie was to die of a heart attack some time later in Whitemoor prison. He had been sentenced to life for shooting dead a copper, a different sentence to the one he'd been on when I first met him in Parkhurst. He had spent some of the time between living in Spain.

I had only been at Gartree for a short period of time when I was told that a PO and one of his staff were coming to see me from Lewes. They wanted to interview me about my move from that prison and to let me know the results of an inquiry about the allegations that I had smuggled a gun into Lewes.

A few days later I was shown to a side office and sat in the presence of the senior officer and one of his staff. They informed me that after extensive inquiries I had been exonerated from all allegations. But, they added, having told you the good news, we now wish to pursue inquiries into a claim that one of the prison staff at Lewes was bringing in bottles of gin and Scotch which he was selling to the inmates. It had been said that I was one of a number who had participated in some of the parties where the illicit drink had been consumed. If I could name the member of staff who supplied the drink anything I said would be confidential, and they in turn would return the favour.

I listened with amusement and said in response that I had participated in hooch parties but that I had 'never, ever seen bottles of gin or Scotch, much to my regret', so I could be of no help.

In many ways they seemed more serious about illicit alcohol than they did about allegations of firearms. I was caught between the two. They told me that I would be returning to Nottingham prison and that made me quite happy.

I do feel, on reflection, that when I went back into the dispersal system from Nottingham to Gartree, there were some who thought it would shatter me. But at the time of returning to Gartree I had made up my mind to enjoy myself and make the best of a bad deal. This seemed to work in practice as I had a reasonably good time. I spent four months there and when I returned to Nottingham I was back among familiar faces and old friends. My stay was going to be quite interesting.

CHAPTER TWELVE

NOTTINGHAM II AND LEICESTER II
1991–1992

I arrived back at Nottingham in the afternoon to familiar surroundings.

I should mention that at Nottingham there was a reasonably sized open-air swimming pool which I had the pleasure of testing out. There was also a small courtyard with handball posts and so I was able to do my pull-ups once more. I would watch football at weekends with my friends; these games were played with inmates on one side and visiting teams from the outside on the other. One time there was a brilliant young black lad from outside and though I never found out his name I'm sure he will go places as a footballer.

Nottingham jail also had a good library, where I would go each morning to read the daily papers. The food was reasonable and there was a good canteen, where we could spend up to £30 a week private cash if one was lucky enough to have it. We were also able to spend our wage at the canteen. We were paid weekly for our jobs. My job was as a cleaner on the ground floor and the showers which were nearby.

There were four landings at Nottingham and it was an old building with lots of character which I prefer to modern prisons. The visiting-room was small and cosy and the staff were reasonable. I found the inmates very interesting. Among those present I spotted my old friend Paul Marcus Morgan, who was on the 4s landing. Mick Ahmed was also on the 4s, and nearby were Ian Monroe and Kevin Rusko, and of course my old friend Harry Roberts. Just after my arrival Blaine Lodgston arrived. I recalled that he had written to me from another jail and in my reply I suggested that he try to get to Nottingham. Blaine was from Manchester and was serving five years. He was a pro-fighter and just before his conviction he had been number 10 in the world ratings at light heavyweight. He had sparred with the legendary Carlos Durane. Blaine and I became firm friends.

I had a ground-floor cell which was very large. It was actually a double cell and so I had plenty of room as the only occupant. One Friday night I was wandering from landing to landing and I fancied a drink. I entered a cell that was situated in the middle of the 4s landing. Paul Marcus Morgan was sitting there with three or four others and lo and behold he invited me to join in a drink of hooch – which made my night. I remembered this gesture of Paul's and returned the compliment when I arranged for some hooch to be taken to the same cell on another night, much to their delight. The following day Paul visited my cell and during a discussion it turned out that he was doubled up with someone who was driving him crackers with his incessant chatter. Paul said it was doing his head in. I suggested to Paul that he get permission to vacate his present cell and share mine instead. This he did. Needless to say we got on like a house on fire.

I got to know Paul well and vice versa. He had been brought up in Nottingham and told me he got his first sentence of five years when he was fifteen years of age. The judge said on sentencing him for robberies: 'You are the most criminally minded young man of your age that I have met, so I am sending you to prison because a juvenile custody will not do you any good.' Paul told me that he was only out for about eight months before he was sentenced to another five years.

Despite the fact he was in prison I found him to be a very intelligent and likeable person. Whenever we had a party he was the best dancer in the group and he was the best soul singer I've ever had the pleasure of hearing. He was also one of the fastest rap speakers I've ever heard. I decided to take him under my wing and do my best to help him and encourage him away from crime. Blaine and others would join us at these parties; we'd have as good a time as possible before bang-up.

Mick Ahmed and his Pakistani friends would often invite me to share their evening and they were good hosts. They prepared curried meals for us and sometimes we were fortunate enough to also share an occasional drink.

If the reader thinks that one truly lives the life of Riley in jail then I suggest they come and try prison life for themselves. It is not all fun, as the following story will show.

One day I was on a visit and in the same room was a man called Bernie Glennon, an old friend of mine from Parkhurst. He was serving a life sentence for murder and had already done a fairly long stretch. Bernie had a handlebar moustache and was from the north of England. He was in his early thirties and proud of the biceps and triceps he had built up at weightlifting sessions. He wouldn't take any stick from the screws. In fact he had just come to Nottingham after having been on a lay-down at another jail for assaulting a screw. In return they had beaten him up severely.

I was speaking to him prior to the visit, and during the visit I glanced over and he seemed deep in thought. I thought he looked a little paranoid. When the visit finished I told Bernie to come round and see me after he was unlocked so I could have a chat with him. He said he would do so.

We were late unlocking. Shortly after, an inmate came to my cell and told me that Bernie Glennon had been found hanging from his bars. He was dead. I found out the following day that Bernie had agreed on a suicide pact with a fellow inmate who was also serving life. They shared a cell and had decided to kill themselves by use of hand-made ropes. Bernie's cell-mate had backed out of the pact during the last few seconds and had watched while Bernie jumped off the chair to end his life.

Bernie Glennon left all his personal possessions to me. I placed them in reception for safe-keeping after having sorted out the contents. I wrote a letter of condolence to his son, who was serving a sentence at another jail, and said I would make all the possessions available to him on his release.

This is the other extreme which may give food-for-thought to many of the preachers and do-gooders both within the system and outside. Prison life is not the television programme *Porridge*, all fun and humour.

One afternoon I was sitting in my cell writing when a knock came at the door and Nigel Benn, the ex-middleweight champion of the world, entered my cell. He was a middleweight contender at the time and six months away from a title shot. He was with Peter de Freitas, his manager, and his entourage. Nigel said he had come to see me. We shook hands and I found him to be a likeable person. We had photographs taken together and Nigel gave me a signed picture. In exchange I gave him a pair of signed punch-bag gloves which I had just received from Charlie Magri, the former flyweight world champion and a personal friend. Charlie also visited me during my stay at Nottingham.

Another time Kevin Rusko came to visit Paul and me in our cell. He was in a bad frame of mind, unhappy that the screws had spoiled his visit for some reason or other. After he left he was talking to people outside the cell. I noticed he had a stick in the waistband of his jeans. He seemed very agitated. I said to Paul, who was my first concern, 'Stay with me. I think it's going to go off.' I was right. Kevin went to the main office and started beating the table top with the stick and shouting loudly. Then the screws got round him and there was a general mêlée of struggling arms and legs. Paul and I were near the office at the time as we followed Kevin. Other cons started banging the plastic windows of the office and kicking the panels of the walls and door. Kevin managed to break free and came out in a rush. I grabbed his arm and pulled him towards my cell. I ushered Paul in and pulled Kevin in after me. I then shut the door quickly. The cons and screws, who had followed in a mixed group, were shouting outside. I said to Kevin, 'You will have to go to the block, voluntary or otherwise. I suggest you go voluntarily and I will go with you to make sure you don't get a kicking.' Paul was wiping the sweat from Kevin's forehead and there were bruises on Kevin's neck. Paul made him a quick cup of tea and Kevin said he would go to the block but wanted to go upstairs first to his cell on the 4s landing to pick up his radio, soap, toothbrush and towel. So I rang the cell bell and when the screw came to the slit in the door I told him that Kevin wanted to collect his stuff and would then go to the block voluntarily. This defused the possibility of a riot. We went upstairs via the iron staircase adjoined to each landing. All the cons were standing on the landings and leaning over the rails asking us what they should do. I kept repeating that Kevin wanted to cool it and go to the block. He picked up his things and we went back downstairs. I walked with Kevin towards the chokey block and the screws gave me their word they would not harm Kevin. They said it was not necessary for me to go to the block with him. Kevin went before the Governor the next day and he received as punishment three days down the block and was then returned to the wing. It all ended well, but it could have been otherwise. The possibility of a riot had been defused. My part in this was only for Kevin's sake.

I get many letters each day from people from all walks of life, so of course some wrote to me at Nottingham. It was on the television, in newspapers and on the local radio that I was back. One letter I received was from Bob Manito. I first met Bob when I boxed him and beat him on points in my first pro fight at Mile End Arena in the East End of London when I was seventeen years of age. He told me he was now training kids at a boxing club in Kent. Another letter I received came from Archie Hall, alias The Butler, who was born in Edinburgh and was serving a life sentence for the murder of his employers, ex-MP Walter Scott Elliot and his wife Dorothy. When he was freed from that life sentence he murdered his brother and his brother's girlfriend and another man. I met him briefly at Parkhurst many years back.

One afternoon Paul and I went to collect our tea at the servery and on the way there two inmates passed us and made a detrimental remark directed at Paul. I didn't hear it but I noticed Paul's expression and asked him what was wrong. He said, 'Them two bastards walking by took the piss out of me. I'll see them later.' So I said we would talk about it. We collected our tea and went back to the cell. Paul said, after putting his tea down, 'I won't be a minute.' I mistakenly thought he had gone to use the recess next door. He came back after about ten minutes and entered very fast with one of the piss-takers following him. As they came in Paul pushed the door almost shut and then hit the fellow about five times on the chin. The fellow was shaken and dazed so I grabbed him by the scruff of the neck and shoved him out of the door. I said, 'Fuck off and don't come back.' I asked Paul why the fellow had followed him down. Paul said, 'I went up to the 2s landing but there were three of them in the cell so I told the biggest one I wanted to see him down here.' He added, 'I thought three might be too many so it was best to get one down here.' I laughed and said, 'Good thinking Paul, discretion being the better part of valour.'

John Dunsford, whom I met at Gartree, also arrived back at Nottingham a week after me. I introduced him to a female pen-pal and they struck up a relationship. John was serving seventeen years and told me that he and his girlfriend planned to get married soon and the wedding would take place at Nottingham. He asked me if I would agree to be a guest and I accepted the invitation. I told John that I would arrange his suit as well as one for myself so that we could look smart on the day. I phoned a tailor, a friend of mine called Barry Scott, and he and his manager agreed to come to the jail and measure us up. At my request they also brought shoes, shirts, socks, underwear and top-pocket handkerchiefs. But just before the wedding I was called up in front of the Governor, who said security would prefer me not to attend the wedding as it would entail too much work. I was going to argue the point but decided otherwise because John was up for parole and I didn't want anything to complicate his wedding. I agreed to step aside and forgo the invitation. Maybe I should start a lonely-hearts club because I have introduced about six inmates to their future wives.

One evening John Dunsford came into our cell and told us he had had an argument with a black fellow. As he was talking this fellow also came into the cell without knocking and proceeded to argue with John. I interceded and said, 'You should have finished the argument upstairs and when you enter my cell you should knock first, so both of you go outside and finish the argument.' But the fellow just carried on waving his arms about and shouting. I told him one more time to get out but he just continued. So I hit him a couple of times with right-hand punches and scruffed him tightly by the neck. As I did so Dunsford slung a punch at the fellow but I got in the way of it. I said to John, 'You're a bit after time, now both of you get out of my cell and sort it out.'

A couple of days later the black fellow and I shook hands when he agreed he had been in the wrong.

Myself, Paul and another fellow would sometimes go to the video room, which was even smaller than a cell and adjoined the classrooms. We would watch classic video films that I had sent in by friends from outside. We enjoyed such films as *Jolson Sings Again*, *The Jolson Story*, *Gordon of Khartoum*, *Lawrence of Arabia*, *The Treasure of the Sierra Madre*, and many others.

One night Paul and I were having a cup of tea and a chat after lock-up when Paul said he could smell burning. He went to the door and stood on a chair to look through a crack. There was a scuffling of feet nearby and Paul said, 'The fire brigade are running about with long hose pipes to the cell on the right.' They were trying to jack a cell door off, which they finally managed to do. By this time I was also up on the chair being nosy watching the activity. It transpired that one of the cons who was a bit mixed up had set his cell on fire in a suicide bid, but members of the Fire Brigade successfully got him out and saved his life. The following day some spoke about it and said the event had brightened the night up.

A woman friend whom I only knew by letter arranged to see me on a visit. After the visit all seemed well but the following morning, very early, I was summoned to the Governor's office, which was in an adjacent passageway off the wing. The Governor said there were two Nottingham detectives who wished to see me. I said I had no wish to see them but he advised me to do so as the lady friend who had visited the day before had been in possession of a firearm. I quickly decided I should meet them; I knew nothing of this and did not wish to get shifted again. I said to the Governor, 'What time do I see them?' He replied that they were in the next office waiting, so I agreed but asked to call another inmate as a witness which I was allowed to do.

I went to the door overlooking my wing and called over the first inmate I set eyes on. I thought I had selected a sound person because Bonzo, another inmate from the East End, had said that this particular person was so during a discussion some weeks back.

The sound one and I sat down with the two detectives and one of them stated, 'Do you know your lady friend was found in possession of a firearm?' I said that was ridiculous. Then the senior detective produced from his jacket pocket what I thought was an automatic firearm. He asked if I had ever seen it before and I said, 'Never.' He said my lady friend had it in her handbag. I asked, 'Why didn't the screws take it off her and arrest her before she entered the visiting-room then?' He replied, 'I was just testing your reactions because this is an imitation firearm cigarette lighter and though the staff knew it was in her handbag they were watching you to see if you were involved in an escape plot.' I said, 'If you check with one of the staff (whose name I gave him) you will know that I've never met this lady before yesterday. In fact the particular screw I just mentioned checked her phone number out for me and he'll be able to verify everything I say.' The detective responded, 'We don't think, after having seen your reactions, that you were part of any plot but we'll have to check with the Home Office to see how they evaluate the situation.' I asked if it was likely they'd move me to another prison due to this unforeseen incident. He said the Governor would let me know tomorrow. I waited twenty-four hours to find out. The Governor told me they accepted my story and I would not be shifted. They had also questioned Diane, who came from Nottingham and ran a clothes shop. They were satisfied that there was nothing suspicious.

It was not quite the end of the story because I was later to find out that the inmate who I was told was a sound fellow, and who was my witness, had actually battered his six-year-old son to death with a billiard cue. It was one more lesson in the so-called credibility of some in jail. I should have known better but I didn't get much time to check him out. It was just another case of sound as a bell, salt of the earth, the terminology used on a daily basis by most inmates when they vouch for someone they know little about.

The church in the jail was quite beautiful and I was given a job cleaning it out, on top of the job of cleaning the passage area and the showers. I would visit the church occasionally and at the end of the service I would enjoy a chat over tea and biscuits and meet students and other people from outside who were visiting on the day.

One time I lost a bracelet that young Brad had given me – Brad being a kid from Doncaster who visited me with his mother, Kim. I put out a £100 reward to anyone who found and returned the bracelet, which had fallen off due to a weak clasp. A foreign fellow finally returned it to me saying he had found it in the passage. I was pleased. Money speaks all languages.

My friend Tony Burns, whom I have known since he was twelve years of age and who is now the boxing coach at the Repton Youth Club, visited me. Tony was a top-class amateur fighter who represented England and Wales; he would have made a good professional but preferred to stay amateur. In my opinion he is the best boxing coach in the country.

Ian Monroe, who used to do tattoos for the other cons on their arms and bodies and was an excellent tattooist, was another who created interest at Nottingham. There was also Harry Roberts, who made wooden jewellery boxes that were works of art; they had coloured pictures on them, usually of a canal with a barge.

One evening after we were locked up Paul and I had an argument. He was sitting to the left and I was on the right when Paul, in his anger, slung a honey jar at me. It caught me on the left eyebrow and split it. As soon as it hit me I pretended to be hurt, although I wasn't, and acted by covering my left eye with both my hands as though I was in pain. Blood began to seep down my face and Paul was full of concern. I relaxed his concern by smiling at him and saying it was a good shot. This reminded me of the film *The Odd Couple*, which starred Walter Matthau and Jack Lemmon. Strangely enough Paul and I had watched this classic comedy on video a few weeks previously. One should remember that close people have arguments outside in society so it's understandable that, due to prison life, arguments also occur between close friends in prison. I saw the humorous side of this incident and stored it away in my memory bank.

But this was not the end of the story. When my eyebrow bled I had to ring the bell to see if it needed stitches. They weren't necessary and one of the medical staff covered the cut with a plaster. I thought no more of it and walked into Blaine's cell in the morning. When he spotted the plaster he asked how it happened. I told him as I saw no reason to lie, but Blaine took offence at what Paul had done and spoke as if he wanted to knock him out. Apart from a great weight difference and

Paul being part of my family, I explained to Blaine that if he respected me he would forget the matter – which he did. I could understand Blaine's attitude to a point but it was the end of the matter. It goes to show how situations can sometimes escalate in jail.

I had a pull-up bar in the cell which I had rigged up and I would do pull-ups there as well as on the yard. I had also hung a table-tennis ball from the light fixture; it hung from bootlaces, the ball having had a hole made in it with a needle. I would use this as a punch-ball and make it rebound in angles from the ceiling. I have used this method to keep fit in other jails.

One day my instinct made me uneasy and I said to Paul, 'Something tells me I'm going to get shifted, and this feeling won't leave me.' After lunch, when we had been banged-up for the usual hour period, and I was lying on my bed and Paul was sitting on his listening to the radio, the door opened and a woman Assistant Governor along with two screws came into the cell and said, 'We want you to come down the block with us.' I asked, 'Am I being shifted again?' The answer was yes. I asked where I was going but they said they didn't know and I would be told in the block. So once again my instinct turned out to be correct, much to my regret. I shook hands with Paul and told him not to worry as I would keep in touch and so would not be far away.

When I got to the block the AG told me that, because of escape suspicions, it had been decided to send me to Leicester prison in Welford Road. I was going under the rule of 'Good order and discipline'.

I arrived at Leicester jail and was taken to the block where I was allowed to make a phone-call to a friend to give my new address. Back in my cell I wrote to Paul and others. On the third day of being locked up for twenty-three hours I was told I could go and join those in the main prison. I said I preferred to stay where I was, as I was quite happy on my own and was fed up with being shifted from jail to jail without reason. But eventually that day I agreed to go on to the main prison.

Unless one has been separated the way I have from close friends during my time in jail it may be difficult to comprehend the terrible feeling of loneliness that comes about from having to leave without forewarning. There is hardly time to say farewell. And then one is taken to a new but similar environment, to a cold bare cell, and left alone with thoughts of those you have departed from. It brings about a sense of loss. I didn't know when I would meet my friends again.

I was placed in a cell on the 2s landing of this old building and was made very welcome by the inmates. They were aware I had arrived because the media had once again made news of it. Because it was a local jail there were not many serving long sentences and some of the inmates were just on remand. As a result I was treated like I was Billy the Kid, and inmates and screws were at my door constantly during the three weeks or so I was there. They came to ask for my autograph or to have various books, written by myself or by others about me, signed.

I enjoyed my stay and found it very interesting, and I enjoyed meeting so many new acquaintances. The staff were reasonable and friendly and the visiting-room was OK, although usually packed. There was just a small courtyard for exercise periods; nearby I could see the security block where I had spent twelve months many years ago. I found some of those on remand interesting because they were fresh from the street. As usual I met a minority who I had previously met in other jails. The food was reasonable and I didn't go short of anything whilst there.

Just as I was beginning to get used to the place the Governor called me up and said it was time for a transfer.

CHAPTER THIRTEEN

BLUNDESTON
1992–1994

In February 1992 the Governor told me I had been allocated to Blundeston prison in Suffolk. I said to him, 'I'm not keen on going there.' He replied, 'You've not got much choice, it's either Blundeston or Dartmoor.' I said I would think about it. He told me I had forty-eight hours.

This was on a Monday morning. I returned on the Wednesday when the Governor had arranged to see me again. He said there could be no deal – it had to be one or the other. So, with little choice, I accepted Blundeston. I left Leicester a few days later.

It was a quick journey by van with an escort and I arrived at Blundeston just before lunch. In the reception area I met Ron Stevens, who years before had frequented the Double R, one of the clubs that belonged to me and my brothers. Ron was serving a long sentence.

Reception was outside the wire compound that surrounded the jail, and after my luggage had been sorted out it was put on a trolley which I pulled down to the courtyard. The wire gate was opened and, along with one of the screws, I entered the main prison. It was a new building with a football field in front of it.

When I got to the allocated wing a couple of cons helped me carry my baggage on to the second floor of the three-storey building. This was to be my home for the next two years.

It was a reasonable jail although the gym was disappointing; there was no punch-bag or punch-ball and the PTIs seemed to have a liking only for weightlifting, football and football. I did use the gym but also did yoga and dynamic tension in my own cell. This was one of the few jails where I kept my cell pretty basic because I wanted to make it clear that I had no wish to stay there any longer than was necessary.

Blundeston turned out to be the most violent jail, other than Parkhurst, I had been in.

Pat Claydon arrived a short time after me. Pat was a good amateur fighter and had fought in the States as well as in Britain. His brother John, whom I met when he visited Pat, had fought for a title at welter-weight and been unlucky to lose. Tony Argent from Canning Town was also there. He was well-built, tall, fit and strong and he could have a fight.

There were a few scousers and a Welsh fellow called Simon Melia. He ended up marrying Lady Alice Douglas, who used to teach drama classes at the prison. I was present one evening at a play put on by Lady Alice, and afterwards Simon Melia, who was acting in the production, asked me to have a photograph taken with them. The photograph was syndicated across the media for the following day along with an article about Lady Alice. She was a very attractive person and one of the nicest people it has been my pleasure to meet. She received some very bad press for marrying an inmate. I believe that some of her family frowned upon the marriage – but I suppose it's right to say that love has no boundaries. I met Lady Alice again about three years later when I was at Maidstone prison and we still remain friends. She is a good woman.

During the time I was with Simon at Blundeston and again

in later years at Maidstone I found him to be a likeable fellow. It was his quest to be an actor. Simon could look after himself; I recall he knocked someone out during his time at Blundeston.

There was excitement on the field one day when Jimmy McGinley had a row and pulled a big blade. A group were trying to take the blade from him. One of his adversaries ran from the side of the field and kicked his feet from under him, but he still retained the knife. A screw eventually persuaded Jimmy to hand over the weapon.

At the time I was watching from my window because this particular morning I had not gone out on the field but had heard the commotion. There were racial problems between blacks and whites and on at least three occasions I had interceded as peacemaker because I didn't wish to see friends from either side in trouble. These arguments ended peacefully but could have ended in violence.

I met a fellow who *always* carried a biro around with him. When I asked him why, he said it was to use as a weapon. If necessary he would stick it in someone's eye then twist it until the point hit the brain. In this way he would be able to kill an enemy. He was not at all a prolific writer – he was almost seventy years of age!

There was also a kid in Blundeston by the name of Kevin who ended up marrying a woman I introduced him to. He could have had a good career in films but despite all the help I gave him through introductions on visits he failed to rise to the occasion. I understand his marriage later ended in divorce. There used to be weightlifting competitions in the gym. Kevin, who was powerfully built, won a couple of power-lifting competitions. Although I helped him considerably, both in and out of jail, he didn't even send me a card when he was released. I have accepted this as part of prison life. A lot of the inmates one meets have no depth.

I came off the field early one afternoon and the Principal Officer (PO) said that George John Gray had robbed the canteen while wielding a large knife. He had taken tobacco and other stuff, and had then run off to barricade himself in his cell on the second landing. This was two cells away from mine on the opposite landing. The PO asked if I would talk to Gray and see if I could get him to surrender as Gray was also threatening to cut his own throat. I said I would see what I could do. I decided to help Gray because at one time he used to run about for me, but this had stopped when I found out he was a junkie. I still felt reasonably sorry for him; one time he had put me on the phone to his mother, and I had feelings for all mothers. So I went to his cell door and talked to him. I pointed out that he would not get a kicking by the screws in retaliation because they were reasonable at Blundeston. He eventually handed the knife over.

This episode appeared in the press when Gray went to court some time later. I wish to point out that though I was asked to give evidence for the prosecution I refused, pointing out that I would not even appear if subpoenaed. I had also spoken to Gray's counsel; we agreed amicably that it would not be in Gray's favour if I was to appear for the defence as this would just highlight the case. I had no ulterior motive when I went to Gray's cell other than to help him, and I am quite satisfied that I did so.

I was summoned to the office one afternoon and told there was a message from my friend Steph King that my old friend Harry Hate-'Em-All Johnson was to undergo a heart operation in Derby. He was suffering from angina. I arranged with the padre to phone the hospital that day to speak with Harry but, sad to say, Harry died on the operating table before I could talk to him. For reasons beyond my control the phone-call was too late.

I thought about Harry and felt so sad, not only because of his early death at the age of forty-six but because he had spent so little time in the outside world. Like his old friend Charlie Bronson, Harry was part of prison folklore. They both found their notoriety to be very costly. I like to think that Harry, wherever he might be, would be pleased to know that he is mentioned more than once in my story and that my mentions will establish his position in the folklore of prison.

Geoff Reynolds was another likeable person but he had a trait in his make-up that made him aggressive after drinking. Geoff liked a drink of hooch but often ended up spoiling his night after he banged-up. At Blundeston there were no toilets in the cells and Geoff would press the night sanitation unit which was used to let the inmates out. He would go to the end of the spur and knock out or break all the windows by punching them. Geoff would end up down the block the following morning regretting his sins of the night before, not of drinking but of its inevitable consequence – the punishment that followed. Whenever he broke the windows he would lacerate his hands. He was a glutton for punishment, not just in a physical sense but also because each time he received twenty-eight days loss of remission. I warned Geoff that he would get shipped out because of such stupid behaviour but he didn't take my advice.

Once Geoff had a good straight fight with a young Scouse fellow called Ginger. The fight took place on a spur of the wing and lasted for about ten minutes. I watched and if I'd have been the referee I would have called it a draw, though Geoff did end up with concussion as a result of taking a head-butt to the face. Geoff was physically strong and used to do weightlift training. He would help me address envelopes for some of the letters I wrote and in doing so sorted out a few of my pen-friends for himself. He was a bit of a ladies' man and I would gee him up by pointing out he had blue eyes like Frank Sinatra!

One night he and a Brummie called Dave got drunk. They both wedged up in his cell and refused to come out. They were hurling abuse at the screws on the other side of the door. As a result they were both shipped out to another jail the following day.

Geoff ended up in Whitemoor prison along with my best friend Bradley Allardyce, whom at this time I was yet to meet. Some years later Geoff arrived at Maidstone prison, where he spent some time with me before his eventual release. But I'm jumping ahead in the story a bit. I'll stop now and get back to the days at Blundeston.

Spence St Pierre was a tall, blond, young fellow. He was well built and used the gym regularly to keep fit. One day he complained to me that he had a spinal injury and the doctor could do nothing about it. This stopped him from using the gym. I said to him, 'I reckon I could cure it with massage and prayer.' He agreed to let me try. I got him to lie on his stomach and I massaged around the spine and said a prayer. I isolated the warmth from the palms of my hands and directed it towards the problem area. I massaged and prayed for about ten minutes. My cure worked and Spence, who could move freely again, was very grateful.

I feel that this gift is something that I have been blessed with and that through it, to a small degree, I can act as a vehicle for the power of God.

Bill Bailey was a nice kid from the Liverpool area who worked in the kitchen. He would get me stuff such as cheese and eggs or whatever else he could get his hands on. I would look after him, making sure he had tobacco. Close by his cell was a burly con who tried to take a liberty with Bill early one morning. I came upon the scene and scruffed the fellow by the neck, slung him against the wall and butted him in the face. He left the jail a few days later when he went on the 'numbers', a term used for those going on Rule 43, to the block seeking protection. He was always shooting his mouth off about his army days and how he had knocked people about. Some years later Bill Bailey corresponded with me from Hornby Road, Liverpool prison.

About nine o'clock one evening, after I was locked-up for the night, I heard a commotion of screws outside the door opposite my cell. I could smell burning. Smoke was coming under my door which was heavy on the lungs. Myself and others went to our windows and shouted 'Fire!' and I breathed in the fresh air. A little while later the screws came and opened my door; they also unlocked the others on the spur. They told us to go to the TV room downstairs until the smoke died down. The burnt-out cell opposite was occupied by a junkie who was without heroin powder this particular night. The need had cracked him up. He had brandished a knife at screws, threatening to cut them unless he was given powder. His demands weren't met and in a rage he had set fire to his cell. Apart from putting his own life in danger, he was not doing the rest of the inmates or myself any favours either. We couldn't prevent the smoke going into our lungs. We were as pleased as the staff that we were minus this junkie for a neighbour. We sat in the TV room for a while and after about an hour we were asked to go back to our cells.

One of the priests who spoke at the chapel services in Blundeston gave some of the best sermons I have had the pleasure to hear. He had very clear diction and got on well with everyone. Some time later, after I had left Blundeston, I learnt that he had been asked to retire as a minister because he was suspected of bringing in contraband for some of the inmates. There was also a chaplain in his seventies who was well liked; his name was Donald Boyce. He would regularly visit me in my cell and we became friends. We discussed all manner of subjects. He was a kind-hearted man who often brought us bars of chocolate.

During a work-out in the gym I displaced a vertebra beneath my neck; this was very painful when I turned my head to the left or the right and prevented me from training for a while. I went sick and saw the doctor, who said he could do nothing and that maybe, in a few days, it would remedy itself. It didn't get any better and in fact began to feel even worse. Luckily someone above was on my side. During a conversation with an inmate I was told that a con on another wing was a healer, an osteopath-type person who was an excellent manipulator of bones and muscles. However, I'd have to get to see him straight away as he was leaving the jail the following day. I raced across to the other wing and my luck was in again when the screw there agreed to let me through to the 2s landing – the majority of screws wouldn't have allowed this.

Having found the healer, he invited me in to his cell and I explained about my injury. He said, 'Sit down and relax. I won't hurt you. It will only take a short time.' He placed his hands on the lower part of my neck and again he repeated, 'Relax.' He then massaged my neck for a minute. I felt his fingers moving gently around the affected area and then there was a slight click. He asked me to turn my head to the left and the right which I did and the movement was easy and free of any pain. I have been grateful to him ever since. I think his name was Williams and he came from south London.

Blundeston, as I've already mentioned, was a very violent jail. I witnessed a number of violent incidents. In my time I'd been involved in some. I didn't relish them. I mention them only to show what it is like in jail and perhaps to deter others from taking the same path.

A young Vietnamese immigrant had a fight on the field with another inmate. This took place behind the toilet area, convenient for fights as it was out of sight of the screws. The Vietnam kid's adversary wore a gauntlet-type glove used in the kitchen butchery area. Although the kid put up a good fight he was eventually knocked out and severely scarred due to the glove. This kid was reason for more talk later on when he tried to escape from a taxi taking him to hospital; he was finally shipped out to Parkhurst.

One day a young, rather cocky inmate arrived from Leicester. He was well built with blonde hair and blue eyes and told anyone who was prepared to listen that he was a karate expert. But it turned out he was no Bruce Lee – someone soon discovered he was a nonce case. About five inmates sealed off the area to the karate kid's spur and hooded themselves up. They cornered him close to his cell, placed a hood over his head and knocked him senseless with sticks and coshes. They also kicked out all his teeth. They continued to beat him until he lost consciousness. His face was lacerated with deep wounds from their steel toe-capped boots. Apart from the gashes he also had a broken nose, broken jaw and broken cheekbones. I saw him staggering along the passage on his way to the hospital.

A similar incident happened a short time later. Another new arrival came to Blundeston. He spoke to me just prior to a visit and he seemed OK. I learnt he was a lifer. After his visit he was sitting in his cell when some other inmates entered and attacked him with sticks. He suffered serious facial injuries and was drenched in his own blood. Despite being barely conscious, he managed to ring the bell in his cell and eventually, although without any haste, the screws arrived. His injuries were so bad he was taken to an outside hospital and stitched up. He was then shifted to another prison. It was later discovered that a mistake had been made and this lifer wasn't a sex case at all. He had been beaten for nothing. Unfortunately, this is one of the perils of prison life.

There was a scag (heroin) dealer at Blundeston who was in his middle fifties. He used to sell scag throughout the prison and take as much as he could for himself. It was well known to everyone. He was given home leave to see a relation who he claimed was ill and then, a short time after, he got his parole on a first application. To me this makes a mockery of the system which advocates against the use of drugs. This inmate was serving a sentence for possession and distribution. Yet at the other extreme I have known many cases of friends and associates who were refused parole; they were clean and respectable, did not participate in the taking of drugs and had everything going for them on the outside – a wife, a job offer, future prospects. It makes me wonder how these decisions are made. How can the parole board, probation, prison officers and padres conclude that a specimen like the scag merchant is more deserving of parole?

The inmates at Blundeston met in the passageway, which was named Bond Street due its length and all the activity that took place there – they would meet on the way to classes or to work.

Matt Spear, a lifer, was an interesting inmate. He used to make very good hooch. He had been on a number of charges for this but carried on regardless. It seemed to give him a buzz and lift him out of the day-to-day boredom. On the same subject, I can remember how in Nottingham an inmate by the name of Digger had constructed a type of pull-down drinking bar above the shelves in his cell. After the screws had been round on their regular searches he would lower the bar and we'd all have a drink!

I continued to take a cold shower every morning at Blundeston; as in most prisons there was never a queue. I found it invigorating and a good start to the day. I also started to study reflexology from books and this has helped both with physical problems and in relaxation over the years.

My brother Ron and I were still corresponding on a daily basis, keeping each other up-to-date on different matters. Ron told me that, through someone else, Michael Jackson had expressed a wish to visit him. A few days later I read of this in a national newspaper; the report seemed to stem from Michael Jackson's public relations department.

I received lots of interesting letters from old and new friends. One old friend I would particularly like to mention was Lenny Peters, who, along with Diane Lee, had many successful hit records. Ron and myself had met Lenny many years ago in the East End of London. Ron was the first to discover his singing talents and helped him in his quest for stardom. Lenny used to visit me and also Ron at Broadmoor. I once got Lenny a night at the Blue Angel club in Berkeley Square. I managed this by speaking to Noel Harrison, the son of the famous actor Rex Harrison, who was himself an entertainer there. Noel was one of the nicest people it's ever been my pleasure to meet. The Blue Angel was packed every night with young Guards officers. I used to go there frequently with my late wife, Frances, and I'd buy her gifts – albums of the resident singers and also soft toys.

A lot of people didn't believe that Lenny was genuinely blind, but he was. He was a quite remarkable person. He had a great perception of presence; whenever I sidled up to him at one of the bars in London, he always knew it was me. Without any prompting he would say, 'Hello, Reg. How are you?'

I recall one night in particular when Ron and I had left the

Kentucky Club with Lenny and Winifred Atwell, the great pianist. A group of us went to the Greengate public house in Bethnal Green Road. Lenny and Winifred played the piano and sang songs in turn; it was a wonderful evening. Sad to say Lenny died some years ago of cancer.

You may wonder why I write of these days in a book about prison life but such fond memories of the past helped Ron and myself to come to terms with life within the confines of the prison walls. There are a lot of inmates who have not been as fortunate as us and have no happy memories to call on; they see the system as having deprived them of any memories of consequence.

Another old friend called Laurie O'Leary used to visit me at Blundeston. Usually he would visit after seeing Ron and in this way messages could be passed between us. We had known Laurie since we were kids. Ron and I had made him manager of the Twist Club, which was on the middle floor of our club Esmerelda's Barn in Knightsbridge. The lower ground floor was a lesbian club called the Cellar Club and the top floor was a gambling room. Ron, during a visit, also put Laurie in touch with the spiritual medium Doris Stokes. He organized a Rolls-Royce for the occasion and also a large bouquet of flowers for Laurie to give to her. Laurie went on to become her manager and the partnership was a great success. Again, sad to say, some years later Doris passed over into the spiritual world. I am a great believer in the universal law that says what you give will come back to you. This is the reason I mention Laurie and his career; Laurie remained a friend when many others had forgotten us.

In February 1994, after I had been at Blundeston for a few years, I made a request to go to Maidstone prison. Governor Dodds called me to his office and told me I would be going there. However, a few days later he called me up again and said

I was going instead to Albany on the Isle of Wight. I argued my case saying that having spent eighteen years at Parkhurst I was not prepared to return to the Island. I understood that Albany's new regime involved the integration of sex cases with ordinary cons and the place was full of grasses. Also, as a lifer, I should have a certain choice of prisons. Governor Dodds listened and said he would do his best to renegotiate Maidstone for me. He was successful and I was told that I'd be leaving for Maidstone in three or four weeks' time. I would like to say that Governor Dodds was a reasonable man who always had time for the inmates. I understood from my conversation with him that his wife was ill and I hope she made a full recovery.

A couple of days before I left, a friend of mine, El Toumier, who came from Tunisia and was serving a life sentence, did me a great favour by lending me ten phone cards. This was quite unusual for someone to do but it was because of the mutual respect we had for each other. I consider him a good friend, as he does me. I recently had a letter off him from Whitemoor jail telling me he was taking the screws to court on assault charges.

The day I left Blundeston I did so with happiness, anticipating my reunion with friends at Maidstone. I was especially looking forward to seeing Joe Martin. But my arrival was destined to be delayed. I boarded a coach along with others on their way to various jails and we had got fifteen miles down the road when it ground to a halt. We heard the PO tell another member of staff that some documents had been left behind at Blundeston. He rang the prison and asked for the papers to be brought out to the coach. So we were parked by the roadside, going nowhere, for half an hour. When we restarted the journey, we were heading first for Feltham and a stop-over for a meal. We were all glad to be on the move again. It wasn't for long. Some distance down the road the coach stopped again. This time it was more permanent – the coach had broken down.

Once again we had to wait, this time for over an hour, until vans arrived and we could be transferred. We eventually reached Feltham and I enjoyed a cup of tea there and met a few of the inmates. The staff seemed very efficient and amicable; I recalled that many years ago Feltham used to be a Borstal for young offenders.

I left Feltham by coach along with other inmates. This time there were no delays. I was pleased to arrive at Maidstone – even if it had taken much longer than expected.

CHAPTER FOURTEEN

MAIDSTONE

1994–1997

When I got through Maidstone reception on to the main Weald wing I was allocated a cell in the corner of the 3s landing. My good friend Joe Martin was there to greet me. Later that evening Joe took me to his own cell, which was two doors down from my own. It was beautifully done out, decorated by himself. There were drape curtains, a pulley for special light effects, a table in the middle of the floor and many small ornaments. Joe asked me to join him for a chat. John Heibner, who I knew from the East End and Parkhurst, joined us, as did Anton Reardon, Adam Barnes, Sid Taylor and little Ron Stevens. We all had a good night.

The following day I was given a job as a cleaner. I went to look at the gym. In fact there was one gymnasium room on the field and another upstairs in a separate building. There was also an indoor swimming-pool. Close to the wing was a small courtyard which was used for the morning exercise period. We would go to the field of an afternoon where inmates would play or watch football, walk around the perimeter, or use one of the gyms.

Maidstone turned out to be the best prison I had ever been

in. The staff were liberal-minded and reasonable. One in particular helped the inmates a lot and that was PO Bush; he helped everyone without exception. Ray Buckingham and Ken Baker were also good, as was a small screw named Bob, who had his leg broken in a car crash, and a screw we called 'Fat Bob'.

In this jail groups of peers would have a certain amount of privacy and other inmates would only join them if invited. We were allowed to wear most of our own clothing and this had the effect of making the inmates less embittered. It was another feature of the more liberal regime. The food was reasonable and there were cooking facilities so we could make our own meals if we wished. Canteen payment was once a week like other jails. There were showers on each landing and on the ground floor. The library was downstairs and outside the wing. Maidstone was a very old jail, historic in that people had once been hanged there. There was a beautiful chapel surrounded by gardens. There was also a small hospital. There were two additional wings, apart from Weald, called Medway and Kent, and there was a separate wing for sex offenders called Thanet. The number of inmates was usually around 450 and most were serving long sentences.

Before I arrived the move was mentioned on TV, radio and the newspapers and I had a great welcome from all. I found the place everything it was supposed to be – a good jail. Blundeston had already marked the censor's card at Maidstone; I was a censor's nightmare! But they handled my mail very well and it was always on time.

Ron and I still had our three-monthly visits when I would be taken to see him. Although it was good to meet I used to come back more stressed than relaxed. I usually had an escort of two or three from Maidstone, exclusive of the driver, and also three Broadmoor staff on arrival. The place allocated for our visits was more of a foyer than a room and the escorts always sat within hearing distance. In effect we had no private visits at all throughout the years, apart from three occasions when they allowed Ron and me to use the main visits room which was very good. Our phone conversations, when we were allowed them, were also monitored. Our mail was read by the censors. From our separation at Parkhurst, apart from those three visits, we never had a private conversation.

Ron had a very dry sense of humour and one time someone had mentioned the allegation that he'd had an affair with Lord Boothby. Ron, who was attracted to young fellows and not old men, said in response, 'I would rather be seen dead than in bed with 'im!'

I met another couple of old friends at Maidstone. Billy Fullerton, who came from Stepney and who I'd met years ago at Parkhurst, was there. We would occasionally work out in the gym together. There was also an inmate on Medway wing called Peter Sharpe. He was of the 'old school' and I knew him from years back. He was serving a life sentence for a shooting and had done some time in Dartmoor. He told me something which I'd forgotten. He said I'd once paid a fine for him which had saved him from doing three months – he'd never forgotten it. He has returned the gesture in full, in lots of different ways, many, many times over. He is respected by all and has impeccable principles; to this day we remain firm friends. He is his own man and a man of standing. I would often see him in church and afterwards I would have a tea or coffee with him.

Ken Holmes was also on Weald wing and became a firm friend. He was from the East End and was a great help to me. He was the best artist I've ever met within prison walls. Young Shane Keeler was another on Weald wing. He was a lifer. Shane had first come to my attention years before when I read in a newspaper that he'd been convicted of murdering an old friend of mine by the name of Charlie Clarke. Charlie, who lived in Chingford, had been a cat burglar and one of the best in the game. While I was at Nottingham, Shane sent me a letter from Maidstone expressing his sorrow and remorse at what he'd done. Shane began his life sentence at the age of sixteen. He was not of criminal intellect but just a kid who had gone badly astray as many do. I hope he gets the chance to start a new life.

Late one afternoon an old friend from the 1950s arrived with his son. Brian Emmett and his son Michael had been convicted of a cannabis deal along with my old friend Joe Pyle. Brian and Michael were both born-again Christians. They were genuine as opposed to some in jail who only claimed to be Christians for their own advantage. Brian had lost a son in a car crash and this had made him turn to God. He would often offer prayer and help to those in need of it. In his earlier years Brian had been a good amateur fighter and had also had bare-knuckle fights. He would teach some of the younger inmates boxing in the gym or out on the field. Michael was a big likeable person, and it was good to see father and son together.

Dean Henry was another I met. Despite his conviction, he was a millionaire and one of very high intelligence. He used to own a helicopter and could also pilot it. Mick Harrington also came on the wing. He was serving twelve years for a shooting.

Despite the better regime and being among good friends, there still seemed to be something missing from my life. One day in June 1994 I went to the gym and was punching the speed-ball when I realized someone had walked in. I turned around and there was a tall kid with a holdall. He was dressed in a fawn jacket and a pair of old grey tracksuit bottoms. He said to me, 'Are you Reg Kray?' I told him I was. He said, 'My name is Bradley Allardyce. I hope you don't mind but would you look after my bag while I go for a run round the field? I'll come back for it.' I agreed and we shook hands and I continued punching the ball. A little while later he came back from his run and we talked some more.

I invited Bradley to join me for a walk and I unwrapped the tapes from my hands as we circled the field. He told me he had been convicted of armed robberies and was two years into a twelve-year sentence. He had recently arrived from Parkhurst. He also told me that his younger brother Andrew had committed suicide just months ago and he was obviously still very upset at the sad loss. He said that a fellow inmate at Parkhurst, Vic Dark, who was known to me, had helped him cope with the bereavement.

Bradley talked about his brother's funeral and how he had helped carry the coffin to the grave. The screws had him on a six-foot dog chain even though the cemetery was covered in police and dog-handlers. There was even a police helicopter hovering above.

Bradley had been convicted at the age of twenty-one. He had turned to crime for a sense of adventure after he'd been kicked out of the Foreign Legion, which he had joined when he was nineteen. He said he had liked the Legion and was devastated when, through no fault of his own, he'd had to leave. He also told me that he'd made a rope ladder in the few days since his arrival and he was going to use it to go over the wall. He had no friends as such and was not getting many visits.

I weighed Bradley up as a sincere and likeable person. I decided to offer him my friendship and to help him. I told him not to try to escape. I said, 'Get yourself over to Weald wing. I'll see you on the exercise yard at 11.15 a.m. tomorrow and we'll talk some more.' We shook hands on this. I did see Bradley the following day but only after he had hesitated to join me because I was in the company of my old friend Pete Gillett and he didn't wish to intrude. When I finally saw him the exercise period was nearly over so again I said I'd meet him

the following day. This time he told me the good news that
he'd be over on Weald wing that evening. He had told them in
the office that he was having problems with someone on
Medway and requested a move to Weald. The PO had agreed
to this.

Bradley joined me that evening in my cell and we had a
long talk and got on like a house on fire. I offered my friendship
to Bradley, which he accepted. I told him I only wanted one
thing off him and I would give the same in return, and that was
his loyalty. To this he agreed and we shook hands on it.

We had a good evening and at 8 p.m. we parted and he
returned to his cell four doors down to the left. This particular
evening was the start of a long-standing friendship; we would
have many such nights, and others would join us or we'd go to
their cells for parties. But the most important part of this
friendship was that I felt a sense of well-being; the fact I could
tutor and watch out for Bradley gave me a new sense of
direction and a new purpose in life. We had deep conversations
on all subjects, which meant I didn't have to put up with the
usual inane conversations that pass between inmates, with a
few exceptions. Like ships that pass in the night, their talk is
often superficial – there is no trust, loyalty or real friendship
there. I felt refreshed and more resolute because of Bradley's
company.

This friendship was the start of many profound happenings
in my life which I will tell you about.

Bradley and I would often train together in the gym, and we
would also socialize together. He was a good singer. He could
imitate Jim Morrison and Kenny Rogers among others; he'd get
hold of a hairbrush and pretend it was a mike and entertain us
all. He also did Jim Morrison's Indian Dance.

I helped Bradley to decorate his cell and to get it in some
semblance of order, although it didn't compare with mine. Joe

Martin and I had the best two cells in prison! My cell was like a study, with curtains on the back windows. I had another set of drapes a yard in front and a bed made into a sofa. The walls had imitation beams painted on them. I also had the cupboards decorated as though they were real wood. There was an armchair covered in green material and a small table. The light was covered by a shade. All in all it looked like the perfect study. Bradley would join me or I would join him for chats and meals outside the bang-up times. We also played snooker and pool and sometimes football together.

Pete Gillett often came over from Kent wing to cut my hair. He was a very good barber but this was also an excuse for him to join us in a chat. A group of us, at exercise periods, would go to the back of the pool, sit on the grass verge and talk. The group would usually consist of myself, Bradley, Pete Gillett, Carl Kay, and various others. Sometimes we swam or sparred with gloves on or wrestled, which made a change from just sitting about. Carl Kay seemed a likeable fellow but on release he murdered a young shop assistant in Woolworths. Carl stabbed the kid when he committed a robbery for just a few pounds. When we heard about the killing in Maidstone we were not happy with Carl. The only mitigating circumstance, if it can be called such, was that Carl Kay had become a junkie. He wrote to me from Broadmoor but I didn't reply to his letter. I do have some pity for him – he was committed to Broadmoor with a life sentence and he has to live with his conscience. Our whole group had the greatest sympathy for the victim's family; we felt sad that a young life had been taken in vain. At a later date Carl was convicted of stabbing the Yorkshire Ripper, Peter Sutcliffe, in the eye with a biro. I do hope that Carl Kay manages to make the best of what's left of his messed-up life. I like to remember him as the pleasant person he appeared to be when he was in our company, rather than to think of him as a senseless killer.

I wrote to Vic Dark and thanked him for being so helpful to Bradley during his time of need. We continued to correspond and became friends. Vic was a karate belt holder and also held belts for judo. He was serving a long sentence after being found guilty, along with some others, of a robbery in Ilford. They had produced shotguns, tied up the staff and left with considerable takings.

During the Gulf War, while I was still at Nottingham jail, I read in the *Guardian* newspaper that soldiers had requested the support of well-known people and celebrities; they wanted these people to write to them for moral support while they were in the front line. I started to write to these soldiers and many corresponded with me; they told me they had taken me and my brother as mascots and had named some tanks, heavy artillery and other weapons after us. One Christmas I received a card from a Commander and his men of a Royal Artillery regiment thanking me: 'I, the Commander, and my men, all respect you for your efforts that have helped to boost our morale.' It was mentioned in the newspapers that although many had not written to the Services, Reg Kray had done so – and this made me very proud.

Bill Curbishley, Roger Daltrey and Gordon Haugh came to visit us one day. Bill, who was also born in the East End, has been a friend for many years and his story is a successful one. It couldn't have happened to a more sincere, loyal and charming person. He started off as manager of Roger Daltrey and the Who, and went on to make the film *Quadrophenia*, to manage Led Zeppelin, and to put the show *Tommy* on in London and Broadway, among many other achievements. Bill's brother Alan is the manager of Charlton football club.

In the gym I used a speed-ball and also a punch-bag. I'd do

pull-ups on the bar, some weight-training and sit-ups. Joe Martin used another speed-ball at the same time. I managed to get two speed-balls and platforms, and also a punch-bag from Charlie Magri's sports shop in Bethnal Green. We would all go to parties in Ron Stevens's cell; he was a character who liked to get drunk. He'd be happy when he was drinking early in the day but when he went to get his lunch at the hot-plate he would usually end up slinging it all in the air. Ron was serving ten years for robbing banks at gunpoint. The gun he used was a replica. He also liked to con people out of cash. Jim Smith, Victor Aderinola, Kenny Holmes, Sid Taylor and Jim Morrison would also join us. Jim Smith got shipped out of Maidstone for being drunk on a visit.

During my stay at Maidstone I had a visit from Charlie Richardson, Frank Fraser, and my brother Charlie. Charlie, at the time, visited me occasionally – once every two or three months.

Another good friend I made at Maidstone was twenty-three-year-old Danny Brown. He got his life sentence at the age of sixteen when he was found guilty of strangling his girlfriend after finding her in bed with his best friend. In many other places it would have been seen as a crime of passion. Danny is not criminally minded and is a good straight kid. He was always clean and tidy and kept his cell spotless, like a little flat. He had made his cell like a home because to Danny it was his home. His grandmother would visit him often and I used to get him pen-friends to write to. Whenever there were parties and the older ones, like myself, would sometimes reminisce, Danny would seem a bit out of place and he would go very quiet. Like a lot of kids in jail, deprived of their youth for whatever reason, he had nothing to contribute. It made me feel sad for Danny and for the others in the same situation. I think I helped to give him confidence; he came out of his shell and he would sometimes sing. It made me happy to see Danny enjoying himself.

An interesting inmate at Maidstone was Dr Bask. He was a qualified doctor but had been convicted of slitting a woman's throat and received a life sentence. Whenever I had any ailments I would go to him, despite the fact the authorities at Maidstone didn't like him giving out medical advice. I was always pestering him to take my pulse while we shared a cup of tea!

One afternoon a fellow by the name of Willie came to Bradley's cell while I was there and started slagging him off, so Bradley hit him on the chin with a right-hand punch. I got in between them and stopped any further trouble. Willie and Bradley were friends before this so I pointed out the error of their ways and they made it up.

There were a number of major events during my time at Maidstone, some good, some totally bad. The first bad thing happened early one morning when I went to Bradley's cell. I always called in to greet him 'good morning' before taking my shower. I noticed that the door was shut and attached to it was a huge black padlock. At first I thought I'd gone to the wrong cell, and I looked for the cell card which had his name and number on it – the card was missing. I was very concerned and I realized at once that he was either down the block or had been ghosted out. Instead of going for my shower I went to the main office to find out Bradley's whereabouts. The staff were not very helpful. They said he had definitely left the prison but they didn't know where he had gone. I felt an emptiness when I realized he was no longer going to be with me. It is hard to describe the loss of the company of a close friend in jail. The previous evening we had had a party with friends and really enjoyed ourselves. Bradley had sung some songs, among them 'Old Friends' by Kenny Rogers, which had made our night. Strangely, even though we'd been having such a good time, I'd had a feeling that something wasn't right. It was an instinct or premonition.

Later that morning I met a good screw by the name of Mick who told me that Bradley had been shifted to Whitemoor. I was upset but I thought I must remain positive and asked to see the Governor and security to find out why. Over the weeks I got no satisfaction but I did manage to get an inter-prison phone call and felt better when he assured me that he was fit and well.

I wrote to some people I knew at Whitemoor and asked them to take care of Bradley and this they promised to do. Vic Dark, Bradley's old friend, and Ron Easterbrook were also at Whitemoor and so he had some good company. Bradley remained at Whitemoor for some time and despite the tough regime he handled it well.

I had to accept that once again I would be wandering aimlessly around the wing at Maidstone searching for friendship and conversation. Though it was hard to get used to I had to be realistic and to make the best of a bad deal.

On one of my journeys through the wing I met and befriended a lifer by the name of Bill Taylor, who was situated on the 2s landing. We got on well and Bill had the qualities I like in friends – good principles and morals. He was very helpful in the ensuing months, and I did my best to reciprocate. Bill and I were to meet again at Wayland prison, but there is more to tell of Maidstone before we move on.

By January 1995 I had not seen Ron for several months but, as usual, we stayed in daily contact by letter. I told Ron that a friend, Mr Duggan, had put me in touch with Father Peter Rookey, who was a priest to a church in Chicago. I had heard that Father Rookey was a healer and so I phoned and asked if he would visit me when he came to London. Apart from wanting to meet him myself, I also expressed a wish for him to visit a little boy in the Nottingham area who was seriously ill suffering from muscular dystrophy. I hoped and prayed that he could help him. Father Rookey kindly said that he would come to see me and that he would journey to see the little boy. I told Ron of this and he said he would also like to meet Father Rookey.

Another important matter cropped up this month when my brother Charlie's chauffeur was stabbed to death by Ronnie O'Sullivan Snr, the father of the snooker champion. Charlie told me all about it and that Ronnie O'Sullivan Snr had been charged with the murder. I phoned my old friend Micky O'Sullivan, of the same family, and arranged to see Mick and Danny O'Sullivan on a visit. As much as I regretted the death of the man, I wanted to make sure there would be no ill-feeling between Charlie and Ronnie O'Sullivan Snr. The meeting took place and it was all resolved.

Shortly after, three books were published which neither Ron nor myself were happy with. All three were consistently inaccurate. They all had the same theme. It was my opinion, and Ron's, that they undermined us both, and Ron asked me to try to put the record straight. I gave Ron my word that I would do this. He knew I'd already written books of my own whereas Ron never had the patience or inclination to write.

The first of these books was written by Kate Kray (as she was known then) and the other two were written by my brother Charlie in conjunction with two separate authors. Ron was so upset by Kate's book that he decided to get a divorce from her. The book was mainly fiction, a product of her own imagination. It upset Ron considerably and he saw it as a double-cross by her. This didn't put him in a good frame of mind and added a lot to the adversity of his everyday life at Broadmoor.

I spoke to Charlie over the phone about his two publications and voiced our disapproval. Charlie told me that because he had been so busy he hadn't had time to go through the manuscripts page by page as he should have done. I pointed out to him that even in the noisy, troublesome environment of prison I had still written five books and made sure that I had gone through every single page of every book, with only one exception. I had been able to correct the mistakes in that book later. I felt he should have been as intense as I was about it, making sure that it was all factual. Ron and I had serious discussions about this.

It was written in his books that the twins brought notoriety to the name of Kray. What did they think we could bring? We never went to university. Perhaps they thought that Ron and I might get silk at the bar!

There is also blame put on Ron in these books. But Charlie was over twenty-one and he could have walked away at any time he chose. It is untrue to claim, as some have, that we were responsible for Charlie turning to crime. Of his own accord he was a fence, handling stolen property, until I put him into various clubs including the Double RR. When Charlie wrote his two books, with the help of co-authors who knew nothing about Ron or me, I thought it was very insensitive – especially as Ron read those books while he was in Broadmoor. Other patients would have been able to get hold of copies and to see how Ron had been criticized and to remark on it to him. Ron wanted me to put the record straight. I can say, without any shadow of doubt, that Ron was blameless as regards these accusations. Some stupid and ignorant people have laid the blame on Ron for my own situation, insinuating that he influenced me, which was not the case. During Ron's funeral service I made it quite clear that I exonerated him from all blame for my own predicament. I have done my best to keep my word to Ron and feel I have been lenient towards others in doing so.

There have been many people who have written untruths about Ron and me. The fiction is too extensive for me to respond to in detail. There are some who write about how close they were to us during the sixties but none of them could ever take the place of big Tommy Brown, alias the Bear, who was with me twenty-four hours a day, or Ian 'Scots' Barrie, who was always alongside Ron.

When Ron and I, along with the others convicted in 1969, appealed to the High Court against conviction and sentence, Tony Lambrianou, Chris Lambrianou and Ronnie Bender made statements against us without our knowledge. This completely destroyed any chances we might have had. However, it didn't do them any good either – the judge dismissed *all* the appeals! Connie Whitehead also made a statement to the police against us. He tried to retract it when he was in the witness box because he didn't think the statement would be made public, but we had already been given copies. I don't feel any bitterness or ill-feeling towards any of them. Bitterness only hurts the person who is feeling it. I decided a long time ago to look only to the present and the future.

Of late many people seem to be out to exploit my name. It gives me an insight into what it is like outside these days. In general, although obviously with some exceptions, people seem to be out to use others. One's word of honour doesn't seem to mean anything.

One day, in the month of March, I received a call that Ron had been taken to Heatherwood Hospital in Berkshire for some tests. On 16 March 1995, at about 6 p.m., I was allowed to make a phone-call from the office at Maidstone to the hospital and I spoke to Ron. He asked if I would visit him as soon as possible. He expected to be taken back to Broadmoor the following day. He said he felt OK but wanted to get back quickly as he didn't like it at Heatherwood. Ron asked if I could contact Charlie and ask him to visit that evening.

After the phone-call I spoke to Paul Marsh, the Senior

Officer, and asked if I could see Ron at the hospital. I asked if he could arrange an escort that night but Marsh said it wasn't possible. I told him I'd known other people be allowed to visit hospital for lesser reasons but he was adamant I would not be allowed to visit Ron.

The following morning I was called to the office on the ground floor at around 9.30 a.m. The probation officer Pete West was present, sitting in a chair near the phone, and he said he wished to talk to me. Paul Marsh then entered and whispered something in Pete West's ear. I instantly had a bad feeling about this. Then Pete West said, 'I'm sorry. I have some bad news to tell you. Your brother Ron died of a heart attack at nine o'clock this morning.'

I found this hard to take in. Then, amidst my troubled thoughts, I just broke down. A little later I asked to make a call to Charlie and he confirmed what I'd been told.

I must mention that Pete West was a considerate man but I had little liking for Paul Marsh.

When I went back to my cell on the second landing other inmates told me they had already heard the news about Ron's death on the radio. They had known before me. I went back downstairs and spoke to the senior officer about it. I told him I wanted to phone Heatherwood Hospital where Ron had been admitted and also make a call to Wexham Hospital, where it seemed Ron had been diverted, for whatever reason, on his way back to Broadmoor. I also wanted to call my friend Bradley Allardyce. All these calls were allowed. The doctor at Heatherwood told me that Ron had needed a massive blood transfusion and had also needed to have an endoscopy on admittance to Wexham – this was a tube placed down the throat. I inquired of the doctors at both hospitals as to why Ron had needed a massive transfusion but they couldn't give me satisfactory answers. There was also no good explanation as to why Ron had been diverted to Wexham. I then phoned Bradley for some length of time and he consoled me over the loss. I called Charlie again and asked him to visit as soon as possible. I told him I would be taking care of the funeral arrangements.

Later that day my old friends Freddie Foreman and Joe Martin were allowed to come over from Kent wing and to bang-up with me over lunch. When they arrived on my wing, the fact that they'd been close to me for so many years made me break down again. We shared some hooch, which helped to relax us, but it didn't take away any of the sorrow.

All of this time is a bit hazy in my memory. So much was taking place. Despite my terrible sorrow I knew I had to remain positive and to make phone-calls regarding the funeral. I had to talk to Paul Keays, the undertaker. I was also responding to calls from the media all across the country, TV, radio and newspapers.

Strange to say, just before Ron's death, Joe Martin was going to be best man at Rab Thompson's wedding in Maidstone prison. I was going to lend Joe one of my suits which was in reception but something, like a premonition, made me change my mind. It was this suit that I wore to Ron's funeral.

After Ron's death I tried not to hug grief but it dawned on me that, whereas I had received letters from Ron via Broadmoor for sixteen years, there would be no more. I also recalled my mother's last words at Parkhurst that I should take care of Ron, so I was going to do so and give him a good funeral, no effort or cost spared. I was pleased that Joe and Fred were in my company. Ron had always thought and spoken highly of them both.

My thoughts went back to a few days before Ron's death when, in the company of others in Ron Stevens's cell, I had made a tape for Ron. I had said: 'We seem to be going nowhere fast – so make the most of the moment and enjoy yourself.' As these thoughts flooded through me it didn't seem possible that

I'd spoken to Ron only two nights ago and that he was no longer with me, although I knew he was still with me in spirit. I remember the letter I received from Ron the week before. He had written: 'If anything happens to me make sure Charlie is OK.' I also thought of the little boy who was seriously ill in Nottingham and how Ron used to send the kid £20 a week.

In the sixteen years Ron had spent in Broadmoor he had read many bad reports on himself by the press. He had spent those sixteen years mostly in what they call a day-room. In this room patients would have to raise their arm for the nurse if they wished to go to the toilet or wanted a light for a cigarette. When I thought of this bleak environment I didn't know how he'd survived so long without totally cracking up. All this was on top of the stick he got from the press.

There were many more thoughts in my head during those days but I prefer not to go over them. It took me some hours to dictate these pages on Ron's death. I was apprehensive of reliving this time but it was something that I had to do.

Ray Buckingham, one of the senior staff at Maidstone, spoke to me and said it would not do my parole chances much good if I made a big occasion of Ron's funeral. He didn't seem to know me as well as I thought he did because my parole chances were the last thing on my mind. I intended to make a very big occasion of 29 March – and I did so.

I arranged for Charlie and the undertaker Paul Keays to see me, along with the stonemason Mr Smith and Dave Courtney, who was to take care of the security. On this visit, which was in a private room, I made all the arrangements for Ron's funeral. I spoke to the stonemason about getting an Italian marble gravestone erected at Chingford cemetery which would be in place six months after the funeral. I also organized the security work starting from the undertaker's parlour in Bethnal Green Road. The procession would start at the undertaker's, proceed to St Matthew's church, and then end finally at Ching-ford cemetery. I arranged by phone from the office on the wing at Maidstone, and by using numerous phone cards, the floral wreaths and tributes. I had to sort out a suit, shirt, shoes, etc., and an overcoat. I was working so hard to put things together that what little I ate, I was eating at the phone.

Carol McQueen was the florist I contacted to arrange the floral wreaths, as I knew her from her shop in Roman Road, east London. She did a good job on the day of Ron's funeral.

I also contacted my solicitor at the time, John Donnelly, and I asked him to get all the medical papers and reports from Broadmoor that he could. The press reports were saying that Ron had died of a heart attack, that he was a chain-smoker and had a history of heart trouble. I knew that Ron hadn't had heart trouble and I intended to prove the statements a lie. When I got the reports I was right; Ron never had any history of heart trouble.

Although I was very busy I found time to read the press reports claiming there had been a speedy inquest and post-mortem on Ron's body. Neither myself nor Charlie had been consulted or contacted about this despite being next of kin. However, I had to let the funeral proceed as all the arrange-ments had been made.

The *Independent* newspaper published an article by Jason Benetto stating that the post-mortem and inquest were probably the speediest in history. Members of a society concerned with inquests said that both had been disgusting affairs and that it was also illegal that Charlie and I hadn't been consulted. As with the news of Ron's death, I seemed to be the last to know anything.

I sought legal advice and John Donnelly sent me copies of the Thames Valley Police reports which stated clearly that Ron had bruise marks on both his left and right wrists. When I delved into this no reasons were given as to why the bruises should be present, except that he was cuffed up prior to his death. My logical response to this, which I stated on Talk Radio a few days later, was that in my experience if cuffs were too tight one would normally ask for them to be loosened. I said on Talk Radio as well that the bruise marks were there because in my opinion a struggle had ensued. I am still of this opinion today.

The Thames Valley Police reports also stated that Ron was agitated on arrival at Wexham. Yet it was also stated that during this period of time the endoscopy was performed – this involved putting a tube down his throat. This left me with two questions. Why was Ron agitated? And if he was, how could he have allowed the endoscopy to take place? The report also said that Ron's larynx was swollen. This makes me sure that the tube was forced down his throat.

Having read these reports my solicitors and I requested that we be able to read on receipt the statements from the escort that was with Ron. We never received such statements. The term for prison and Broadmoor escorts of this kind is 'Bed Watch'. This escort would have been with Ron all the time, even accompanying him to the toilet. To my way of thinking it seems ominous and sinister that we were not given the benefit of being able to read these statements.

The chief doctor of Broadmoor came to visit me. His name was Dr Romero and I found him to be a kind and considerate man. He asked me if I would give him the details of my last conversation with Ron, which I was happy to repeat to him. I formed the impression that Dr Romero found it strange that Ron had died so suddenly. He gave me the impression that Ron was quite a strong person during this time and he knew, as I did, that just months previously Ron had nearly strangled a fellow patient when he used a head-lock on him. This patient had been taunting Ron and bullying some of the other patients and Ron's patience ran out. This man was over six feet and of a burly build, and it took eight charge nurses to break Ron's grip. The man was nine seconds away from death. The *Star* newspaper ran a front-page report on the incident.

When I stated all this on Talk Radio, on TV and in the newspapers, no one contested what I had to say. I was asked on Talk Radio if I could give specific names of those who might be involved in a plot to kill Ron. My reply was that I could not do so because it was possible that innocent people could be caught up in a web of intrigue.

During the talk on the radio with James Whale he said, after listening to me, that questions had to be asked.

Common sense and logic seem to indicate that Ron didn't die from natural causes. Although a lot of newspapers reported that Ron was a chain-smoker, my reply is that there are many chain-smokers throughout the world who don't die of heart attacks. My grandfather Jimmy Lee was one and he lived until the age of ninety-seven.

Dennis Arif, Vic Dark and Cyril Burkett at Whitemoor asked where they could send wreaths, as did Ray Gilbert. This is something I will never forget because their kind thoughts gave me good feelings. They were all very shocked and very sympathetic.

A little while after Ron's death it was arranged that I should be escorted from Maidstone prison by car to go and see Ron's body at the funeral parlour in Bethnal Green. I was cuffed up on the way there. One of the escort was Debbie Rogers, a senior female staff officer. Her husband was the top security man at Maidstone.

When I arrived Debbie Rogers kindly gave permission for the cuffs to be removed and I was allowed, with my brother Charlie who was waiting for me, to see the body. Ron was dressed in a suit and looked at peace. I stayed some minutes with Ron. I felt his shoulders, which still seemed to be in good shape, and I said a few words.

At the time I didn't think of looking at his wrists for bruises or examining his body for any other marks. It was not until later that I received the Thames Valley Police reports.

On arrival at the funeral parlour the press had been waiting and they were still there when I came out, taking photographs.

On the way back to Maidstone a strange thing happened to me. The word 'repose' came to me for no apparent reason. Although I wasn't familiar with the word I felt quite sure that it meant 'at peace'. When I got back to my cell I looked it up in the dictionary and it verified what I had thought. It gave me an inner feeling of peace knowing that Ron was 'at peace'.

Another strange thing kept happening to me over the next few days. I called Anton Reardon, Ron Stevens and others to my cell so they could witness it. Repeatedly, I felt an intense heat across my shoulders and back. It was not an uncomfortable heat, nor an unpleasurable one, and it seemed to signify that Ron's spirit was with me. The others were quite amazed by the strength of it. At this period of time I used to sleep on the floor. Whenever I lay down the heat would be present on my back.

I knew that Ron had wanted six black horses and a hearse for his funeral. I asked the undertakers if they could arrange this. They weren't sure if it was possible. Somehow the press got to hear about this and the story was reported. A few days later another undertaker sent a fax saying he had six horses and a hearse at their disposal if I wished to use them. This made me very happy. I put them in touch with Paul Keays.

I spoke to Charlie and told him about my plan for six horses and a hearse and Charlie said that he didn't think there'd be sufficient time as it would slow up the procession from Bethnal Green to Chingford. I said to Charlie, 'Fuck worrying about the time. I'm not going anywhere and I don't care if it takes a week. I'm going to make sure Ron's wish is granted.' I also arranged that there would be twenty-six Rolls-Royce and Daimler cars in the procession. The car I was in, which was to follow behind Ron's hearse, was a prison-acquired car.

Ron's funeral took place on 29 March 1995. That morning I left Maidstone early by car with my escort – the PO Dave Bush, Debbie Rogers, and a staff member called Bob. I was cuffed and had an overcoat over my arm. When we arrived at the funeral parlour the press were waiting, along with photographers, and many onlookers. The security people were also there, as well as the police.

I met Charlie and friends inside. I was also greeted by Superintendent Wildman from Limehouse police station, who was in charge of police security. He introduced me to a woman police officer who was a member of the police Public Relations Office. Both were polite and cordial and we shook hands. Superintendent Wildman said to me: 'Your security people seem to be making a good job at the start of the day, so I'll leave the main security to them.' I recalled suddenly that Ron and I had spent some time, in the past, in the cells below Limehouse police station!

I was taken by escort once again and for the last time to see Ron's body. The small room had bouquets and vases of flowers around the coffin, and a candle was burning. As on my previous visit, Ron looked at peace. I stayed a while, kissed him on the forehead and said a few words. I had one last look at Ron and then left the room.

As soon as I got back into the main room of the parlour I had the most amazing surge of energy. It was as though Ron was saying to me, 'Keep strong and do your best on this day.' Charlie, unseen by the escort, poured a small bottle of Scotch into a glass of orange juice and I quickly drank it.

I had arranged with Mr Bush and Mrs Rogers that I be allowed to put on my overcoat so I could wear it at Chingford cemetery. We proceeded by car to St Matthew's church, where the service was to take place. My car and the others followed Ron's hearse to the church and on the way we passed by my old house in Vallance Road. I spotted a number of people I knew from the past in the crowd. One was Sid Smith from Bethnal Green. He was walking fast alongside the car, waving to me. He banged on the window and shouted out, 'Do you want me to take those cuffs off so you can go?' I replied, 'No thanks, Sid, I'm OK.'

When I got out of the car there was clapping and cheering from the crowds. I noticed there were kids and teenagers standing on lamp-posts and lying on the rooftops of buildings close by. They were all shouting, 'Kray twins!' and 'Free Reggie!'

We went into the church and I met the two priests who would be conducting the service, Father Christopher Bedford and Father Ken Rimini. I also spoke to the choirboys and shook hands with each of them and kissed them on the forehead. Flowers, bouquets and wreaths, filled the entrance to the church. I walked along the pews and was greeted by old friends and new. Most shook hands with me and some I was able to speak to. A team of cameramen from London News Network was on the balcony of the church. I had given permission for them to film the funeral.

I sat close, just to the left of Ron's coffin. Charlie and his son Gary sat to the right. I was cuffed throughout the service, which started at twelve noon.

The order of service was:

ST. MATTHEW'S CHURCH
BETHNAL GREEN

In Loving Memory

of

RONALD KRAY

BORN 24th OCTOBER 1933
DIED 17th MARCH 1995

OFFICIATING PRIEST
FR. CHRISTOPHER BEDFORD

WEDNESDAY 29th MARCH 1995
at 12 NOON

Organ music

OPENING SENTENCES

'MY WAY'
sung by Frank Sinatra

PRAYERS

'*Reg and Charlie would like to include in this service friends
who cannot be here today, friends from Broadmoor and
prisons. They are young Charlie, Mohammed, Joe, Paul,
Bradley, Anton, Jim, Rab, Ron, Pete, Lee, Andrew and all
others, too many to mention. They are with us in spirit.*'

HYMN
'Morning Has Broken'

MESSAGES
read by Sue McGibbon

INVICTUS
*Out of the night that covers me
Black as the Pit from pole to pole,
I thank whatever God may be
For my unconquerable soul.*

*In the fell clutch of circumstance,
I have not winced nor cried aloud;
Under the bludgeonings of chance
My head is bloody, but unbowed.*

*Beyond this place of wrath and tears
Looms but the horror of the shade;
And yet the menace of the years
Finds, and shall find me, unafraid.*

*It matters not how strait the gate,
How charged with punishments the scroll,
I am the master of my fate.
I am the captain of my soul.*
                    William Ernest Henley

A WAY OF LIFE

A MESSAGE FROM REG AND CHARLIE
*We wish for only good to come from Ron's passing away and
what is about to follow is a tribute to Ron. It is a symbol of
peace in that the four pall bearers will be Charlie, Freddie
Foreman, Johny Nash and Teddy Dennis. Each one
represents an area of London: North, South, East and West.*

SILENCE

MESSAGE FROM REG
*My brother Ron is now free and at peace. Ron had great
humour, a vicious temper, was kind and generous. He did it
all his way, but above all he was a man, that's how I will
always remember my twin brother Ron.*

God Bless, Reg Kray.

SCRIPTURE READINGS AND PRAYERS

HYMN
'Fight the Good Fight'

FINAL COMMENDATION
*Do not stand at my grave and weep
I am not there. I do not sleep.
I am a thousand winds that blow.
I am the diamond glints on snow.
I am the sunlight on ripened grain,
I am the gentle Autumn rain.
When you awaken in the morning's hush
I am the swift uplifting rush
Of quiet birds in circled flight
I am the soft stars that shine at night.
Do not stand at my grave and cry,
I am not there; I did not die.*

'I WILL ALWAYS LOVE YOU'
sung by Whitney Houston

Organ music

As I stood close to Ron on this day I also *felt* very close to Ron. After the service they carried Ron's coffin down the aisle and out of the church. Myself, Charlie, Freddie Foreman, Frankie Fraser, Teddy Dennis, Johny Nash and the rest of the congregation followed. Once again there was clapping and cheering. In fact it was so noisy that the horses in front of the hearse seemed to be startled, so I motioned to the crowd with my hands that they cool it a little as I was afraid the horses would bolt.

I got into the car with the escort and the procession started off towards Chingford cemetery. There were huge crowds all the way from the East End to Chingford. In fact, on this day, Ron's funeral brought London to a standstill. The traffic congestion in the East End ultimately affected the traffic everywhere else. For the entire journey, from St Matthew's to Chingford, three young boys ran beside my car, talking to me through the window. There were two white kids and one cheeky little black kid. One of the white kids raised his fist and said, 'Stay strong!' The other said, 'You know my uncle Tony Burns.' The little black kid shouted out, 'You know my grandfather don't you?' As he spoke one of the security team walking beside the car ushered the kids away but I motioned that they should stay and I said to the kid, 'Yes, I do know your grandfather.' At this his little face lit up and he said to the security, 'See, I told you!' There were lots of girls and women, both young and elderly, waving to me. One woman passed a small bouquet of flowers through the window of the car, and two others passed through little golden hearts which I put in my pocket.

All the while, the police escort, on bikes and in cars, led the way and followed behind us. Some of the police also walked beside the car, alongside the press, who took constant photographs. There were TV cameras along the route and police helicopters in the sky above.

People clapped and cheered, and elderly and young men tipped their hats and caps in respect. As I looked out I saw many people at the windows of houses and flats and shops. Again I spotted kids on rooftops and up lamp-posts.

We eventually reached Chingford cemetery gates. The hearse and the cars stopped at the end of the lane where Ron would be buried in the family plot alongside my late wife and my mother and father. I got out of the car and went round and patted the horses. Just before the service began I walked across to the gravestone where Frances lay and also to the gravestone of my mother and father, and I kissed each stone and placed a bouquet of flowers at the foot of each.

We all gathered around the empty grave. The service was read. There was a chanting from the priest which seemed to have a calming effect on me, as did the incense that he waved about. I looked up into the sky and it was clear and blue and the sun was shining. I said to myself, 'Ron's probably looking down, watching over us.' I recalled that only the day before it had been grey and raining yet today the weather was beautiful. Ron's body was lowered in the coffin and the first handful of earth was thrown by the priest. I lowered a bouquet of flowers, as did Charlie and others.

Once Ron had been laid to rest I was led back to the car, where I shook hands with Charlie before the car left the cemetery to take me back to Maidstone prison. We travelled back without problems. I went through the reception area and returned to Weald wing.

I watched all the news bulletins of Ron's funeral early that evening. Everyone said, from what they'd seen on the television, how well the day had gone. They also said they were proud to have been part of the day. All of my friends at Maidstone, and some inmates whom I didn't even know very well, sent wreaths to the cemetery. One was in the shape of a boxing ring. Bradley sent a wreath with the word 'Godfather' on it, and there was one from New York. Van Morrison, Barbara Windsor, Mike Reid and other celebrities too many to mention also sent wreaths.

I learnt later that a street party had taken place in Paddington in respect to Ron, and there were other similar respectful days throughout London. I was told that the kids from a Bethnal Green school had asked to be allowed out to watch the funeral but they had been refused. They had walked out of school and followed the procession.

Later, I contacted the East End local newspaper, the *Advertiser*, and asked them to trace the three kids who ran beside my car. This was done and I arranged for them to visit me at Maidstone. They were called Kevin, Gary and Lance. As a return gesture, on the day they visited, I arranged for them to go to Charlie Magri's sports shop and pick up some trainers and tracksuits.

A few days after Ron's funeral I heard a song on the radio, 'Help Me Make It Through the Night', and I thought how appropriate this song was. Even now I often find myself thinking, after having learnt some interesting news, that I must phone or write to Ron. I suppose this will remain for ever.

I was sent a press cutting from a Canadian newspaper that had a lengthy report on the funeral. Part of it read:

In a funeral befitting a President or Prime Minister, notorious East End gangster Ronnie (The Colonel) Kray was buried on Wednesday. Thousands lined the streets of working class Bethnal Green to catch a glimpse of the elaborate cortege and his mobster twin Reggie who was let out of prison to attend his brother's funeral. The pomp was spectacular. Six jet black horses outfitted with plumed head pieces drew the flower-bedecked hearse. A black Daimler in the cortege was topped with a portrait of the twins. On the side a message formed from white chrysanthemums read: 'To the other half of me.'

The media, the TV, newspapers and radio all said that Ron's funeral was comparable to that of Winston Churchill.

Kate Kray, whom I prefer to call Howard, attended Ron's funeral. I spoke to her on the day out of courtesy and respect for Ron. But I haven't been in touch with her since. I have no wish to contact her as in my opinion she has made a career out of Ron's death. It would not be so bad if what she wrote was even factual. An editorial in a local newspaper about one of her 'stories' even stated that Kate wrote about Ron as though she lived on another planet – or thought her readers did.

Many thieves and villains as well as celebrities attended Ron's funeral. The thieves from Hoxton and all parts of the East End respected Ron and did not forget what he had done for them. In the early 1960s Ron, Jimmy Kensit (Patsy Kensit's father) and my brother Charlie were charged by the police with what was then called SUS. It was a charge of suspicion and loitering with intent. It happened when they had parked the car and were using a phone-box nearby. The police pounced and arrested them. Ron went to great lengths to prove their innocence.

When the court hearing took place at Old Street Magistrates Court, Ron had a top QC. He was able to prove that the horn on the car, which the police claimed was used as a signal, was broken and in need of repair. Ron proved the police to be unreliable on so many points that the magistrate of the day, after hearing all the evidence by prosecution and defence, slammed down his notebook and said, 'It is apparent that someone is lying.' He then dismissed the case.

The point of this story is that at the time all the thieves in the area were periodically put on a charge of SUS by the local police and took their three months' imprisonment without fighting their case. Innocence was hard to prove and so the sentence was just accepted, like an occupational hazard, whether they were guilty or not. After Ron's case, however, all the thieves came to Vallance Road for advice on how to beat the charge and their solicitors quoted the dismissal of Ron Kray as part of their defence!

The top echelon of Scotland Yard watched in dismay. They knew it was a test case and that the outcome would be important. After Ron's victory the regular SUS charges stopped. So, on the day of Ron's funeral many people remembered what Ron had done for them.

Some people tried to say, and wrote in books, after Ron's death, that he was mentally ill when he shot Cornell dead. This is not true. I was with Ron on the night, ten minutes before Cornell's death and shortly after. Ron was in sound mind and didn't have a single drink before he went to look for Cornell at the Blind Beggar. Ron would be the first to agree that he made the decision with a clear head. I do not like people saying that Ron was not of a sound mind that night. I know the truth. He made a decision and accepted full responsibility for it. That decision cost him half his life in prison and in Broadmoor.

Just after the funeral some photographs taken of Ron in his coffin appeared in the *News of the World*. This was the first knowledge I had that these pictures had been taken while he rested in peace. I contacted the *News of the World* to protest. They said they had received the photographs anonymously. To give them credit they did then send the photographs on to me. I checked with the security people but they said they did not know how it had happened or who had taken the pictures. So it was, and still is, a mystery. I can't accept that they were sent anonymously but I will probably never know the full story. Perhaps someone, somewhere, will one day come up with an answer.

Shortly before Ron's death I was visited by Father Peter Rookey, the healing priest from America. He also spoke to Ron on the phone and blessed him. He said the miracle prayer that offered Ron peace and happiness. Just a couple of weeks later, on 17 March, St Patrick's Day, Ron died.

A lady from Broadmoor came to see me after Ron's death. She was the senior social worker and her name was Mrs Carol Hames. She emphasized that Ron received the best treatment he could at Broadmoor and that he was quite happy. She told me she was sad at Ron's death.

It was only during the later part of Ron's stay at Broadmoor, after he nearly killed another patient, that he took a dislike to the place. This was because he was shifted from the ward he was used to on to the dreaded Norfolk ward. Ron told me that while there his medication had been stopped – to do this to someone who suffers from paranoid schizophrenia is the worst type of cruelty. Norfolk ward is the same ward where our friend Charlie Bronson suffered so much.

I myself, although finding the visits stressful at times due to the lack of privacy, also have fond memories of Broadmoor. I was always made welcome there by the staff and was given good meals when visiting. On a couple of occasions it was arranged by Wilf Pine, a friend of Ron and me, that we had a huge platter of food, lobster, mackerel, chicken, different cheeses, and fruit. Some of it I gave to the screws who took me there. I also recall that whenever I went to the toilet area, to clean my teeth and have a wash, the soap I used had a nice aroma. Whenever I come across similar soap it always reminds me of visiting Ron at Broadmoor.

I told all this to Mrs Hames and thanked her for coming to see me. It was considerate of her.

I started to work on a documentary video revolving around Ron's funeral, which I produced from Maidstone jail through phone calls and visits. The documentary was called *The Epilogue of Ron Kray*. Shortly after it was released it was banned from WH Smith's. I found this hard to understand. There was nothing sinister in the content. Nor was there anything injurious to anyone, other than possibly myself, as I had produced it from inside prison. This documentary is still on the market today. I would have liked the documentary to have been perfect but it was difficult to organize from within the confines of prison walls. I wanted to have it ready for the first anniversary of Ron's death in March 1996. I knew it could have been better given more time but it does capture most of the poignant moments of that special day.

A few weeks after Ron's funeral a con on the wing came to my cell one Sunday morning and hesitantly passed me a copy of a newspaper. He said, 'I think you should read this, Reg.' I turned the pages and found a big article with the headline, 'Ron Kray's Brain Down the Drain.' The article said that after Ron's death a pathologist had removed his brain for experimental purposes. This was the first I had heard about it. Just as I had been the last one to know of Ron's death, I had no knowledge of this either. I believe that the next-of-kin should have been notified. I phoned Charlie and asked if he knew anything. He said he hadn't been consulted, just as I hadn't. Apart from taking Ron's brain, which naturally upset me, I also didn't like the insensitivity of the newspaper report.

I consulted my solicitor and told him to take the appropriate action to ensure Ron's brain could be buried with him. I arranged for it to be collected by Paul Keays, the undertaker, and put in a special wooden casket and placed in Ron's coffin. I consider it was an illegal act, removing Ron's brain, as the only time parts of the human body should be removed after death is either if the person has agreed to donate organs after death or with the permission of the next-of-kin.

The other aspect that upset me was that we would never know for sure if it was Ron's brain that had been returned. All of this adds to the original mystery of Ron's death, and the speedy autopsy and inquest that followed. It leaves a question mark as to why anyone should wish to examine or experiment with Ron's brain unless it was linked with the mystery of Ron's last hours. I know that Ron must have been terribly lonely, that he had no one to turn to for help. He must have been cuffed up for almost the entire time, even when he was receiving blood transfusions and the endoscopy. I imagine it was a time of terrible adversity for him, a time of awful claustrophobia and pain.

I ask the reader to consider, with an open mind, the circumstances of Ron's death. I ask the reader to deliberate on the issue, to weigh up the facts and to think about them carefully. My conclusion is that Ron didn't die from natural causes.

Some months after Ron's death, Robert Gardner and I took part in a Lifers Moving On course. This entailed intensive training, swimming, speed-ball, punching the bag, using weights and doing pull-ups in the gym. All the inmates during the two-week session were videoed. We enjoyed ourselves but at the end of the course Robert and I were the only ones not allowed a copy of the video and photographs taken. When I inquired why the Governor said it was because I was too high-profile. This seemed ridiculous and very unfair to Robert – the only reason he wasn't allowed a copy was because he had done all his training with me and so the video showed us together. We complained on the grounds of blatant discrimination but the Governor told us that both the video and photographs would be placed in our boxes in reception until whenever we were released and only then would we be able to have our copies.

Almost one year after Ron's death there was another sad and terrible event. Charlie's son Gary died of cancer on 8 March 1996. Gary had been ill for some time. I had phoned Charlie a short period before and he had told me that Gary, who was just forty-two, had only a matter of weeks according to the doctors. Charlie arranged a visit and Gary was brought down by car to Maidstone. He was in a wheelchair and, even though the authorities knew the situation, he was still searched before going into the main visiting-room. Gary looked gravely ill. When Charlie told me about the search I was very angry but out of respect to Gary I didn't cause a scene. I knew I wouldn't be seeing him again. When I said goodbye I was extremely sad. As Charlie pushed Gary's wheelchair away, I stood by the door leading back to the wing, and couldn't prevent the tears from streaming down my face.

After his death, I told Charlie that I wanted to arrange the funeral and would also see about getting a gravestone. I saw it as a privilege and honour to be able to do these things. When the funeral took place I didn't ask to attend. I knew such a request would only be turned down.

Gary was buried at Chingford cemetery in the family plot. The funeral service was held at St Matthew's in Bethnal Green, the same church where Ron's service had taken place. Charlie was terribly upset. He and Gary were like brothers and friends as well as father and son. They used to drink together and go on holiday together. His loss was a great blow to Charlie.

Gary was only a kid when I was sentenced to life in prison.

Both Ron and I had the highest regard for him. Ron expressed this in a phone conversation I had with him just before he died. My mother, Violet, brought Gary up from childhood and thought the world of him, just as my father did. I recalled playing in the back yard with him, teaching him how to fight and generally having a laugh with him. He left lots of good memories.

At the funeral service the priest said that Gary, throughout his illness, never once complained. He said that Gary's courage was an inspiration to all his family and friends. I arranged for an empty car to follow behind Gary's at the funeral procession, to signify that although I could not be present physically I was still with him in spirit. I also had a six-foot message made up of white carnations and red roses that read, 'Though not present I am with you in spirit, God Bless, Reg.'

A few months later Bradley returned, after having spent a year at Dartmoor and other prisons, and this was one of the highlights of my stay at Maidstone. I had missed Bradley's company, especially the deep talks we used to have on all subjects. We resumed punching the speed-ball together, playing football and going swimming. I had his cell painted and decorated and some cupboards put in. I also got a fish-tank to put in his cell. I ended up with three fish-tanks in my own cell as well. Sometimes when I would go out on exercise on the field Bradley would drop a line, with coffee and biscuits on the end, from the window in the tailors' shop where he worked!

I had been suffering from stomach trouble for some time and a check-up was arranged for me at Maidstone General Hospital. On arrival at the hospital the press were waiting on a corner near the entrance and I spotted them right away. Also in the company was a detective who stood out a mile. The press photographers started clicking away with their cameras. I went through the admittance area and had an X-ray taken. The doctors and nurses were very kind and sociable. They told me the result was negative so I was very, very pleased. As I left the hospital the cameramen took some more pictures and then I was driven back to Maidstone.

The following day a photograph of me appeared in the newspapers showing me cuffed up to the escort and getting out of the car outside the hospital. It could only have been someone in authority at Maidstone who had alerted the press to the date and time of my arrival. I had no prior knowledge of it for security reasons. The newspaper headlines said: 'Reggie Kray let out for cancer test', and 'Hospital dash drama'. To allay any fears of my friends and supporters I got a statement in the newspapers that I was A1 fit.

There was another incident with the papers. One Sunday I read a report that claimed I didn't wish to be in contact with Patsy Kensit because of her relationship with Liam Gallagher. The report said that friends of mine had told her to stay away as she would be bad for my reputation! This was completely ridiculous. I wasn't able to contact her to put the record straight and a spokesman for Patsy then made a statement that she had *never* been in contact with me. This was also incorrect. I forwarded a card that Patsy had sent to me to the newspaper and a part of it was published. The situation had been created in the first place by an untruth – as is often the case. I like Patsy and wish her all the very best for the future.

While I was in Maidstone Dave Courtney and Lennie McLean had a falling-out. Dave asked me if I could mediate between the two of them as normally they got on OK. I went to the office and asked the PO, who was a reasonable man, if I could phone McLean and he let me do so. I acted as a peacemaker and both of them, finally, agreed to be friends again. Some time later when I was working on the documentary about Ron's funeral, *Epilogue*, I phoned Lennie from one of the phones in the passage and asked him if he would speak a few words about Ron on the documentary – but he said he was too busy with his TV work. I wasn't very happy about this as I had got him the TV work in the first place! I had introduced him to Mike Reid on one of my visits. Then he went on to say over the phone: 'Will you stop sending the Firm round and stop asking them to ring me.' I said: 'There's not been a Firm, as you call it, since the time I was convicted. That sort of talk doesn't do me any good. You are a liar and you know these phones are tapped.' I knew that the only people who had been in contact were those selling tickets for a charity Supporters' Night. He went on to say, 'Don't put me in touch with the one who wears a knuckle-duster round his neck any more.' I realized he meant Dave Courtney because he used to wear a miniature gold knuckle-duster on a chain. I told him: 'If you mean Dave Courtney why don't you phone him up and tell him yourself instead of telling me.' At this point Lennie McLean slammed the phone down and we never spoke again. After this I decided I would never try to act as a peacemaker again!

The month of August came and I had a phone-call informing me of Charlie's arrest. I phoned the police station where he was in custody and they told me he would be remanded to Belmarsh prison. The following day the newspapers reported that Charlie had been remanded after a short court appearance, charged with involvement in an alleged £78 million drug smuggling charge. Through the office at Maidstone I arranged a phone-call to Belmarsh. Charlie told me he was innocent and would be making further court appearances.

Around this time a friend of mine called Donna Baker visited. She was an attractive girl. On this particular day Bradley was also in the visiting-room. I introduced him to Donna and then he went back to his own table. After about ten minutes he came back. His face was flushed and he looked flustered. Knowing him as well as I do, I knew he had something on his mind. It soon became apparent what it was. He said, 'I think you've done enough chatting with Donna – what about me sharing her company for ten minutes or so?' It dawned on me instantly that he had fallen in love with my young friend. I laughed and said, 'Don't get agitated. Donna will join you at your table. I'm sure she'll agree.' Donna did agree and they spent the rest of the visit together chatting away like two love-birds. I was to find out later that Donna's regard for Bradley was the same as Bradley's for her. They had fallen in love!

I used to get great pleasure in watching Bradley and Donna when they had a visit on the same day. It was good to see them so happy together. When they went up to the canteen to buy drinks and crisps he would hold Donna's hand and walk her in and out of all the tables in circles. It was a nice act of love, and it made me think about how long he had been deprived of his freedom. Bradley had received numerous knock-backs on parole and yet he had everything going for him, a home to go to, a good future and good friends. In contrast I have known people be given parole who were not self-reliant, had no job to go to and no home.

About a month after Bradley met Donna he proposed on a visit. She accepted. He had made up his mind to marry Donna but still asked my advice if he should or not. I told him he couldn't wish for a better person to marry. I was especially pleased because I had introduced them to each other. Bradley and Donna set the date for 24 October 1996. Bradley asked me to be best man. I asked Bradley if he and Donna would let me have the honour of making all the wedding arrangements as a gift. They agreed and thanked me.

Around the same time I met a very attractive, intelligent and elegant young lady who had come to visit me. Her name was

Roberta Jones and steadily we became very close. I recall on her first visit I said to her, 'You are a very good-looking girl so it must be my lucky day!' Rob agreed to help me with the wedding arrangements for Bradley and Donna. This pleased me a lot as I was getting quite serious about her. We had started courting, although this was a bit tough on Rob due to my situation.

On the day of Bradley's wedding I arranged, with the help of Rob, for a large candle to be delivered to the chapel at Maidstone. It was blue in colour and had been placed in a bowl with the words *Bradley – Donna, Affection, Reg*. We also arranged for a large cake, a basket of fruit and chocolates, and several bouquets of flowers – one for the buffet table, one for the altar next to the candle, and one of red roses for Donna to carry. I organized a CD player on which, after the service, some favourite songs were played: 'Simply the Best' by Tina Turner, 'I Will Always Love You' by Whitney Houston, 'Tougher Than the Rest' by Bruce Springsteen and 'My Way' by Frank Sinatra.

I walked Donna down the aisle. The service went off well. I later made a speech saying how happy I was for both of them. Bradley also made a short speech saying he was proud I was his best man, thanking all the guests for being there, but mainly saying how happy he was to be married to Donna. Among the guests were Tony Burns and his wife Barbara, and Donna Cox. Half-way through the reception I asked one of the women screws if she would allow Bradley and Donna a few minutes together on their own in one of the side rooms but my request was refused!

On this same day I had organized two light planes to do a fly-past over Chingford cemetery out of respect for Ron's birthday. The planes carried a banner each with seven-foot-high words reading, 'Ron Kray – Never To Be Forgotten'. Family, friends and supporters had gone to the cemetery to lay wreaths for Ron and the rest of my family on this special day. The planes, on returning from Chingford, flew over Maidstone prison yard. This took place at 11.15 a.m. so I was able to see them from the exercise field. That evening, in the TV room, we were able to watch the Chingford fly-past on Sky TV.

All in all it was a great day. I couldn't have had a better birthday gift than being best man at Bradley and Donna's wedding. That evening we were joined by all our friends and they helped us to celebrate the occasion.

Just after the wedding I arranged a charity party for kids at the Repton Boxing Club with Tony Burns as the host. Animals were taken there so the children could see and hold them; these included rabbits, snakes, monkeys and a hawk. Pie 'n' mash was delivered in containers so the kids could have something to eat. Later, I also put on charity events in Nottingham for the elderly and for some local kids.

Also in the month of October a stupid article appeared in one of the Sunday newspapers claiming that I was walking round the yard in Maidstone wearing Red Indian clothing with feathers on my head! I saw Governor Malcolm Jones, who substantiated by letter that this was complete rubbish. I issued a denial that appeared in the *Daily Mirror*.

It is one of my ambitions to be recognized as a song-writer and for some time I have been writing lyrics. I arranged to see Tony Mortimer and Brian Harvey of East 17. We got on well and became good friends. Tony later split from East 17 and went solo. He looked at my lyrics and chose 'Falling Rain' to put music to. This will be on an album in the near future.

The following year, 1997, was the twenty-ninth year of my imprisonment. It began quietly. I had an article published in the 'My Cultural Life' column of the *Guardian*. I wrote about my trips to La Scala, the opera house in Milan, my love of radio, and my favourite singers. During the following month I was in touch with Caesar on Talk Radio. Over the next few nights a number of people phoned in to the radio programme. With a few exceptions, they mostly believed that I should be released.

In March I visited Charlie in Belmarsh prison. On the same day my two solicitors, Trevor Linn and Mark Goldstein, arrived at Maidstone for a prearranged legal visit. The prison, due to 'security reasons', had not informed them that I'd be travelling to Belmarsh and so they had a wasted journey. I would like to say that Trevor and Mark are two of the best, in fact *are* the best, solicitors that have represented me. Both are more than just solicitors. They are also very firm friends.

When I left Maidstone I was double-cuffed to a screw. A driver and another screw were present in the van. Before leaving I was strip-searched. We passed through Beckton Heath and I saw, through the misted windows, the beautiful houses in the area and a large forest. I thought to myself how nice it would be to walk through the trees at my own leisure, to smell the scent of the leaves and pines, to feel freedom.

On arrival I saw the ominous walls of Belmarsh. We entered through the main gate and passed through four other gates within the prison walls. There were cameras and razor-sharp barbed wire. The van was driven to what is known as the sterile area. One of the staff of Belmarsh came and looked inside the van. I was told by one of the screws that the van and its occupants, for security reasons, had to stay in this area for fifteen minutes.

I was finally taken inside, where I had to have another strip-search. My clothing was X-rayed. I was escorted upstairs through corridors and various doors, barred and bolted, to a small room that had a table in the centre. There was a video camera to the right and I presume the room was bugged. I sat in the presence of three Maidstone screws and a couple of Belmarsh staff. The Belmarsh staff were polite but serious. My brother Charlie entered in casual clothing. He looked haggard and drawn, as if the claustrophobic and sterile environment had taken its toll on him. We had an emotional reunion.

Charlie had brought a flask of tea with him. When we had finished it I asked if we could have another cup. Charlie replied that it was a standard-sized flask; he was given it at 5 p.m. each evening and it was all he could use until 8.50 a.m. the following morning. I told Charlie that I found it disgusting. During my years of imprisonment I have been in two security prison blocks, for a six-year period at Parkhurst and for one year in Leicester, but Belmarsh is the most extreme in its conditions. It's hard to describe the suffocating feelings that come from being there. At this time Charlie had endured eight months of this caged existence. My opinion is that the regime in Belmarsh is deliberately harsh and is designed to obscure clear thinking. I have heard that certain medical professionals are looking into the adverse mental effects on those imprisoned there. Those on remand, who are supposedly innocent until found guilty, can only spend £30 a week. This has to cover phone cards, toiletries, cigarettes and any additional food that the prisoner may want. When locked up in a cell for a long time one gets depressed, has bouts of anxiety and becomes irritable. The stress factor makes one more hungry and increases the desire to eat and drink.

I was worried about the effects on Charlie's health. Under these conditions he couldn't possibly concentrate on his forthcoming trial. The visit was over in a couple of hours.

We said our goodbyes and I was led back out of the prison. I returned to Maidstone that same day.

17 March 1997 was the second anniversary of Ron's death. I made a special taped message to be played during the service at the cemetery that day. Prayers were said and then five white

doves, representing my parents, Ron, Frances and Gary, were released to fly up into the sky. I also arranged for a Spitfire to do a fly-past above Ron's grave. This was followed by a light plane with a banner that read 'Ron Kray – Legend'. These planes also flew back over the exercise yard at Maidstone. I was out walking with my friends Bradley, Spider Armstrong and Anton Reardon.

I had another good friend at Maidstone called Vic Devenish. He was a person who only ever saw good in others. I had never known him to speak badly of anyone. Occasionally, on visits, I would meet his lovely wife Wendy and daughter Kerry. They were a close family and loved each other very much. Vic complained about stomach pains when I went to his cell one day. Although he persisted in telling the staff of the prison and the medical people, it was weeks before he was even allowed to go to an outside hospital for a check-up. He was diagnosed as having an ulcer but continued to suffer because his treatment was inadequate. Another time I went to his cell Vic was lying on the bed in so much pain that his eyes looked glazed. He was holding his stomach. I rang the bell until a screw appeared and I insisted that a doctor came to see him. Eventually two of the medical staff arrived to take his temperature and examine him. One of them sent away for a stretcher and when Vic was put on it Bradley helped the screws carry him down two flights of stairs. However, after yet another trip to the hospital, he was returned to the prison. This time he was allocated to a cell on the ground floor. Only a short period of time passed before Vic became very ill again. Before he was taken back to the hospital he gave me his wife's phone number and asked me to let her know what was happening.

There was terrible news to follow. Something went very wrong. After an operation Vic died suddenly in the hospital.

The circumstances of his death are still not completely clear. At the time of writing, his wife Wendy is fighting for the truth. An inquiry is going on.

I had known Vic in Parkhurst. He was completing a thirteen-year sentence at Maidstone. His death was a great loss. On 17 April Rob and Donna attended his funeral.

About the same time I lost another friend. Mick Morris came from Bethnal Green. He was a likeable person and also a good friend of Ron's. Mick had just finished a sentence and was only fifty years of age when he died. The only consolation was that he died outside the prison walls. At the time of his death I believe Mick was courting the daughter of one of my other friends, one of the Great Train Robbers, Tommy Wisbey.

The General Election was approaching and I expressed the opinion, via the media, that people should vote Labour. I used the quip, 'Love thy neighbour, Vote Labour!' The *Daily Mirror* ran an article revolving around my words. In the days that followed there was a humorous cartoon showing Tony Blair sitting at his desk pointing a finger at two hoods in dark glasses. There was also a little figure that was supposed to be John Major, trussed up and in a concrete block. Tony Blair was saying, 'Tell Mr Kray thanks but we don't need any help.'

A large article also appeared in the London newspaper the *Evening Standard*. It was by a journalist called John Gibb who had come to visit me. Included in the spread was a piece I had written myself. Earlier in the year it had been suggested that I might move to Wayland prison as a Category C prisoner. A de-categorization from B to C had been recommended in December 1995 but since that time nothing had happened. I was reluctant to go to Wayland for a number of reasons, including its bad reputation. It was known as a volatile prison and a very violent one, with numerous muggings and stabbings. After waiting so many years for a progressive move I had no wish to go and live in such an unstable atmosphere, despite the fact that it was stated by a Wayland governor and one of his senior staff that it was possible, if I went there, that I could be released at the end of my thirty-year recommended sentence.

Another prison, Erlestoke, was eventually suggested and on 30 April I had an interview with the Governor. One of the first things he asked me was whether I was over the death of my brother Ron. I thought this was a ridiculous and insensitive question. He went on to mention that my record showed I had been known to have the occasional drink of hooch. I said to him, 'My conviction was not drink-related, but I do like an occasional drink. There has been none about for a while but if there had been I would have had some.' He replied, 'Because of the number of years you've been away I don't think your capacity for drinking would be the same as it was.' So I said, 'You wouldn't want to bet on it. If you got me a bottle of Scotch we could see!'

Some weeks later I was informed by my solicitor Trevor Linn that my application had been turned down.

On 8 May it was my anniversary of twenty-nine years. I celebrated, along with friends. Thinking about it, celebrated is probably not quite the right word!

Conditions at Maidstone started to deteriorate. A new Governor had arrived from Albany to take over. His name was Mr O'Neill. There were far more early bang-ups during the week. Inmates were often locked up from 5 p.m. to 8 a.m. the following morning. There were some peaceful protests about the situation but nothing changed. At the same time a new rule was introduced that inmates should only embrace and kiss their visitors at the beginning and end of a visit. I can only imagine they were supposed to sit at attention for the rest of the time! Many inmates were warned for sitting too close or for kissing their wives or partners when they weren't supposed to. The screws patrolled the tables checking that everyone was behaving 'correctly'. It was all completely outrageous. It felt like Gestapo tactics.

Maidstone prison had always had a fairly liberal regime and I considered it the best jail I had ever been in. The staff were reasonable and everything ran in a smooth and orderly fashion. Mr O'Neill, however, thought differently. He was a born-again Christian and kept his Bible to hand during adjudications. When someone was on a charge, he would quote texts at the inmate. This was all very well but the general opinion was that Mr O'Neill might do better to check his dictionary and delve into the word 'compassion'.

After a few months it appeared to me that more inmates than usual were being put on charges for alcohol or drug abuse. I checked this with the medical staff and found it to be true. I concluded the obvious, that with the stricter regime and the long hours of bang-up, more inmates were turning to drink and drugs. This was down to frustration, stress, bitterness and anger. The inmates were being forced into a corner where they needed a crutch to lean on. The young ones especially couldn't cope with the long bang-ups, especially in the summer, and their stress and frustration often pushed them towards drugs. It was likely they would become dependent on this crutch, which would cause them problems when they eventually left the prison environment. This was a cycle of events that would eventually cost the taxpayer money. These inmates would return to prison because their need for drugs would criminalize them even more.

A further problem came about with the introduction of Mandatory Drug Tests. This pushed the inmate more towards the use of heroin rather than cannabis for the simple reason that cannabis stays in the system much longer and so is more likely to be detected. A positive test result could mean extra weeks added on and the loss of certain privileges.

I would suggest that the Home Secretary delve into the effects of a harsh prison regime. It is possible to have a milder regime that is still orderly and effective. Maybe then those people released back into society would be more responsible and worthwhile citizens. If anyone doubts this I suggest they examine the idea of cause and effect.

The person who spoke the most sense about all these issues was Judge Tumin. After he had conducted an inquiry into the causes of the Strangeways riots he said in effect that inmates should be allowed more contact with their families so they could maintain relationships. However, in many prisons, there seems to be a completely opposite policy.

I had an interview with Governor O'Neill and requested that I be allowed to stay in Maidstone and take up my Category C there. His reply was that I 'had no need to speak any more', meaning that as far as he was concerned he was not willing to grant my request.

Mr O'Neill issued a directive for inmates to sign. It was a compact between the prison and the prisoner and included a number of conditions that the inmate should uphold. I didn't need to be told to treat my visitors with respect, as I always did so anyway. This was just one among many ridiculous suggestions. Another was that prisoners shouldn't participate in the drinking of hooch. I told Mr O'Neill, in the presence of senior officer Bush, that I wouldn't be signing the paper as I was not a hypocrite or a liar and that if there was any hooch available I would gladly drink it.

Mr O'Neill said he had a joke to tell me. He said there was a seven-horse race and the last of the horses turned his head round to the jockey and asked, 'Why are you whipping me? There are six horses in front.' I took this to mean I was going nowhere fast. After I'd told him that it was against my principles to sign the compact, he uttered the words, 'Is a piece of paper worth dying for?' I replied that I intended to keep my principles regardless of the cost. I took his words, rightly or wrongly, as an innuendo or threat that because of my attitude I might die in prison.

I was notified by Charlie that the defence might wish to call me as a character witness in his trial that was to take place shortly at Woolwich Crown Court. His representatives contacted me and a meeting was arranged. Following a very short discussion I was informed that they intended to call a number of people with criminal convictions to give evidence. I expressed my opinion that this was not the best defence tactic! I couldn't deal with matters in detail as we had very little time but I said I was willing to attend if it would help Charlie.

Following the meeting I had time to reflect and consider matters fully. I discussed everything with my own lawyer. Upon advice received from him I decided not to go to court. I did not believe that any evidence given by me would assist Charlie in his case. Although I wanted to help this didn't seem the right way.

In June Charlie was convicted on drugs charges and was sentenced to twelve years imprisonment. Charlie told me that Fields, his co-defendant, had been advised not to give evidence on Charlie's behalf. Fields had been informed that if he did he could expect a much longer sentence. Charlie went back to Belmarsh from the court and a few weeks later he was transferred to Long Lartin prison in Evesham.

On 18 June I had a visit from Rob accompanied by James Whale of Talk Radio and his wife Melinda. I enjoyed the visit very much. I arranged with James to talk on his radio programme via the phone on the wing at Maidstone. I delved into Charlie's trial and conviction and also talked about some recent allegations that had been made regarding my brother Ron and the late Lord Boothby. I challenged those who made the allegations and said I would refute them in any court in the land. I am still waiting for a response but do not expect one. I wrote a letter to the *Independent on Sunday*, where an article had appeared regarding these issues, and it was published:

> Having read the article by John Pearson regarding the Lord Boothby/Ron Kray connection, I suggest that he confers with MI5 and gets his facts straight. Some time back I read a report which clearly stated that MI5 had checked out the allegations and that there was no substance whatsoever in them.

The day after I talked to James Whale on his show I was placed on report, charged with contacting the media by phone. I was taken down to the block but the case was adjourned. I contacted Trevor Linn, my solicitor, and my barrister Pete Weatherby and they got in touch with Maidstone prison regarding the charge. A few weeks went by before I was called into the office and told that the charge had been dropped.

At the time I contacted James Whale the law was still ambiguous on the subject of inmates contacting the media. The issue had yet to be resolved. Since that time it has been established that no inmate will contact the media without prior permission. Without permission they will be put on a charge.

At the end of June I had a visit from Johnny Armour, the bantam-weight champion. I found him to be a nice kid and in the near future he could become champion of the world.

Roberta and I had originally made the decision to get married in June but due to various hold-ups, mainly prison paperwork, we finally set the date for 14 July 1997. The Maidstone priest, who was one of the Prison Service Chaplaincy Team, was called Stephen Edwards. He and I had clashed in the past. One morning when I went to church he had said to me, 'I'm really surprised to see you here. What's the occasion?' I told him there was no occasion. 'What I'm here for is personal.

Why are you surprised to see me in church? Am I so different from others, especially those who come to church to get a tick for parole?' Because of our differences I didn't want him to marry Rob and me, and I requested a priest of our own choice. We chose our good friend Ken Stallard, a very courageous man and a good orator. The reason I say he's a man of courage is that many years ago he smuggled Bibles behind the Iron Curtain at great risk to himself.

Before the wedding took place I had a meeting with the security staff and Stephen Edwards. It was agreed by security that we could have photographs taken of the day. Then Stephen Edwards said, 'Isn't there an issue about these photos?' A discussion followed and security then sided with the priest. For a while it looked like we weren't going to get any photographs at all. I told them I would ring my solicitor to sort it out. Eventually it was agreed that we could have photographs but they would be taken and developed by a prison photographer. I resented this because I realized he would be no David Bailey! But security would not change their minds.

On the evening of 13 July, the night before our wedding, I had arranged with the help of our friend John Redgrave for a laser display to be put on outside Maidstone jail. I told a few close friends inside the prison what was going to happen and told them to be up at their windows after bang-up. The laser show was due to take place at 10 p.m.

Bradley had recently been shifted on to Kent wing, opposite my own wing, Weald. We were both on the top floor and I was able to shout across to him, 'Are you ready for the show?'

It began just after 10 p.m. Bright lights flashed and the laser beams cut through the sky, just above the roof of the prison chapel. Wedding bells were projected along with the message, 'Reg and Roberta – Married in the morning.' It was a great spectacle. There was also a rainbow. I chose this because my mother Violet used to sing 'Somewhere Over the Rainbow' to Ron and me when we were kids. I knew on that night that my parents, Ron, and all the rest of my family who had passed away were with us in spirit.

All the inmates were looking out of their windows, shouting out and enjoying themselves. I heard a banging on my cell door and a screw, who was not the jolly type, told me to get down from the window or I would be put on a charge the following morning. Of course I ignored his ludicrous demand. I had already wedged my door and put some cardboard in the spy hole so he couldn't see me. All the inmates were told the same but nobody took any notice. They were having a good time! We all had a most enjoyable evening. It was something unusual and it broke the routine. It was a night none of us will forget.

As it turned out we were not charged for being at the windows, although I'm sure they thought about it. No one in authority within the prison knew the laser show was going to take place – it probably put them in a spin. Although it had no sinister aspect to it I'm sure it will be held against me in the future. My philosophy is that it should be possible, even when in prison, to keep a sense of humour and to enjoy the occasional glamorous event!

The day of 14 July came and I was set to marry my soulmate Rob. The morning didn't start off well. About 9.30 a.m. I was called to the office, where I was met by the priest and one of the governors. They told me they wanted to go over the final details of the day. When the subject of the photographs came up the priest said that he was not going to allow photos to be taken. I remonstrated and finally stormed out of the office and contacted my solicitor Mark Goldstein. He put a call in to the prison and sorted it out. After a short debate it was established, finally, that we *would* be allowed to have photographs.

I had arranged for two large bouquets of red roses to be

placed in the chapel, one at the front near the altar and the other at the back where the buffet would be placed. I also sent red roses to Rob at home. A friend of mine called John Irving had made a lovely large blue candle which was placed by the altar to be lit during the wedding ceremony. The wedding cake was delivered to the prison in the morning. A buffet was also prepared inside the prison and laid out on a table.

As a wedding present Bradley gave me a special gold bracelet with the word *Legend* engraved on it. There are two sapphires, one each side of the writing. When I say I'm proud to wear it, I don't mean it in an egoistic way.

There were twelve people on the guest-list, including Bradley and Donna, Tony and Barbara Burns, Donna Cox, Len Gould, Dave Webb, Danny Brown, and my Turkish friends Kubilay and Ray Hussein. Last, but definitely not least, were my solicitors Mark Goldstein and Trevor Linn. I had also asked Dr Fais, who was the resident doctor at Maidstone, but unfortunately he wasn't able to make it. Dr Fais is the nicest of men, gentle, understanding, a real professional in his field, and a true gentleman among men.

Early in the afternoon I was escorted to the chapel where I changed into my suit. Shortly after, Rob and Donna and all the guests joined us. Rob looked beautiful in her wedding dress; we were able to talk for a while. We had some photographs taken outside the chapel and then the ceremony commenced.

I waited at the altar while Bradley walked Rob down the aisle to the music of 'Amapola', a track from the film *Once Upon a Time*. Ken Stallard spoke and then recited the words of the wedding service. We made our pledges. It was a very emotional moment. I took the ring and placed it on Rob's finger. She then placed a ring on my finger. Ken Stallard pronounced that we were man and wife. I then kissed the bride!!

We sang the hymns 'Morning Has Broken' and 'Amazing Grace'. I stretched my arms around Rob, Bradley and Donna while we said prayers. We remembered those in our families who could not be present – but were with us in spirit. Ken finished with some beautiful words. We signed the book and then as Rob and I turned to walk back down the church, friends showered us with confetti made from the torn-up petals of fresh flowers.

We mixed with our guests and talked for a while. I stood and made my speech and thanked everyone for being present. Bradley then delivered his very touching speech.

He and Ray had agreed to perform the song 'Imagine' by John Lennon. Bradley sang while Ray accompanied him on the guitar. I have nothing against anyone's religion and though I strongly believe in God and Jesus I feel the world would be a better place if there were not so many different religions. The only way that could be is if there was no organized religion and every man was allowed to simply believe in whatever he wanted to believe in. Rob and I sat together and quietly listened to the music. It was another special moment.

We rejoined all our guests for the buffet. Unfortunately there was no champagne but we had tea and soft drinks! Danny put on a tape of some songs that I'd had specially prepared. The first one, 'My Mother's Eyes', was dedicated to my mother. While we enjoyed the conversation and sandwiches we also listened to 'Simply the Best', 'Have I Told You Lately That I Love You?' and 'My Way' among other songs. It was good to be surrounded by all my friends and to share in their company. I talked to the guests. We relaxed and enjoyed ourselves. It made a change to smoke ordinary cigarettes in contrast to the usual roll-ups. Later, Rob and I cut the cake and passed round the plates.

When our time was almost at an end I took Rob's hand and

we danced slowly to 'Strangers in the Night' by Frank Sinatra. I felt a mixture of sadness and joy. I remembered the first time I had met Rob when I said to her, 'This must be my lucky day' – and it was still my lucky day! It was the happiest day of my life! Rob also danced with Bradley and I danced with Donna. Then Rob and I danced together again until the music stopped. Our special day was over. We embraced and kissed – and then we had to say goodbye.

Bradley, Danny, Ray, Kubilay and I were all returned to our separate wings. Donna drove Rob home and stayed with her for the evening. I was glad she was with a special friend. When I got back on the wing I was greeted by my friends there and that night, after ringing Rob, I watched the coverage on television and listened to the radio.

Shortly after the wedding I was interviewed by a visiting forensic psychiatrist called Dr Sugarman. He was affiliated to Maidstone prison. He prepared a report to be included in my parole papers. This included a comment which has been reported in some newspapers: 'there were short periods when the prisoner made strong, even intimidating eye contact, and conveyed a feeling of suppressed aggression or defensiveness, with a paranoid or contemptuous flavour.' What he didn't mention, however, is why I gave him these looks. On one occasion he asked me, 'What date did your brother die?' I thought this was completely insensitive and I couldn't see the point of the question. He continued to inquire about Ron's death and also raised the issue that I might be at risk of criminal activities if I was released! He asked me if I had had any confrontations during my sentence. I couldn't think of a more ridiculous question – did he think I was living in a nunnery?

Dr Sugarman went on to declare in his report that I was 'oddly grandiose' about my artistic talents. As he had neither read nor heard any of my song lyrics I suggested he reserve his judgement. Surely it is better to strive for something, for a sense of achievement, than to sit back and do nothing?

Despite some of his comments he still concluded that he would 'support a series of progressive moves through lower levels of security'.

I received the sad news while in Maidstone that my old friend Tommy Brown, alias the Bear, had died. Tommy used to drive me about in the early sixties and I had known him for many years. He was the most powerfully built man I have ever known. He was over six feet tall and was an ex-heavyweight pro-fighter. One time he had assaulted eleven coppers when they went to arrest him in the house where he lived in Tottenham.

At 11.15 one morning I left Weald wing to go on exercise and a con approached me whom I had not seen before. He said he had a stiff (a note passed from con to con rather than sent through the post) from Ronnie Knight, who at that time was at Blundeston prison. He told me that any reply should be sent to Blundeston. I said there wouldn't be any reply. When I got back on the wing I read the stiff Knight had written. He said that he was going back to Spain on his release but not a lot else. I had made up my mind instantly not to reply. This was because a stiff is usually only used for one of two reasons – because the sender doesn't want the content read by the screws (which would happen with an ordinary letter) or if the sender is afraid of the recipient's name turning up on his records in case this affects his parole chances. As there was nothing of interest written in the stiff I had to conclude it was the latter that bothered him.

There was also another reason why I wouldn't reply. I had been told by more than one inmate who had journeyed from Blundeston to Maidstone that Knight had befriended John Barry. Barry was among those who gave evidence against me at my trial and also against Ron and Charlie and Freddie Fore-man, to name a few. I thought that Knight should not mix with someone who had been a prosecution witness. My reasoning was that Knight had only done it to get noticed, so he could get a tick in his favour for the parole board. I was told that, when asked, Knight said he wasn't sure that Barry had given evidence. But Knight was fully aware of it. He was fully aware of the London circles. Yet he was telling other cons he wasn't sure about what had happened. Knight would also have known that Barry had been under the protection of the police for many years. In fact I believe Nipper Reid spoke up for Barry during his drugs trial.

I have contempt for Barry but I don't bear him any malice. I am sure I was and still am a much happier person than him. At least I have kept my dignity and honour.

As for Knight, I also have contempt for him, perhaps more so, because many years ago Ron and I were friendly with him. We had even stayed at his mother's flat in Dalston while we were on the run from the army. I have known Knight for a long time and though he hadn't been in touch with us for many years he should have remembered that friendship and not forsaken it for a chance to ingratiate himself within the system.

As I said with Barry, so I say the same about Ronnie Knight – I bear him no malice. I am happier within myself than he will ever be on the Costa del Sol.

It is my conclusion that the inmates of today are better all round than those of yesteryear and this includes many who refer to themselves as the 'old school'. Experience has taught me that the so-called 'faces' in jail, compared to what they term the ordinary cons, are the biggest screamers when they are doing bird. I am told by other cons that Ronnie Knight did not stop grovelling and moaning about his seven-year sentence. Yet he had ample money from the crime he was sentenced for. The so-called ordinary cons, a lot of them just kids, do it better behind the door.

On occasion, I reflect back to the last holiday I had before I was imprisoned. That was in 1966. My brother Ron, Ian Barrie, and a female friend of mine called Christine Boyce joined our special friend, the one and only Billy Hill, in Tangier. While we were sitting by the lido one day Billy said, 'I'm going to start up an illegal gambling game in London and if you and Ron want in you can be.' We told him we'd be pleased to accept. I asked him if it would be OK if we pulled a few quid out for Charlie. Bill answered, 'It's your money, do what you like with it.' Ron and I did declare Charlie in on it, just as we'd done over the previous years in the thirty-three clubs we'd owned. Some of these were small and some were big. They were mainly drinking and gambling clubs. It has been claimed in various books that Charlie was responsible for setting up many of these ventures but the truth is that it was always down to Ron and me.

Unfortunately our holiday in Tangier was cut short. One day two detectives came to the flat and produced a green card saying that Ron and I had to go to the police station in the centre of the city. There we were told that we had to leave the country within twenty-four hours. When we left the station we rang Billy Hill and he was able to get us a short stay of execution. We were allowed forty-eight hours.

We were truly sorry we had to leave Tangier. It was such a beautiful place and very biblical. I remember all the colour and scents and the bustle of the kasbah. We had intended to buy a bar there but alas it was not to be.

Two Moroccan detectives arranged to meet us at the airport to make sure we got on our plane. The senior of these two men was called Dreis. They were very polite and gentlemanly. They told us that the orders had come from above, via Scotland Yard.

After Ron died I had a difficult job in getting boxes of Ron's personal possessions out of storage and into a safe warehouse. This is where they remain today. Due to my situation I've never been able to look through them. I have no idea when I'll be able to do so.

I will relate a short story of Ron's sense of humour. When Ron was in Broadmoor he had arranged to have credit from the store. Ron was very generous; to his way of thinking money was only for one thing – and that was to spend. One fine Sunday afternoon some visitors arrived and after a good visit, as they were about to leave, Ron asked one of them, 'Do you mind taking care of a small bill I have to pay on the way out?' His friend said, 'Sure, Ron.' The friend, thinking the bill was for about £50, was shocked when the manager of the store presented him with a bill for £1,500! When Ron told me this story I saw the funny side of it but Ron, with his dry sense of humour, just related it as though he was stating a fact. I learnt later that the bill was paid.

As well as receiving mail from many people out in society, from all over this country and abroad, I also get inundated with mail from other inmates. These are my favourite letters because we obviously have a lot in common. Most are young offenders, some already sentenced and some on remand. Nearly all of them, as well as expressing their support for me, ask me for advice on how to cope with their time in jail.

So I'll take this opportunity to give you, the inmates, the advice that has helped me most to cope with my own situation. Although I have sometimes steered away from my own philosophy I always go back to it. Prison life is all a waiting game; we wait for the start of each day, we wait for meals, we wait for visits, we wait for bang-up, and we wait for the termination of whatever sentence we are doing. My advice is to do your best not to play the waiting game. Look upon each jail as a cheap hotel until you get a better one! Keep yourself occupied and keep as fit as you can. Keep constant contact with your family and friends and use the phone as much as possible. Stay away from the use of Class A drugs. Remember that the distance of the mile has to be travelled, be it a short or a long journey. It is better to walk the path in a happy frame of mind as far as possible; it is negative and counter-productive to do otherwise. Try to live each of these days, that you might otherwise consider a loss to your life, to the full. Enjoy yourself in the gym or in doing whatever gives you most pleasure. By doing this you turn disadvantage to advantage – you will regain that day of your life. Last but not least, remember the words written by the philosopher Kahlil Gibran:

Cast off the shackles of self-imposed burdens.

If your mind is free then you will be free.

As well as letters I also receive many gifts from different people, some of whom I don't even know. Due to the lack of efficiency of the censors, the name of the sender on the parcel is often ripped off and I have not been able to thank them for their kindness. So I would like to take this opportunity to thank all those whom I have not been able to reply to. One particular gift I received was a beautiful white lambswool Red Indian dream-weaver, which is supposed to capture all your dreams. Strange to say I had good dreams after placing it on the wall above my bed. For this gift I would like to say a special thank you to whoever sent it.

The day after my wedding to Rob, Bradley was transferred to Elmley jail. It was another parting. By this time it had been decided that I would also leave Maidstone to go to Wayland prison in Norfolk. I would finally get my Category C. It had only taken twenty-nine years!

The last few weeks passed slowly. One good day I remember was when Tony Mortimer came with Rob on a visit. We talked about the song we were writing together. Tony is a very talented composer and a very good friend.

During another visit with Rob and Donna, about a month after the wedding, we were told that we could finally see our wedding photographs. They took us through to a back room where five screws were standing around. Laid out across several long tables were all the photographs that had been taken. There were probably about eighty in all. We were told we could pick ten! That was all we would be allowed. It was ridiculous. There was no proper explanation as to why this should be. While we looked at the pictures the screws followed us around as though they were terrified some of them would disappear! I'm surprised they didn't provide an armed guard. We didn't understand why we would only be allowed ten. What were they going to do with the rest of them? All our memories of the day were in those pictures and they were giving us minutes to make an impossible choice. The prison had already insisted that all the photographs would be Crown Copyright, which meant none of them could be copied. Other inmates were allowed to take and keep as many wedding photographs as they wanted. An exception was being made, as usual, in my case. We looked at the pictures for a while and then we chose ten but told the screws that our solicitor would be in touch about the others. Rob wasn't allowed to take the photographs home with her and they remained in the prison. They remained there for the next fifteen months! It wasn't until October 1998 that we were finally permitted to have the ten photographs.

I should mention, as a matter of interest, that before and after the wedding I was allowed to have regular photographs taken by the prison, both alone and with other inmates. This highlights how illogical the system is.

Security would not give me an exact date for when I was leaving but I sussed it out to the very day. They told me at 8 p.m. the night before just before bang-up that I would be leaving early the next morning. I arranged for a friend to ring Rob and let her know. I had already had my going-away party with my friends, including Danny Brown, Charlie Simpson and Ernie Bird. Ernie was a lifer like myself. He had a great sense of humour. He was a specialist at making cakes and once a week, on a Friday evening, he'd make a meal for us of pie 'n' mash.

I had said all my farewells by the time I left Maidstone and I was in sunny Wayland just before lunch on Tuesday, 26 August 1997.

CHAPTER FIFTEEN

WAYLAND
1997–1998

In the reception area of Wayland prison one of the screws asked me, 'Are you apprehensive about going on the wing?' I replied, 'No, why should I be? In fact I'm quite relaxed and happy to be here.'

I left reception with a trolley which had my bags of personal possessions on it. C wing had been designated as the place I would be staying. Bill Taylor, who I knew from Maidstone, helped me with my things. He was also on C wing. I was put on the ground floor on B spur, cell 42. This was convenient because the showers were just a few yards from my cell, as was the telephone and the hot-water boiler where I could fill my flasks before being locked-up. I learnt that C wing was considered to be the worst of the four wings because of the violence that erupted fairly regularly. It was known as the Bronx!

Shortly after I arrived I was told a screw wanted to see me in the room just off the entrance to B wing. I went to see him. I knew what the screw was going to say even before he said it. I had already figured out that putting me on C wing was intended to stress me out. My instinct was right. The screw said, 'I'm marking your card. Some blacks are going to mug you for your jewellery.' At the time I was wearing a cross and chain that Ron had left me with a small gold boxing glove attached to it. I also had a pendant with a photo of Ron on one side and of my mother and father on the other, an Omega watch, a gold ring with a stone that Ron had also left to me, and my 'legend' bracelet.

I told the screw I wasn't interested in what he had to say. My opinion was that someone was trying to stir up racial conflict, which could have happened if I'd believed the screw's words and acted on them. I knew many blacks as well as whites in the prison whom I had met before and who were friends of mine. I said nothing about this incident except to a few close friends. I left the matter at that although, as always, I was on my toes. On reflection it was possible that this particular screw was an innocent participant, as on the other occasions I bumped into him he came across as fairly decent.

A couple of days later Governor Woods and PO Griffin called me to the office for the general chat they had with all new arrivals. Governor Woods said, 'We're a bit concerned for you.' I asked him why. He said, 'Because there's talk of some people taking your jewellery off you.' I replied, 'No need for your concern. I can take care of my own problems.' It seemed to me that, despite their concerns, they weren't actually doing anything about it and this just heightened my suspicions. I left the office and got on with my life on the wing.

I found the structure of Wayland prison to be to my liking. The exercise yard encircles two sets of wings, A & B and C & D. The gymnasium is reasonable and the PTIs are all right. There is also a good library run by a very likeable lady. I find the medical facilities and the medical staff at the hospital to be helpful. Dr Mackenzie is very good. In particular I like the pretty little chapel, which has beautiful lighting effects. I often go there to get peace of mind. I can sit there or in an adjoining room and have a cup of tea. I go to the chapel to say a quiet prayer on many occasions.

I got on with the majority of inmates and staff at the prison. However, what I had heard before leaving Maidstone turned out to be true – there was a very volatile atmosphere in the place and it often turned into trouble. There were many instances of violence: one inmate got his face cut with a Stanley knife in the passageway near the library; four inmates attacked another con with sticks as he sat in the TV room; an inmate scalded another with hot water from a jug and then hit him in the face with the jug; two inmates were attacked by eight others in a cell as they were talking; there was a fight in the exercise area when two inmates attacked each other with sticks; a thirty-year-old con was mugged by three others on the field when they put a blade to his neck. Very recently a con was snookered when another con hit him over the head with a pool-cue! These are just a few examples.

I couldn't fathom why the prison authorities allowed Stanley knives to be sold from the canteen to any inmate. They were supposedly bought for the purpose of hobbies but were used more often as weapons.

There were also frequent arguments due to people jumping the queue at mealtimes and some of this behaviour led to fights. There were no notices not to jump the queue and I never saw any member of staff intervene. However, there were notices all over the prison saying, 'If you know of any bullying please inform us as it affects us all.' It made me laugh, although not in a very humorous fashion, as each day I watched the staff sitting on the table-tennis table chatting merrily to one another while the bullies pushed to the front of the queue for their meals. It seemed the governors and staff were quite content that the law of the jungle rule at Wayland.

I knew that someone would eventually be killed because of

all the random violence. I told my wife Rob that this would happen, and sad to say it did. An inmate by the name of David Colley, who was forty-eight years old and serving a short sentence for growing cannabis in his garden, became involved in an argument with another inmate, Junior Van Brown. Junior had apparently been talking on the phone and complained about the level of noise coming from the TV room where David Colley was sitting. Colley was the nearest person Junior could see and so he took the brunt of the complaint. It is alleged that Colley kicked the door shut and that Junior then left the phone, went into the TV room, and punched Colley on the back of the neck. David Colley was knocked out and fell to the floor. Despite efforts by the screws he couldn't be resuscitated and died of a brain haemorrhage. It is not clear yet whether it was a freak punch or if Colley already had a weakness there. Van Brown was charged with the manslaughter of Colley.

I knew both of these men. David Colley came across as a loving family man and had once talked to me about his children. Junior was also a family man; he was a singer and had several songs on albums. He was due to be released a couple of days after the incident. It was a terrible thing to happen to both families. Unfortunately the stress and frustrations of prison life can often spark off arguments and sometimes, as in this case, the results are tragic. A few days later I went into the TV room and found two bouquets of flowers from David Colley's family. I thought to myself how sad it all was. The inmates had a collection and raised some money for David's family.

I should also mention that on the same day David Colley met his death, there were two stabbings on A wing needing hospital treatment. One inmate had his stomach cut, the other received a wound to the hand.

My old friend Bill Taylor is what we call a *Listener*. He can be called out at any time of the day or night to help another con who has a problem. Many inmates get stressed up or upset in prison and Bill will go to their cell and listen to them and offer advice to help them cope. Other friends from the past I have met again are Andrew Allder, Lou Warner, Peter Spelling and Shane Crossfield. Andrew is a young lifer who has been in prison for thirteen years, since the age of sixteen. He is a very talented artist, a sculptor and a painter. Despite the fact he could have a good future if released he seems to be going nowhere fast. There are many like him who are languishing unnecessarily in prison. I first met Lou in Maidstone. He told me how he had gone to America from Spain as he was wanted for questioning on a murder charge. He had been brought back in a body belt to Wandsworth prison. Lou was recently reading my book *Born Fighter* and came across the story of when Ron and I went to the fairground boxing booth when we were children. One of the fighters we watched was called Slasher Warner and Lou told me that he was a close relative. It seemed strange that I was in jail with Lou all these years later. Peter Spelling was also in Maidstone. When he was on the run from prison and living in Spain he sent me some Indian trophies and kept his word by doing so.

I had some problems with the Governors because I sometimes arranged visitors for my friends inside. I wanted to introduce them to other friends outside who could help with jobs and somewhere to live on their release. It was because of this, in my opinion, that my 'enhanced' status was temporarily taken away. This meant the loss of certain privileges, including one extra visit a month and being able to wear my own tracksuit. The reason the Governors gave for their decision was that certain allegations had been made by staff. These were based on suspicions and were not factual. I told them that I believed these allegations were just a smoke-screen because I refused to concede to their wishes and stop arranging visits for my friends. It was all completely illogical.

A forty-two-year-old neighbour of mine, serving a life sentence, was nearby when I was on the phone to my wife one day. I asked him to say hello to her, which he did, and I noticed that he was very shy and timid. I asked him how long it had been since he had talked to a woman, other than a screwess. His answer was seventeen years. I thought to myself, that's one for the *Guinness Book of Records*! I also deliberated on the fact that one reads so much about training and preparing inmates for their return to society – this was another fine example of their training efforts!

In the January following my move to Wayland I went to see Charlie at Long Lartin. It took three hours to get there and three hours back and I was only allowed to stay for two hours. The second time I visited, five months later, I was able to stay for five days. I found Long Lartin to be a very laid-back jail and a well-run place. The staff operate on a system of mutual respect, unlike Wayland, where many of the screws treat the inmates as if they are in a Borstal. Charlie was fit and well. While I was there I met Charlie's friend Naz and he became my friend too. Naz is serving twelve years and is a Kurd by nationality. The three of us had some good chats together.

Ever since Charlie got his sentence of ten years for being an accessory after the fact in the McVitie trial it has been claimed by some that we had a detrimental effect on his entire life. Though I don't really want to delve into personal family history I wish to put the record straight about this, especially as Ron is no longer able to do so. Charlie had a good fifteen years with Ron and me and shared a lot of profitable and enjoyable times. Although Charlie lived, to some extent, in our shadow this never had to be the case – it was his decision. Often our lives do not take the direction we might have liked or expected but we all make our own choices and we all have to live with the consequences.

The famous poem *If* by Rudyard Kipling sums up many of my sentiments about life in this regard.

Shortly after I arrived at Wayland I made a trip to West Norwich Hospital to have my eyes examined. I was told I would need to have an operation on both eyes to remove cataracts. About a year later I finally had the first cataract removed from my left eye. I was taken to the hospital in handcuffs. The operation was short and successful. The consultant Ted Burton and his staff were very kind and considerate. Later, I had the second operation and my eyesight is much better now.

I still write a lot of letters from jail. They are on my own headed paper with a photograph and beneath the picture are the words 'Life is not a rehearsal ... make the most of it.' These words are my philosophy. But they are probably held against me when it comes to parole reports because in jail it appears that one must not have any philosophy other than to be regimented and to be a number.

I receive lots of letters from young offenders all over the country. Many of them seem to have no chance in life and rapidly become just products of the system. They have very little help and very little future. The thing I would really like to do is to organize good youth clubs all over the country, but especially in the East End of London and in Nottingham. These clubs could help keep the kids out of trouble. I'd like to get the best training facilities for them, as well as good sports equipment, a gym, pool and snooker tables. I'd also like these clubs to have a music studio so the kids can realize any musical ambitions they have. I would try to make sure that celebrities and sports personalities visited periodically so they could talk to the kids and help them. There are many businessmen and women who could help in a venture like this. If any of them wish to join me they should contact me in whatever jail I am in. I'm sure they would get a great deal of pleasure, as I would, from creating a brighter future for all the kids. As the saying goes: To give is to receive.

During the first few months I was at Wayland I had a couple of articles published, one in the *Stage* and the other in the religious newspaper the *Universe*. The *Stage* article was all about my love of the theatre and my memories of long ago. I recalled the derelict theatre Ron and I used to play in as children, my grandfather Jimmy Lee who danced and sang and could lick a white-hot poker, my friendship with Judy Garland and my visit with Frances to La Scala in Milan where we watched Madame Butterfly.

The article for the *Universe* was as follows:

Reggie's Triumph of Love
God works in mysterious ways. If I had not been sentenced to life I would not have met my wife Roberta who I married on
14 July last year.
One should count one's blessings on a daily basis and, it should be remembered, there but for the grace of God go I.
I strongly feel, as my late brother Ron's poem *Coloured, White or Jew* says, we should all live in harmony:

We are all born the same
From God we all came
Coloured, White or Jew,
We are all God's children,
Not just a few.
We should all be brothers
And think of others
Coloured, White or Jew

Then to God we will all
Be true.

It would be a much happier world if we all loved our neighbour. Instead of waiting for the world to be a better place we should do this immediately and the world will become a better place.

If any doubt the power and love of God and Jesus, they should hear a story I learned of what happened in a prisoner-of-war camp, and of the triumph of love over brutality:

There was a soldier of high rank who was repeatedly beaten senseless by his enemy and each time this happened the soldier told the man the story of Christ and how it gave him strength to overcome the beating and the great adversity he was suffering.

When the soldier was released from captivity he went back home and some time later in his new-found freedom, on one special day, he was greeted by the arrival of his former enemy who told him he had become a born-again Christian.

My friend Fr Peter Rookey said when he visited me that the Mafia in Chicago pay him sums of money towards the church. This indicates that although there are doubters we all know in our subconscious that there is life after death.

Though some hesitate and suppress the spiritual because it is not seen to be physical or visual, we know that instinct is most often supreme.

My late brother Ron, although I hesitate to use the word 'late' as he is with me spiritually, once wrote to me that I should always strive to do good, to keep principles and keep respect and dignity – that those were above all. Ron always found great solace when he turned to God in the face of adversity.

During my many years in prison I have lost a family – yet once again God has worked in mysterious ways in that I have met and gained a family with my beautiful wife Roberta, my friend Bradley Allardyce, his wife Donna, Paul

Marcus and Danny, who join my brother Charlie who is still with me.

I am fortunate, whereas some are not, in that I know my family of the past are with me spiritually each day and that my family of the present are also with me daily, so I am completely happy. Each day at the break of dawn I say the special prayer my mother taught us as children.

I recently made a tape to be played in the prison church and I state on this that I have met many champion fighters: Rocky Marciano, heavyweight champion of the world; Henry Armstrong, champion at three different weights; Sonny Liston, heavyweight champion of the world; Barney Ross, junior lightweight champion of the world, to name but a few. And then I learned about another fighter, who fought in his own way many battles, and he to me is supreme of all world champion fighters – his name is Jesus Christ.

My ultimate happiness has come about by marrying Roberta in that I now have total joy. It reminds me of the adage that the supreme force is love.

God bless,

Reg Kray

The greatest lesson I've learnt is to count my blessings and to remember that none of us are exempt from life's problems. We should meet them each morning and treat both the problems and the day as an adventure; we should do our best to solve the problems and to enjoy the day.

A typical morning for me at Wayland will begin at 4 or 5 a.m. when I wake and start to get ready for the day. I can usually hear the ducks and the birds. It gives me a sense of freedom. Later I listen to the seven o'clock news on Radio 2. I have a cold shower at 8.15 a.m. when the doors are unlocked. Sometimes I play table-tennis or go to the gym. I also punch the table-tennis ball I have hanging in my cell and, of course, I go out on the field at exercise time. The exercise area is very spacious and has green lawns. Often inmates can be seen doing somersaults, handstands and cartwheels. Others wrestle on the grass. Some of the inmates walk alone and others in groups. It is a very fast prison, the majority being young inmates. I write many letters and often sign ten or twenty signatures at the request of other inmates. I phone Rob as much as possible and also ring friends, phone cards allowing.

There are several pay-phones on every wing at Wayland and we are able to use them whenever we're unlocked. There are sometimes queues and we have to wait. A PO recently had a notice typed out that if people hogged the phone he would take 'draconian action' to stop it! Despite his draconian threat people still hog the phone and nothing has changed. However, the PO liked his notice so much that he had it placed in a frame near his office! There is always a lot going on at Wayland. The screws, on a daily basis, do their best to persuade inmates to be Judas against their neighbours. They offer them greater chances of parole and even phone cards and tobacco if they will give the names of people participating in drugs or the drinking of hooch. To my way of thinking this is immoral and does not come into the line of thinking of 'Love thy neighbour'. What makes it even more immoral is that the screws do not ask for information for moral purposes but only to get a feather in their own cap and to increase their chances of promotion.

I know of a recent case where a young inmate of twenty-two was mugged by three others. His locked cupboard in his cell was forced open and then he was attacked. They knocked him to the floor, opened his legs wide and forced a spoon into his rectum to pry out cannabis they thought he had hidden there. Afterwards, the kid was very bruised and shaken. He went to the office and asked staff if he could be shifted to another wing. He was told he could only have a shift if he

Right: Bradley and Donna Allardyce's wedding, HMP Maidstone, 24 October 1996.

Below: Bradley at Ron's grave, Chingford Mount Cemetery.

A rare picture of Reg in his cell in HMP Maidstone.

Reg in training, Maidstone.

Above: Roberta in Norfolk, springtime 1998.

Right: Reg and Roberta on their wedding day, 14 July 1997. *(Crown copyright)*

On the thirtieth anniversary of Reg's imprisonment, a small plane flew over HMP Wayland trailing the banner 'Reg Kray Political Prisoner 1968–1998'. *(Alan Donohoe,* East Anglia Daily News*)*

Polaroids of Reg taken at Wayland, and with Richard Reynolds (centre).

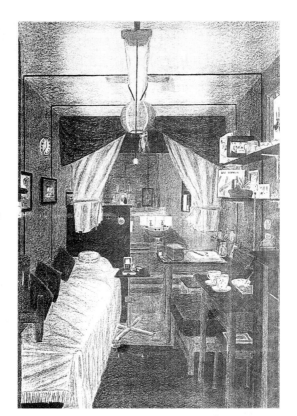

A drawing of Reg's cell at Maidstone by a fellow inmate.

A 'special edition' dollar bill featuring the twins designed by Wesley Harrhy, who died tragically in a car crash. His mother Norma sent this to Reg.

Reg's favourite photo of Ron.

Huey Morgan of the
Fun Lovin' Criminals wearing
his 'Free Reg' T-shirt, Reading
Music Festival 1999.

Official identity card
prepared for Reg when he
went to visit Charlie in April
2000. Note the warning on
the reverse!

The order of service for Charlie's funeral, 19 April 2000.

ST. MATTHEW'S CHURCH
BETHNAL GREEN

In Loving Memory
of
CHARLES JAMES KRAY
Born 9th July 1926
Died 4th April 2000

Officiating Priest: The Reverend John Scott

WEDNESDAY 19th APRIL 2000
AT 12.00 NOON

Reg and Roberta at Charlie's funeral. Reg's friend Paul Marcus is to the left of Roberta, and Freddie Foreman is behind him.
(Johnny Munday, Hackney Gazette*)*

Reg leaving Charlie's funeral.
(Alexs Woods, Rex Features)

Above: Reg at the Norfolk and Norwich Hospital, September 2000. *(Dave Hogan, News of the World)*

Left: A floral tribute to Reg on the funeral hearse.

provided them with names. The kid obviously didn't want to be branded a grass. It would only put him in even more danger and would lose him any friends he had on the wing he wished to move to. The staff remained adamant that unless he cooperated he had to remain where he was. One can imagine the awful fear and anxiety this kid felt, but luckily he sought out my friend Bill Taylor, the Listener, and Bill helped to calm him down. I was present when the kid came back to see Bill and we both talked to him. We told him the best thing he could do was stay on the Bronx (C wing) and that we would talk to the muggers and watch out for him. We knew his attackers reasonably well and were able to reason with them and stop any more conflict. We pointed out that the kid hadn't gone on the numbers (this is the term used for those who stick up names and then go on protection down the block) and that they should admire his strength of character.

On the subject of drugs, more especially cannabis, I feel that the public should be reminded that when it was suggested that the staff in all prisons be given random drug tests the screws, and those above them, protested loudly. Why should that be? Many cons, some of them long-termers, who are found guilty of taking cannabis have had their release held up indefinitely. Yet I know from general information, from talk and from newspapers, that the taking of cannabis is prevalent in society today. It seems there is one rule for some and another for the rest. I don't condone the taking of drugs but I don't like hypocrisy either.

I think that those who seek out drugs for instant gratification should remember the words of a wise man who said: 'If one wishes to stand on the top of the mountain, one should take the trouble to walk up it first.'

There is not much social life on the Bronx or other wings. Inmates walk to and fro along the passageways asking whoever they come across if they have cards, tobacco, puff or powder (heroin). There is no privacy. They continuously walk in and out of cells like rabbits in and out of their warrens. They are always asking 'Have you seen Tom, Dick or Harry?' There are also regular spins on all the cells by screws looking for another feather in their cap. I recall one screw saying to me that because drink is much more visual than heroin or cannabis they tend to seek it out. The fact that most screws are lazy by nature makes this understandable.

From time to time we observe a screwess walking the passageways a little intoxicated which we find humorous, especially as the allegation that I drink alcohol has been used as a reason not to release me!

Despite the fact that in the past I have had an occasional drink of hooch, I stopped after my first month at Wayland. I have no intention of drinking hooch any more. I have decided that drinking goes against me keeping fit. Also, I started smoking again two years ago after stopping for ten years – but I intend to stop again!

There are decent screws in any prison, men and women who are helpful, polite, humane and considerate. There are also bad ones. Really bad ones and moderately bad ones. Some screws, when they have finished serving food at the hot-plate, fill themselves up with what should rightfully have been given to the inmates. In fact one screwess has been seen to be eating porridge on a daily basis, gulping it down! Perhaps the Home Secretary should hold an inquiry – his employees obviously can't afford a decent breakfast of their own.

On a few occasions they have run out of toilet paper in the prison and we've been told that we'll have to wait a week for the new stock to arrive. A few of us were going to complain about this but in the end we decided otherwise. We all came to the conclusion that it was a waste of time as nothing ever gets done. The end result is always a knockback or a rejection. There are many small irritations in prison as well as the bigger aggravations. Sometimes the little things can wear you down just as much as the greater ones. Some rules and regulations seem to change continuously so that one day you are allowed something and the next you are not. I was recently forbidden to use headed paper with my name and address on it and told it was against the rules. This was despite the fact I have been using the same paper for over two years!

Wayland is always buzzing with rumours: so and so is going up for appeal, so and so has gone on the numbers, so and so is a 'smackhead'. It all livens up the day! There are various forms of art practised in the prison including painting, drawing, sculpture, the making of artificial roses, Fabergé-type eggs, and little vases of flowers made from hardened bread. Although it is illegal, tattooing also takes place. One inmate will do the drawing and then another the actual tattoo. Both will receive some payment for this. The inmate on the end of the needle sits on a chair or lies prone on the bed while the needle is connected.

One day I walked into a cell and saw Frank Fraser's picture on the wall. Then I went to another, Mick from Chingford's cell, and had a cup of tea; wrapped around the toilet seat were a pair of women's knickers! All these things help make the day that bit more interesting!

Frank Fraser has always voiced in public that it is time I should be released and this pleases me. My mind goes back to the early sixties, to a day at Vallance Road, when Albert Dimes (alias Italian Albert) and an associate knocked at the door. Albert told Ron and me that he had just been to visit Frank Fraser at Brixton prison where Frank was on remand, along with Joe Wilkins, for allegedly demanding money with menaces from Harry Rogers, a Jewish fellow who lived in Brighton and ran a candy-rock shop. Ron and I knew Wilkins as well as Frank. Albert said that Frank was really stressed up about this charge as he had just come out of prison and was not looking forward to another sentence; neither was Joe Wilkins. He asked if Ron and I could get Rogers to change his evidence or to not appear in court so they would get an acquittal. We told Albert that we'd work on it right away.

Ron and I decided it would be me who contacted Rogers because some six months earlier I'd met him at his shop in Brighton with my late friend George Osbourne, alias Duke. We'd gone to see him about opening a rock shop of our own in the area, or joining Rogers in his, but nothing had ever materialized. However, we'd got on reasonably well with Rogers and I felt I could sway him from prosecuting. I spoke to Rogers and shortly afterwards he changed his evidence. Frank and Joe were acquitted of the charge, which pleased everyone concerned. When Frank speaks on my behalf it is possible he still remembers and appreciates that Ron and I more than likely saved him and Joe from a five- or seven-year sentence.

Frank Fraser is the one out of all my old friends who has been in touch most regularly over the years.

One day, walking round the prison, I noticed a wild long-haired Scotsman; he was stark naked with a slogan hanging round his neck saying: 'Kill the bastards'. He was shouting and gesticulating. I watched a group of young screws advancing on him. Near to me was a member of staff, a physical training instructor by the name of Adrian Jones, who I knew to be a reasonable man. I quickly walked over to him and said: 'Would you tell the young screws not to tackle the Scotsman because he's not doing any harm. If they get hold of him they'll just force him to fight back. I know you have more experience.' He agreed with me and told the young screws to disperse and to let the Scots fellow walk round. I've mentioned this incident because I feel that PTI Jones's response stopped what could have become a very bad situation. If the screws had grabbed hold of the Scotsman then other inmates would have joined in.

One of the best evenings I have had at Wayland was listening to Sunday Half Hour on Radio 2 while lying on my bed. The last shafts of light were coming through the window and I was listening to hymns. At the same time I could hear the banging of windows and doors because the World Cup football was being played. I thought to myself that despite the fact we were all locked up we were, in our different ways, enjoying ourselves and on this particular evening I felt quite content, snug as a bug in a rug!

I am very fortunate in that I can sleep any time I feel like it, day or night, without the need for alcohol, drugs or anything else. I can honestly say that I sleep easily with a clear conscience. I wonder if the same can be said of those who claim I should remain in jail.

Quite recently I heard on Radio 2 that the painter Lucien Freud had sold two of his paintings for 2½ million pounds. I recalled how Lucien used to come to Esmerelda's Barn, our gambling club. He offered, as an act of friendship, to paint a portrait of my late wife Frances and me. For various reasons we never got round to doing it. On reflection it is a pity because to have a portrait by such a renowned painter would have been something to treasure.

My friend Norma Harrhy from Cardiff, whose son Wesley died tragically in a car accident, sent me a beautiful little book entitled *Words on Hope*. She had marked a page for me that read: 'Two men looked out of the prison bars; the one saw mud, the other saw stars.' It was written by Frederick Langbridge. Norma said that she thought the words were appropriate as I always looked up to see the stars. I thought it was a nice sentiment.

I remember another evening when I was walking on the field. There was a beautiful sky, very clear and blue, and I was watching a group of inmates. Two were playfully practising karate whilst others stood in a circle and watched, clapping and cheering. There were many other inmates just walking to and fro. It was a happy night with a good atmosphere.

An inmate told me a funny story about a group of schoolchildren that had been brought on a tour of Wayland. He was working near the outside gate when the kids trudged past him on their way out. One kid, with his hands in his pockets and looking very dejected, said, 'It's not fair. We wanted to see Reggie Kray!'

I've been asked many times by friends and strangers how I have survived thirty years in prison – in effect, what makes me tick and what my thoughts are when I'm behind the door, particularly my thoughts at the loss of my family during this time. I have been hesitant to write about these things for two reasons, firstly that I didn't wish to relive all those thoughts and times and secondly that I, and others in the same situation, accept it as a way of life. I see nothing exceptional in the instinct of survival. I have only decided to tell of these times because I have been repeatedly asked to do so.

There are no simple answers to the questions because they are complex ones and my thoughts are complex in response.

I have pointed out previously that indignation seems to give me energy and the ambition to survive. The indignation stems from many causes, mainly the loss of my family. For instance, I often say to myself when I'm alone in my cell, sometimes pacing, 'We'll show the bastards, Ron!' I know that Ron's main dream was to see me free. Anything I achieve, anything I do, is for the both of us. I also hold on to the thought that I am a blessed person, especially when I think of those less fortunate than myself – for instance my late wife Frances, who died at the age of twenty-three. Just the other day I was listening to a CD of Maria Callas, the soprano, singing *Madame Butterfly*. Frances and I watched this opera together at La Scala in Milan. I thought how sad and ironic it was.

Although I could get bitter towards the Establishment and the staff in prisons, I do not let it get to me because it could only affect me adversely. I don't take drugs as obviously they would have a bad effect too. I suppose the little things that we take for granted in jail are all part of the survival process. Many years ago I used to split matches and we all glued stamps on to envelopes that had come through the post without being franked! Little things like this were necessary.

For about fifteen years of my sentence I was a loner and I believe this helped me to get through. As the old saying goes, 'He who travels alone travels faster.' It is easier to keep a sense of direction. Another thing that has helped me survive this sentence is that I usually go to sleep early in the evening, sometimes as early as 8.30–9 p.m. When I met Joe Louis, the former heavyweight champion, many years ago, he told me that before a fight he would sleep for thirteen hours a night. I know that sleep helps to recharge the batteries. I always rise early as I feel it's essential to have some time to get my head together before the door is opened in the morning. I can honestly say that I haven't had a lie-in in over thirty years.

I work hard on different aspects of survival in jail. So many kids throughout British jails write and inspire me. I feel I owe it to them to lead by example. There are a lot of mind games in prison, both from staff and some of the cons, so it's important to stay on one's toes. I suppose it's best to treat it as a game. Personality clashes between inmates can be very stressful and uncomfortable but it has to be accepted as part of prison life. From time to time there will always be confrontations.

I find that the sexual urge becomes very strong, especially

after having been away for so long. Although we all have times when we have to fantasize, a lifer once wrote in his book that it was advisable to try to switch off these thoughts if one didn't want to go crazy. For what it's worth, I feel that I'm more virile now than I was many years ago!

Yoga and meditation help me to relax. I sit on the bed in the lotus position with a cushion at my back. I place my wrists on my knees and make sure the thumb and forefinger on each hand are touching. I then do my best to switch off and to meditate. It's possible to fall into a trance-like state. The relaxation this brings is better than using any drug. I usually do this alone in my cell but sometimes my friend Richard Reynolds, who comes from Essex, and I practise the yoga exercise when we have nothing else to do.

Like most inmates I am usually pleased to get behind my door at lock-up times. It's a time when I reflect back on the day's events and tidy up my paperwork, which includes incoming and outgoing mail. I try to get it all in some semblance of order using the pyramid system of priority, dealing with the most important things first. I answer as many letters as I can, often while listening to Radio 2 or playing CDs and tapes. During the day, two of my friends, Richard Reynolds and Geoff Jones from Wigan, help me to address the replies. I tend the three plants I have in my cell and make sure I take my vitamins, multi-vitamins, B and C, cod-liver oil and garlic. I also do dynamic tension exercises, yoga, sit-ups and leg exercises.

I feel it's important to try to keep a sense of humour and I sometimes think of the amusing things that went on before bang-up. For instance, if someone asks me if I have any puff (cannabis), which I don't participate in myself, I usually say to them: 'Have a cup of cocoa, it's cheaper!'

Once a week I'm in the habit of rinsing my hair in vinegar – which is supposed to be good for it. One evening when my cell light was out and dusk was settling I picked up the bottle and poured it over my head. It took me a moment to realize it was the wrong bottle and I had picked up the pepper by mistake!

I start each day with a prayer and try my best to figure out, before the door opens again, what I want to do throughout the day. Behind the door we all have our private thoughts about those we love and of our friends in and out. Sometimes I think back to when Ron and I were kids, about six years old, when we both had whooping-cough. We were very ill and I remember how well my mother looked after us and helped to make us better. My wife Rob has the same qualities as my mother. These thoughts help me to stay strong.

I often think about my old friend Billy Hill and I recall one time I had a meet with him in Mayfair. It was outside a large building site that had been fenced off. There was a uniformed copper on his beat nearby. Billy said to him, 'Will you watch my car for a minute and make sure I don't get a parking ticket?' He casually gave the copper a £1 note. This was typical of Billy's easy way of doing things. After the murders of Cornell and McVitie Ron and I went to see Billy Hill at his flat in Bayswater. During our conversation we told him that we'd been responsible. Billy said: 'You must trust me a lot to tell me that.' I replied, 'We would trust you with our lives.' Billy appreciated that we meant this. Ron and I looked upon Billy Hill as a Godfather figure. In fact I rate him as the ultimate Godfather in the annals of British crime.

Just before Ron died he told me that his favourite pastime was sitting in his cell thinking. It has now become my favourite pastime too. All of us, whether we are serving long or short sentences, try to evaluate our situations and to look at where we might go from here, if anywhere. In jail, just as outside, our frame of mind can change according to what happens. Those you mix with during the day can have a good or bad effect on one's way of thinking. My advice to young inmates is to choose their company very carefully. Although perhaps the best piece of advice is that which I mentioned earlier – that one should count one's blessings because there is always someone worse off.

Indignation has been my choice rather than bitterness. This has come at many times, such as when both my mother and my father were seriously ill. I couldn't call them because at that time phones were not available in prisons. When I went to my mother's funeral Ron and I, though both together in the church, could not be close to each other. We were cuffed up on opposite sides. We were not able to see our mother for the last time in her coffin because it had already been sealed. After the service we had to remain in the church while our mother was buried in her grave.

I've had to pick up the pieces, as Ron also had to, and start all over again. The incentive came from within myself. I knew I had to carry on. An example of this is that when I first got my life sentence all my phone-books were taken away. Now I have got twelve of them! I had to fight to keep up with and make new contacts. At times I auto-suggest myself. For example, I could be eating a meal of stew and as long as I enjoy it and auto-suggest that it's the best meal I've ever had, it seems to become as good as caviar and steak might be to someone on the outside. If one practises this on all aspects, forgetting that there is a society outside, then it's easier to accept the conditions, food and environment of prison.

I have already mentioned that I avoid loud and aggressive people because they are a vexation to the spirit. One has to work on this type of thing and not be lax about it. It's the same as showering and shaving every morning – some hardly bother at all. It's not because I want an audience; it's to do with self-respect. It also helps me greatly that I have a beautiful and loyal wife in Rob and this gives me the incentive I need to stay strong.

My sense of direction is guided by the need to survive and maybe one day, God willing, I will be free.

The parole board was due to sit in March 1998 and there was a lot of speculation in the papers about the result. Most of them thought I would and should get parole after thirty years. Simon Heffer, writing in the *Daily Mail*, said: 'Above all, justice must be seen to be done. If a judge decides a man should be punished with 30 years in prison, so be it. Once a man has served those years, and once it is established there is no psychiatric reason for detaining him further, he must be released.' He ends the article with the words, 'If we as a society believe in justice and the rule of law, we can – whatever we might think of Kray – raise no complaint about his being allowed the liberty for which, over 30 years, he has unquestionably paid.'

The Labour MP Harry Cohen also urged the Home Secretary to set me free. In a letter to Mr Straw he wrote: '. . . he has now effectively served his sentence. He should not be punished beyond that.' Even Nipper Reid told the newspapers, 'He has now done the length of time that the court felt was right for his crimes. I see no objection to him being released.'

Included in the parole dossier were two independent reports, one from a Home Office approved consultant psychiatrist, Dr Trevor Turner, and one from Dr David Nias, Senior Lecturer in Clinical Psychology at St Bartholomew's Hospital in London. The psychiatric report to the Board concluded: '[Mr Kray's] current mental state is entirely stable, he has shown no evidence of at-risk behaviour for many years, and he has appropriate insight into his current status. His discharge from prison would involve minimal risk to the community.' The psychological report of David Nias, which included detailed psychometric testing, also concluded that there was no risk in releasing me. 'It is difficult to argue with the claim that he is as fit as he will ever be for a return to the community.'

Other reports were also being prepared by the prison staff. I told Rob that despite the positive psychiatric and psychological reports I still felt I would get a knock-back. After thirty years I didn't expect anything else. The best we could hope for was a move to a Category D prison. My thoughts were confirmed when my solicitor Trevor Linn told me that Jack Straw had not even asked the Parole Board to *consider* release.

Just after my parole reports had been sent off governor Martin and I had a clash. This came about when he spoke to me, among other things, about the issue of getting friends of mine to visit other inmates. He said it was all part of my behaviour pattern and related to whether I got good or bad reports. I concluded, rightly or wrongly, that there was a form of emotional blackmail going on – I knew, even though the parole reports had already gone off, that he could send a further memo to the Board. I said to him, 'I don't like the way you use blackmail so you can put another cross against me in your reports.' I then walked out of the office. This was another reason I never expected to get parole as I will not be a participant in the mind games played by these devious people. It is my opinion that those who run prison establishments do it by playing mind games all the time; these have been a form of mental torture to me over the years.

Lisa, the probation officer, also saw me just after the parole reports went off. During our discussion she said words to the effect, 'whereas most of the other inmates I see tell me to fuck off (and she did specifically use the words 'fuck off'), you are polite, which is unusual. You come across as different due to your polite ways. This is also mentioned in other reports about you. It makes me feel it is more difficult to sum you up.' After I had finished the meeting with her I thought to myself that if that was the case then I would make it easier for them to reach a conclusion for their so-called unbiased reports and so the next time I had a clash with a screw I told him, 'You are fucking stupid!' I was then put on a charge of being abusive to a screw! I was cautioned by a governor called Mr Philips who is quite a reasonable man.

I told Mr Philips, in mitigation, that it was down to cause and effect, that I was a victim and product of my environment. I told him of my discussion with Lisa and that it was my intention to make it easier for everyone to read me by using the language they were all used to. Mr Philips said it was an interesting point. I added that because I was from the old school my polite ways were perhaps somewhat out of date! At the end of my adjudication Mr Philips said, 'If I was you, I would revert back to your original way of being polite.' I saw this as sound advice. I had intended to do so anyway rather than to sink low as they expected.

A couple of days after the adjudication I met Lisa again in the passageway, and she bade me 'good morning' and I returned the greeting. I also said, 'I was speaking about you the other day to Mr Philips.'

She asked, 'What was that about?'

I replied, 'If you ask Mr Philips I'm sure he'll tell you,' and left her standing there.

Talking about Lisa reminds me of another issue she raised during our previous meeting. She asked me, for some reason, what I thought about sex-offenders. I made it quite clear that I did not see them as the salt of the earth. When I described them as scum she rallied to their defence and asked me why I was so against them. I said, 'Where I come from in the East End, there were none there, we wouldn't tolerate them.' The reader may find it interesting to know that on the sex-offenders' wing conditions are much better than those on the main wings. They have benches on the lawn area where they exercise whereas we simply sit on the grass. They also have a putting-green. There are no cameras in their visiting area. The building they are housed in is modernized and has more amenities. I think too much of a liberal attitude is taken with these perverts and that is what I told Lisa.

Around this time I heard that my old friend Lesley Joyce had died abroad. He was a professional crook and was on the run after escaping from Maidstone prison. There was some more bad news; another of my friends, a sweet old lady called Peggy Jamieson, also died and then, not long after, an old friend of many years, Mavis Shippey. Then, just two weeks later, I received a letter informing me that Bill Shippey, Mavis's husband, had also passed away. These were four more friends that I would never see again. It was a very sad feeling.

On 1 April 1998 (April Fool's Day) I returned to the wing after a visit with Rob and was given a message by Bill Taylor that Governor Martin wanted to see me as regards my application for a town visit. I went to the office and Governor Martin was sitting at the desk. Lisa, the probation officer, and PO King were also present. Governor Martin handed me a piece of paper. It was the result of my parole review. I read it quickly as I don't like being in the office with staff; they always seem to wind me up with their mind games. This was another example. They had called me to the office on the pretext of discussing a town leave and I had been passed a piece of paper informing me of a two-year knock-back on my parole. I read it so quickly I had to ask Martin, 'Is that a Cat-D knock-back as well?' He acted as if he wasn't aware of the contents although it was perfectly obvious he must have read it before he gave it to me.

Lisa was staring at me as if she was waiting for a reaction. I wouldn't give them the satisfaction. I just said, 'Thanks very much,' and left the office.

It was what I had expected. I knew that I'd been judged and crucified not on the reports from the professionals, the psychologists and the psychiatrists, but on the reports from prison staff. It was some of these who claimed I manipulated the system and that I was devious. Yet Dr Nias, a psychologist and a man of eminent standing, said in his report '. . . he appears to be an individual who is open and frank in describing his feelings and behaviour'. The prison staff were not able to provide any examples of my so-called devious and manipulative behaviour but their accusations were taken as fact. Some of these members of staff have only served three or four years. They have no degrees or real experience in psychology or psychiatry. In fact one of those who made this allegation was actually a motor mechanic before joining the service! He is the type of man who comes round and counts the number of clothes-hangers in a cell in case there is one too many. He makes a career out of it.

The Parole Board is obviously more impressed by these people than the real professionals in the field of human nature. It is my opinion that they ignored the professionals because they weren't saying what they wanted to hear or to believe.

Another reason given by the Parole Board for turning me down was that I had admitted to drinking alcohol. I have always been honest about the fact that, in the past, I would have the occasional drink when it was available. I have never been disciplined for drinking and there have been no incidents of disorderly conduct or violence arising from it. I would not be a hypocrite and lie – although I easily could have. If I was 'devious', as *they* claimed, I could have easily claimed that I never drank because there was no evidence that I did.

A further reason given for refusing me parole or D-Cat was that I had failed to do offending behaviour courses. Yet I had been told over and over again that I did not *need* to do them. I was told it was all a bit late in the day and that I would not now benefit from them. In August 1997, just before I left Maidstone, a report was prepared by Jane Darling, the prison probation officer. She states in this: 'The Internal Lifer Review Board held here on 20:10:94 agreed that it was unrealistic to undertake offence based work with Mr Kray after so many years.' When I arrived at Wayland I was told by my probation officer that I *would* be expected to do a course and, despite everything I'd been told previously, I said I would be willing to do so. However, shortly after this I was again told by a Principal Officer that there *wasn't* a need to participate in any of these groups. In a further report prepared by another officer for the Parole Board it is said that 'it has not proved realistic, given the length of time that he has served, for Kray to become involved in offending behaviour programmes'. There were contradictions everywhere. It was another example of the mind games they have been playing for thirty years.

When a date was finally set for the course I wasn't informed the day before which is the usual custom. Instead, I was on my way to the gym one morning when I was stopped by a screw and told I should be going to the offending behaviour class. I hadn't been given any time to prepare for it. I went up to the class anyway, where I was then told I wasn't properly dressed and would have to go back to my cell and get changed. At this point I got in an argument and they told me I had an unreasonable attitude! I wasn't allowed into the class.

Later, I received a piece of paper saying that I would not be allowed to join the group and that there was no intention of allowing me on the offending behaviour course in the future.

Although all the reports had already gone into the Parole Board a late memo was sent to them saying that I had refused to do the course.

The majority of inmates who take offending behaviour courses view them as farcical. They go away to their cells afterwards and have a bag (heroin), a puff (cannabis) or a drink. These courses are only usually taken by people because they have to do them but they have very little credibility. For the most part they are ineffectual and achieve nothing.

After Jack Straw's visit to Wayland, where he visited the sex-offenders' wing as well as the main part, he was quoted as saying that he was satisfied the offending courses helped the rapists and sex offenders. Myself and other inmates here saw this as completely ridiculous. If psychiatrists and psychologists are not successful with the likes of Sidney Cook, then what possible effect can ordinary prison staff have?

Shortly after the Parole Board decision was made public, my wife Rob went on television campaigning for my release. There were two telephone opinion polls, one in Norfolk and the other in London, and in both cases over 80 per cent of the people said that I should be released. In London over 30,000 people voted. Rob also went on Talk Radio and other radio stations and the response was very positive on my behalf.

After one of the television interviews with Rob there was also an interview with a Parole Board representative. She gave a list of reasons why a lifer should remain in prison . . . and none why they should ever be let out! She especially mentioned the issue of remorse, although this was not an issue in my case at all. She also talked about all the things that would be taken into consideration including the inmate's level of literacy. I believe she was probably talking about qualifications. I have written five books, produced one documentary, *The Epilogue of Ron Kray*, and, God willing, this will be my sixth book. None of this will count as a credit to me. In fact, knowing the system, it will be another debit.

I received hundreds of letters after my parole application was turned down. They came from all over the country and were very supportive. Many of them said that they couldn't believe paedophiles such as Sidney Cook were being allowed out and yet I was being kept in. They also wrote to the newspapers and complained about the decision. Richard Stott wrote a column in the *News of the World*. He said, 'The reasons given by the Parole Board for refusing to release Reggie Kray or even send him to an open prison are spurious and cowardly . . . He is a victim of a spineless conspiracy.' Lord Tebbit in the *Mail on Sunday* also joined in the debate. He expressed his disgust at the release of the Irish prisoners while I remained in prison. He wrote, '. . . it does not just look hard, it stinks of injustice . . . Poor old Reggie – perhaps he didn't kill enough people to qualify for parole even after 30 years.' Simon Heffer in the *Daily Mail* wrote again about my situation, calling it 'an affront to the rule of law . . . The latest excuses wheeled out for his incarceration are comical.'

After I read the Parole Board decision I was reminded of when the Wayland staff had come to interview me at Maidstone. They informed me that after I had been there for about eight months I would get town leaves and then home visits. They also foresaw that I would be released after about eighteen months. All these promises have been broken. But I'm not surprised.

When I was at Lewes prison some years back a probation officer said to me, 'One of the reasons they don't want to let you out is that they can imagine you turning up to report to your probation officer in a Rolls-Royce!' She said this would be seen as the wrong image for someone who had been away for so many years. Ron and I have often been criticized over the years for being photographed with celebrities. Yet it seems that members of the Establishment can be photographed with celebrities and there is no criticism whatsoever. There are so many double standards in society today that it is hard to keep up with them all!

On 7 May Rob was interviewed live by Sky television at 7.30 in the morning. It was the launch of the campaign to have me released. I had spent almost thirty years in prison. I knew that the interview was taking place and so I arranged the previous day that I would be able to watch the programme in the TV room along with some friends. When I went into the room I discovered that the TV was set to the wrong channel. I went upstairs to the office three times and asked if they would switch it over but to no avail. They wouldn't do it. They deliberately denied me the opportunity of watching. Nevertheless, throughout the day there was massive coverage on the TV and radio and I was able to see and hear some of it. There were a number of debates on the radio and many people rang in to say I should be released.

That evening some friends held a small party for me to celebrate the fact I had almost completed thirty years! There were sandwiches and cake, peanuts and biscuits spread out on a table as a buffet. On the table, alongside the food, was a large note with the words '30 years completed. Reg Kray. Respect.' They decided to hold the party on this night instead of the following one as, quite rightly as it turned out, they expected there to be a number of cell spins (searches) on the 8th.

On the Friday morning I played a tape of the music 'Amapola'. This had been played at my wedding and seemed appropriate for the completion of my 30 years. It turned out to be a smashing day. Rob and I had arranged for a small plane to fly over the prison. This was piloted by a friend called Jim Stephens. Attached to the plane was a long banner with the words 'Reg Kray. Political Prisoner. 1968–1998'. The letters were in red on a white background. The sun was shining and the banner trailed through a pale blue sky. I was out on exercise when the plane arrived. Other inmates cheered, clapped and whistled. They came from all four wings. They came over to shake my hand and to walk beside me in a show of support.

As soon as the plane appeared there was a gathering of screws on the field. One of the staff in the office was overheard to say that the plane was trespassing! Another tried to get the cameras on the plane so they could take down his number. Jim circled the prison for about twenty minutes until we were all taken back inside for lunchtime lock-up.

About a month after this I was told that the Lifer PO wished to see me. She said that my town visit application had been rejected even though probation and one of the governors had agreed to it. After my parole result I wasn't surprised by the decision. I had a further application for a town visit turned down eighteen months later. As escorted town visits are part of the so-called 'rehabilitation' of a prisoner it was obvious that I was going nowhere – in every sense. This application was rejected on the grounds that the police were concerned it could lead to 'large crowds and possible public disorder'. It went on to claim, 'This would not be in the public, Prison Service or indeed your own interest.'

Since arriving at Wayland, I have had the pleasure, along with my wife, of making some new friends. One of these is Rob Ferguson, who runs his own music and technology company in Bedford; he's been a good friend and very helpful with the campaign. Mick Gallagher, who created the internet site (www.thekrays.co.uk), is another I must mention. He has given up a lot of his time and it is appreciated. I have also got to know and become good friends with Alex Carey, who fought in Iraq and showed great bravery. When he visits he tells me his stories of these times and I am always enthralled. Greg Bone is another friend I've made, a very talented composer, who has been working with me and putting my lyrics to music. He is currently working on some songs with the Fun Lovin' Criminals.

My wife and I enjoyed a visit with Huey Morgan, lead singer of the Fun Lovin' Criminals, and their manager Jonathan Block. We discussed the lyrics I had written and they expressed an interest in putting together a single and then an album. A few months later I also got to meet Fast and Mackie, the other members of the band. We all got on really well. At the Reading Festival, Huey dedicated their popular song 'King of New York', about John Gotti, to me. He changed one of the verses to 'Hey Hey Free Reggie Kray' and got the 70,000 crowd to sing along.

My good friend Bill Curbishley visits when he is not jetting off to other parts of the world; he sometimes flies down from London by helicopter. Bill is a very special person, warm and genuine and full of life. He has excellent principles and has always been here for me throughout my sentence. He has great love for his family and his children. I know he is the type of person who would have remained the same even without his success. His friendship means more to Rob and me than words can ever say. Wilf Pine, the entrepreneur and former manager of Black Sabbath, also visits; he's a good friend and was a good friend to Ron as well. Two other pals who have been campaigning for my release are the King of the Gypsy fighters Bartley Gorman and the gypsy Tommy Lee. Jools Holland and members of his band have also been to visit, as has the singer Matt Goss.

Some of the other people from way back I keep in touch with are Flanagan, the first Page 3 girl from the sixties, and Helen Keating, who is in the series *London's Burning*. Barbara Windsor, though I haven't seen her in recent years, has been supportive in the campaign for my release. I also keep in touch with Johnny Nash. I would like to thank Johnny for visiting my late parents, after my imprisonment, and making sure they were OK. My mother and father always looked on Johnny as a good friend, as did Ron, Charlie and I.

John Pearson, who wrote *The Profession of Violence*, has been to visit with his wife, Lyn. We discussed many things about the past and the present. It was good to see them both again and we have kept in touch. John and Mel Redgrave are also welcome visitors; I'm always pleased to see them. In addition, I must mention Stuart and Marcelle Garratt and their lovely children, Tanya, Kirsty and Sian. They have both been excellent friends to Rob, as well as myself, and she has had many happy days in their company. I also had the pleasure of meeting them in Wayland. I often think how nice it would be if Rob and I could have dinner with all our friends one day in the future.

A fellow lifer called Kevin, who was on the same spur, became a friend too. Kevin and I would have tea or coffee together and he would talk about his life story. He used to live like a recluse. For five years he lived in a forest a few miles from Plymouth in the area of Plympton. He had survived by eating trout, snake meat and berries of all kinds. He had been content living this way and had the peace of mind that comes with no financial or emotional worries. I reached the conclusion that many would envy his way of life. Kevin didn't miss the neon lights but instead saw the beauty of the moon and the stars at night. He would awake to the morning dew and the soft pitter-patter of rain on the leaves. It seemed a shame that he had been denied this tranquil sanctuary.

Mr Platts-Mills, the QC who defended my brother Ron at the trial, surprised me with a visit one day. Although he is now ninety-four years of age he is still a very active and lively person. He said he wanted to help if possible and voiced his disapproval that I had not yet been released by Jack Straw. I said I would confer with my solicitor Trevor Linn and thanked him. I asked Mr Platts-Mills the secret of his longevity and he said that he took a cold bath each day and also ate a quantity of lemons. At the end of his visit we bade each other goodbye. It was sad to think that this would probably be the last time we'd meet. I'd grown fond of him over the years and Ron had liked and respected him a lot.

Recently I was shattered when I learnt that one of my best friends had died from a heart attack. His name was John Copley. He was serving a life sentence at HMP Kingston in Portsmouth and had been in prison for over twenty-years. John was seventy-two when he died. We first met in Lewes and had corresponded ever since. He was a great letter-writer and a very intelligent and perceptive man. Much to my regret the final phone-call I was able to make to John was not satisfactory. I was allowed to contact him at the hospital but the line was very bad and as the call also took place in the presence of the prison governor and a PO it made it difficult to say the words I would have liked to say. He will be sadly missed.

Many of the friends I have made at Wayland, apart from the ones I have already described, have asked me to mention them in this book. I am pleased to do so. They are: Huggy, Ollie, Shuby, Chris, Rick, Ali, Mick, Roy, Nitty, Logi, Patrick, Kevin, Tich, Darren, Dean, Bart, Phil and Leroy. I would like to make special mention of Mr Hall, a Rastafarian, who walks the field at exercise every day. We always bid each other good morning. He is a man of very good principles and is liked by all, black and white. Patrick Grant has also been very helpful to me during my stay at Wayland. Newton Barnett, another friend, used to be a good pro fighter. He had fifty-nine fights and narrowly lost on points to Kirkland Laing. Newton still trains hard.

During weekend exercise periods on the field I have sparred and shadow-boxed with my companions Danny Woollard and John Waites. Danny is one of the 'old school' who had many street fights and knows everyone worth knowing in London. He has written a book called *Nothing to Prove*, which I'm sure will be very revealing because when Danny reminisces everyone listens intently. John Waites has been a considerable help, addressing envelopes to people all over the country who have written to me.

One Friday morning there were three fights, which were linked together, out on the field. An Irish kid had his lip badly bitten and was in a state of shock. At one point there were two men fighting against one so Danny Woollard scuffed hold of one of them and evened up the odds. He didn't like to see a liberty taken. This fight gave the inmates something to talk about for the rest of the day.

My friend Ray Gilbert, who is on the same wing and spur, shared a journey with me to Norwich prison for a chest X-ray. This was because an elderly lifer on the spur had been discovered to have TB. We were taken to Norwich cuffed-up. I'm glad to say that the results proved negative. Around the same time there was also an Aids scare. A visiting dentist was alleged to have treated an inmate with Aids and failed to sterilize his equipment after. He had gone on to treat a number of other inmates. I had recently visited the dentist to have my teeth cleaned but was relieved to discover that the event had taken place four days after he had treated me!

Quite recently Ray saved my cell from being burnt out. Early one night, as I was talking to Ray in the corridor, he smelled burning. He rushed over to my cell. I had placed a pillow-slip over the bulb of a table lamp and it had caught alight. He grabbed the pillow-slip and slung it into the sink and opened the window quickly to let the smoke out. It was quick thinking on Ray's part. I followed him into my cell and noticed that all my paperwork was near the lamp, which could have made matters even worse!

Despite the setbacks, I have mostly enjoyed my stay at Wayland. I have been shown the utmost respect from all the cons, most of whom were not even born at the time of my conviction. This prison is not really a good place for lifers but I have tried to make the best of it.

One particular memory that stays in my mind was a Lifers' Day that took place in summer. We were allowed to have a visit from 9.30 a.m. to 3.30 p.m. and for the afternoon they let us go outside on the field. They put up a small marquee and provided food and tea and soft drinks. It was a great day. I was joined by my wife, Rob, Bradley, Donna, Paul Marcus, Chris Rowlands and his young son and friend, and my old friend Georgie Woods. We were able to sit together, talk, eat, walk freely, and kick a ball around. Bradley, Paul and I did some sparring. Later they played some music and Rob and I had a waltz to the music of Charles Aznavour's 'Dance in the Old Fashioned Way'. To round it off Rob and I sat on the field alone; Rob massaged my forehead and I felt totally relaxed, more so in fact that at any other time in thirty-one years.

It was shattering when everyone had to leave. It was worse when we got back on the wing. We felt, even more than usual, the tension of the environment we actually lived in. On the field, with the people we cared about, we had experienced our first sense of freedom in many years. It was the first time we had walked freely with our loved ones. I thought of all the years that had passed me by. When we were banged-up from 5 to 6 p.m. for evening lock-up it was more claustrophobic than ever and that single hour seemed like an eternity.

I'm sure you will find what I'm about to tell you a strange sequel to the day I enjoyed on the field. For some considerable time before this event, when I'd been in my cell and wanting to relax, I had thought of an idyllic scene where I was sitting on a lawn with Rob, surrounded by my close friends, feeling completely happy. It was a dream of mine. Thinking about it always helped me. It dawned on me, after this special day we had spent together, that the scene I had envisaged for so long had eventually come true, although I had imagined the scene to take place on a lawn somewhere in the country – perhaps that part will follow one day in the future! I still think back to those ultimate moments when I was on the field with my eyes closed, with Rob massaging my forehead, and my friends close by. But I also count my blessings and am thankful for the day that was given to me.

A few months after this my old friend Georgie Woods died of a heart attack. I was glad we'd had the opportunity to spend some time together. He was a true gentleman and will be missed by everyone who knew him and especially by his daughter Sharon.

During 5 p.m. bang-up I usually sit at the window of my cell and on sunny days get the benefit of half an hour of sunshine. I find this very relaxing. The other evening I observed something I would have liked to photograph. There was a pale blue sky and a light breeze. Outside my window pages of newspapers were being blown across the grass. In some strange way I related it to the inmates who had been recently shipped out of prison or who had been released at the end of their sentence. Just as yesterday's newspapers were yesterday's news, the passing cons, like ships in the night, were also impermanent. It was an odd eerie scene. There is a window two cells away to the right of me which used to be occupied by a kid called Red. He had been shipped out a week earlier. Over a period of time I had got used to him calling my name through the window. Yet he was there no more. I guess I am also part of this continuous flow. Others will take our place in this ongoing cycle.

The reasons given by the Parole Board for keeping me in prison are no more than excuses. It is my opinion that the authorities and the Establishment have no intention of ever releasing me. I have had to come to terms with this. But I am still determined to enjoy the moment and to live day by day. The following words by Helen Milliebat sum up my attitude to life:

I AM

I was regretting the past and fearing the future, suddenly my
  Lord was speaking.
'My name is I AM.'
He paused. I waited. He continued.
'When you live in the past with its mistakes and regrets, it is
  hard.
I am not there, my name is not I WAS.
When you live in the future with its problems and fears it is
  hard.
I am not there. My name is not I WILL BE.
When you live in this moment, it is not hard. I am here.
My name is I AM.'

I have a positive attitude and I am realistic about my situation. This leads me to the fact that I owe so much to so many. Firstly, to my wife Rob for her sustained love and support, also to Bradley and his wife Donna, to my brother Charlie, to Trevor Linn and Mark Goldstein, to those others close to me whom I consider family, to so many good friends and to all the supporters who have never failed me. I thank them all because I know that Rob, and all the others I have mentioned, will continue to fight for my release.

I know that Ron is watching over me as are the rest of my late family and my late wife Frances. Ron is with me in spirit and so we walk as one. Now that my thirty-year minimum has been reached I remind the reader that Ron travelled most of this journey with me. He is still with me.

If I am ever released I want only to live with my wife Rob, to be with close friends, and to just relax. This is my interpretation of freedom.

On this Friday, 8 May 1998, at the completion of my thirty-year sentence, my thoughts are with Ron.

I hope the reader has found *A Way of Life* to be of interest.

No truth is ever a lie. Truth will always prevail.

Some did not believe that I would ever make it, but I did. And . . .

I DID IT MY WAY!!

A FINAL NOTE

Two years later and I am facing another Parole review. The Wayland Prison staff have produced very negative reports. I have been in the system too long to be surprised. I have had interviews but find myself reading yet another set of bizarre and twisted parole statements, words I have never said, conversations that have never taken place. I have done everything that was asked of me at the last parole hearing but it is still not enough. A Governor suggested during a meeting that I should do an 'Enhanced Thinking Skills' course. This had not been put forward at the last review or in the intervening two years and was simply a new hoop they wanted me to jump through. It was held against me when I objected. When I saw the Governor again on his own he said 'between the two of us' he didn't see any reason why I should do the course!

During an interview with an internal probation officer, she asked: 'What do you intend to do about controlling the media?' I thought the question was naïve and ridiculous. I replied that even Frank Sinatra didn't have that kind of control!

I have been criticized for many things including giving signatures and writing to other inmates, for writing to Mike

Tyson, for writing song lyrics and for seeing the band Fun Lovin' Criminals on a visit. I have been especially criticized for choosing to see an independent psychologist rather than the prison psychologist. Despite Dr Gudjonnson being one of the top psychologists in the country, a man known to and respected by the Prison Service and the Parole Board, it was inferred by the screws that I would be seen as trying to 'buy' a good report. I think a man of Dr Gudjonnson's high standing and integrity would have something to say about that! It has been my experience that prison psychologists only serve their own master – and that is the Prison Service.

I am not optimistic about a positive result. I have served over thirty-two years in prison but obviously, for some, it is not enough.

In March I heard the news that my brother Charlie had been admitted to hospital from Parkhurst. He only stayed a few days before he was returned to prison but continued to feel unwell. I had already put in a request for a visit and when Charlie was re-admitted to St Mary's I was told I would be allowed to go and see him.

I left Wayland at 8 a.m. on 18 March with four screws as an escort. One of them was driving the van. As we pulled away from the prison a red Ford car followed us. I thought it was the law but one of the screws told me it was the press. We could see the feller holding a camera. The car followed us all the way to Winchester prison, where we stopped at about 11 a.m. The driver made good time and provided all of us with boiled sweets along the way! There was also a box full of ham and cheese sandwiches, crisps, apples and cartons of milk. Although there were no smoking signs in the van, I was allowed a smoke – which was a relief.

At Winchester I was put in a small cell and the staff were polite and cordial. I had no cause for complaint. They gave me sausage, egg and chips for lunch with a cup of tea. Someone had pencilled *Chelsea FC* on the table and on the chair someone had written *Ritchie Boy Smith*. There is always graffiti in cells.

As we left Winchester at about 12.30 p.m. the press tried to get a photograph. The reporter ran across the road with his camera. I'm not sure if he got his picture but he took some more shots as we were getting petrol a few miles on. When we reached the ferry at Portsmouth the photographers had a field day and another car joined the one that had been following us. The ferry men chased them off but not before they had taken plenty of shots of me in the van. When we arrived on the Isle of Wight the press continued to follow us all the way to Parkhurst until we passed through the large gate. Instead of entering the main building we left again and the van travelled to St Mary's Hospital just down the road. The press stayed with us and took yet more pictures as we left the van and went into the hospital.

We went straight to Newport Ward to see Charlie. He was pleased to see me just as I was to see him. He was sitting up in bed. There were two screws in the room; these were part of his bed-watch, a team who stayed with him for twenty-four hours a day. Charlie looked very ill. We talked for half an hour before I had to return to Parkhurst.

I was met at the gate by two screws who had retired. They were called Mr Shepherd and Mr Drury and had been with me at my mother's funeral years before. They are two gentlemen. I was put in Charlie's cell on C-wing. It used to be the psychiatric wing and, a long time ago, I had spent three years there with Ron. I met my old friend Noel Travers there and a friend who had visited Ron in Broadmoor by the name of Mick Glass. I also met one of Charlie's friends, Pete Grayston, who was a pro kick-fighter and a karate black belt, and Fossie, the only survivor of the Iranian siege. When I first arrived one of the medical team saw me to make sure I was OK.

I visited Charlie again on the Sunday morning and on the Tuesday of the following week. Each time the press were waiting outside the hospital and once a television reporter shot some film which was later used on *Meridian News*. Charlie was getting progressively worse. He was in a wheelchair and had to take regular oxygen. His legs had swollen to twice their normal size. I spoke to Dr Baski, who informed me that Charlie had heart wastage. I was told his condition could result in heart failure. At the same time I heard that the Prison Service and Home Office were saying he could still be going back to Parkhurst, either to the Hospital Wing or C-wing, which not only upset Charlie but seemed to me totally inconsiderate and inhumane.

The last time I saw Charlie was on Tuesday 4 April. I saw him early in the evening and he died later that night. It was heartbreaking. His eyes were shut. He had an oxygen mask attached to his mouth and was breathing heavily through it. He had never once complained even when the doctors told him he had less than eight months to live. They did everything they could for him and, along with the nurses, were kind and considerate. My friend Wilf Pine was like a rock during this time. He visited Charlie every single day and even stayed overnight towards the end, keeping him company if he woke, making sure he was never alone. The bed-watch escort was also very considerate, allowing Charlie some privacy. I was told that the doctors, along with Charlie's close friends, had tried to get Charlie compassionate parole so he could spend whatever remained of his life at home. This is normally granted when the inmate is terminally ill. In Charlie's case it was to no avail. Jack Straw obviously rejected their letters of appeal. Charlie was hopeful for a while; he thought he might be shown some compassion. But it was not to be. Compassion is obviously reserved for the likes of Saunders, the Guinness criminal, and General Pinochet.

The night before Charlie died I was rushed to St Mary's Hospital because his condition had deteriorated. It was about 8.15 p.m. and raining hard. The press were still waiting outside the hospital. It felt strange to be out in the darkness. The flash-bulbs were popping. I couldn't remember the last time I had been out at night.

When I saw Charlie he seemed to know he was going to die. He said, 'I hope Diane gets here soon – please God she gets here in time.' Charlie's prayers were answered. He passed away peacefully the following night holding Diane's hand. Diane was Charlie's regular girlfriend over the years. She was with him till the last.

Three staff came to my cell at Parkhurst to tell me that Charlie had died at 8.45 p.m.

On 18 April I was taken from Wayland to Belmarsh prison, where I was to spend the night before Charlie's funeral. The inmates and staff were helpful and friendly towards me. I had visited Charlie there a few years before when he was on remand. It brought back some memories.

From Belmarsh I was taken to Bethnal Green Police Station the following morning. The police left nothing to chance. There were over two hundred on the streets, with a motorcycle escort for the funeral procession. There were also helicopters above. I arrived at W. English & Son, the funeral directors', at around 11 a.m. There was already a large crowd and I spotted some familiar faces – friends like Bartley Gorman and Peter and Lyn Tansey – to name just a few.

Inside the funeral parlour Rob and I spent a few quiet

minutes with Charlie. I laid a photograph beside the coffin, a picture of Charlie, Ron and me, and said a silent prayer. We then left for St Matthew's.

The streets were packed and the cars moved slowly through the crowd. My prison escort were very pleasant – I couldn't have asked for better. I looked out of the window at all the people. They smiled and waved. I felt very emotional. The sun was shining and it was a beautiful day. It was also a day full of sadness.

Inside St Matthew's we made our way to the front of the church. Sitting close to me, to my left, were my old friends Wilf Pine, Bradley and Donna Allardyce, Paul Marcus, Frank Fraser and Marilyn Wisbey. Behind were many old and new friends. I saw Eric Mason and was reminded of the time we spent together in Wandsworth prison – he has always been a sound person. Roberta sat to my right. My wife and I have been through a lot of adversity together over the past few years. We have endured many trials and tribulatons. Rob's loyalty to me has never faltered and, as a result, she has got to know me better than anybody else.

Fathers John Scott and Ken Rimini conducted the service. I would like to express my thanks to them, for their kind words and compassion. They were a comfort to me. I would also like to thank Paul Keays and his wife Terri, of W. English & Son, for organizing the funeral. I appreciate all their hard work, their kindness and consideration. Thanks should go as well to Richard Grayston, who organized the security on the day – he, along with his men, did an excellent job. Thanks as well to my friend Flanagan for all her help.

After the service the cortège wound its way to Chingford Cemetery. On the way I was reminded of a letter I received just days after Charlie died. It was from a young kid called Lance who I had first met at Ron's funeral when he ran alongside the car. He wrote and told me he couldn't be present at Charlie's funeral and enclosed a photograph of himself and Charlie that had been taken a few years ago. He asked if I would place it on Charlie's grave and I did this for him.

At Chingford I laid flowers on the graves of my mother and father, of Ron, of my late wife Frances, and my nephew Gary, Charlie's son. I dropped a red rose on to Charlie's coffin. I stood for a while beside my wife and friends. My mind was full of many things – the past, the present and the future. It was yet another ending, another farewell. After Charlie's funeral I went back, with my escort, to Bethnal Green Police Station. Later that evening I returned to Wayland prison.

Sad to say on 29 April my little friend Paul Stapleton also passed away. He was just thirteen years of age. He had suffered for many years from muscular dystrophy. His mother Maria brought him to see me at Gartree prison when he was only four years old. I will always remember his courage. He fell over again and again in the visiting-room but continued to get to his feet and to keep on smiling and laughing. Little Paul was a lovable and precious child and I will never forget him. I'm sure he is in heaven. I would like to thank everyone who helped with donations while Paul was alive. He will be missed by many, especially by his family, and I pray he is now happy and at peace.

This will be the sixth book I have completed and now I will take a long rest. I feel at peace with the world so I cannot complain.

HOW DO WE SAY GOODBYE?
(Dedicated to Charlie)

How do we say goodbye?
Do I sigh or do I cry?
All that goodbye means
I find so hard to comprehend,
Hard to imagine this as the end.
Maybe we'll meet again one day,
A new beginning and not the end.

Reg Kray

EPILOGUE
by Roberta Kray

One final chapter to this book was always intended. Reg might have expressed many things in it – joy, sadness, hope, disappointment or expectancy, perhaps only the vision of some distant light at the end of an impossibly long and dark tunnel. They were words that were waiting to be written. They would have reinforced, as he so badly wanted, the message that there are better ways to spend your life than behind bars. They would have spoken, although never explicitly, of determination, courage and pain. Above all, they were words that would have revealed a little more about the man who wrote them.

What I never envisaged, *could* never have envisaged, was that I would have to write this final chapter myself. Reg died of cancer on Sunday, 1 October 2000, just a few weeks short of his sixty-seventh birthday. He died a free man although he had little opportunity to enjoy his freedom. For a brief period only the door was opened and the future given back to him.

It is hard to know where the end begins. There may be certain defining points, facts delivered or truths spoken, but there is nothing absolute. Reg's illness was not sudden. He suffered for a number of years. He asked for help from the only people he could ask – the prison medical staff. He saw them frequently. He described his symptoms. They examined him and took notes. Their conclusion was that he had Irritable Bowel Syndrome (IBS). They prescribed Milk of Magnesia, enemas and paracetamol. Despite the lack of any improvement they persisted with the same treatment.

Things grew particularly bad during the last nine months of his stay at Wayland Prison.

Based on the conclusion of the 'experts', we tried to find ways of easing his symptoms by reducing stress and improving his diet. Neither of these was a very realistic objective in the circumstances. Steadily his health deteriorated, the pain and discomfort increasing with each passing week. After keeping fit for so many years he stopped training or going to the gym. The only exercise he continued, when he felt up to it, was his daily walk.

In January 2000 Reg was eventually taken to the West Norwich Hospital where a few tests were carried out. The doctors came to the same conclusion as the Prison Service. Reg was told once again that he had IBS. By this time our feelings were mixed, a combination of relief and frustration. His symptoms were getting progressively worse but the diagnosis remained the same.

On visits Reg was constantly uncomfortable and in pain. He saw the prison doctor or nurse most days but to no effect; they continued to dole out the same ineffective medication. Around this time reports began to circulate in the press that he was very ill and might have cancer. I wrote to the specialist at the West Norwich Hospital who had treated Reg to get confirmation of their results. I wanted to put Reg's mind at rest and to refute the newspaper articles. Reg received a definitive letter from them dated the 3rd of February stating that there was no reason to believe he had cancer of any sort.

I believed them ... and that will always be my greatest regret.

Reg's parole review, due in March, was postponed due to Charlie's illness. He was thankful he was able to go to HMP Parkhurst and visit his brother in the local hospital. It always preyed on his mind that Ron had died alone. However, even while Reg was staying there he was often unable to make the short journey across the road to St Mary's due to 'staff shortages'. Other inmates at Parkhurst were very supportive; they welcomed Reg and treated him with kindness and consideration. Reg knew that Charlie would not recover. He realized it was only a matter of time.

Sadly, Charlie died on 4 April 2000. The funeral took place on the 19th. Reg attended along with his prison escort and an extraordinarily large police presence. It is hard to say why the police were out in such force, with hundreds on the streets in addition to helicopters and a motorcycle escort.

It was a terrible day for Reg. He found some consolation in revisiting those parts of the East End that were special to him: Bethnal Green Road, Vallance Road where he grew up, Pellici's café, and St Matthew's where the service for Ron had also been held. He saw the thousands of people out on the street and felt their love and sympathy for him. In his grief he was comforted by the knowledge of their affection.

We were together for only a brief time that day. He arrived at the undertakers, W. English, chained to his escort. All his emotions were displayed on his face. We had a stiff whisky and Coke waiting for him. Charlie was the last of his immediate family. He had lost his mother and father, his twin brother Ron, his nephew Gary and now Charlie, all of them taken from him while he was in prison. If people ever imagine that Reg wasn't punished enough for his crimes, then they should think again – the loss of all his family was a punishment that went beyond his many years of incarceration.

Before we left, Reg asked me to go with him to the chapel of rest. The prison escort accompanied us. In that small room Reg took my hand and said a prayer over Charlie's coffin. I was aware of the stillness, the scent of the flowers and Reg's terrible sadness. But above all, I was aware of the presence of strangers. Even in grief, even within the confines of that tiny room, he was not allowed a moment's reprieve.

Six months later I would stand in that room again. But this time there would be no hand in mine. There would be no comfort.

It wasn't until 3 July 2000 that Reg finally got his Parole Board interview, a long and inexplicable delay, even taking into account the circumstances. The Board itself would sit at some point during the following weeks. Reg never really believed he would get a positive result. He knew the best he could hope for was a move to an open prison but he felt in his heart that it wouldn't happen. He was undoubtedly right. It had taken twenty-seven years to progress from an A-category to a C-category prison so it wasn't likely he would be allowed the luxury of hope after only three years at Wayland. Why this should be is an important question.

I remember the Lifers' Day at Wayland, just as Reg does in this book. It was a special day, and a very emotional one. But I remember it for another reason as well. It was the time I talked to a number of staff, including his personal officer and some governors, and they all said exactly the same thing, that there was *no* reason for Reg to be turned down for an open prison at his next parole review. He was doing well. Everything was fine. They were reassuring and encouraging.

However, when the review finally came around numerous reasons for refusal materialized in staff reports. He had suddenly and mysteriously ceased to be suitable. They all, without exception, recommended Reg should remain in C-category conditions for a further period of time. They all suggested he should do another prison course, a psychology-based favourite entitled 'Enhanced Thinking Skills'. Their recommendations were made with the same suspiciously familiar phrases.

I remember a story that Reg related to me around this time. He had been called into a meeting to discuss his review, and the prison psychologist (a young woman with little knowledge or experience of prison life) suggested he would benefit from this course. He told her that, with all due respect, she would probably benefit even more from doing it herself. It was not a wise thing to say but it was a response born of anger and frustration.

This was a man who was already sixty-six years of age and had spent over thirty-two years in prison. This was a man who nobody in the system had bothered with for over thirty years, and who no one had *ever* asked to complete a course in all that time. This was a man who had been left to deal with everything himself. And then, predictably, when the end was in sight, the Prison Service decided it would take an interest.

The whole issue has already been chronicled in this book. I only raise it again because of its importance. In addition to his basic punishment, his thirty years plus of incarceration, Reg also faced the perpetual torment of Prison Service psychology.

It is right that society should be protected from dangerous people. If there is overwhelming evidence an inmate will re-offend then their release should be very closely examined. If an individual's release will erode public confidence in the judicial system then that issue must be addressed. Naturally the Home Office will not go around releasing terrorists who have blown up or maimed thousands of people. Obviously the Home Office will not sign the release papers for unrepentant, vicious and persistent paedophiles. That any of these people should be released before a sixty-six-year-old ex-gangster, who had already served over thirty-two years for the killing of a fellow-criminal, who had shown he had no intention or inclination to return to a life of crime and who held no existing violent tendencies, would be an anomaly so perverse as to be laughable. Wouldn't it?

After Reg was turned down for parole in 1998, his solicitor Trevor Linn released a press statement claiming that the Home Office was handing him a 'death sentence'. They were prophetic words. Had Reg been released at this time there is every possibility his cancer could have been detected at an earlier stage.

It was because of Reg's previously bad experiences with prison psychologists that his solicitor suggested we once again arrange for an independent psychologist and psychiatrist to make assessments and write reports for the 2000 Parole Board review. We chose two high-ranking and esteemed professionals. Dr MacKeith, a forensic psychiatrist, and Professor Gudjonsson, a psychologist, were men whose integrity could not be called into question. The Prison Service and the Parole Board were informed of our intentions.

Reg received a lot of criticism from prison staff over his decision to ask for independent opinions. The amount of resistance in relation to these two experts, both highly regarded by the courts, seemed indicative of the way the parole review was likely to go.

Both experts spent long periods of time with Reg. Their reports were detailed and well-balanced. Dr MacKeith concluded that he should be moved to 'open' conditions and released in three to six months. He expressed his belief that there was now a 'window of opportunity' for a well-managed release into the community. Professor Gudjonsson also expressed the opinion that Reg was ready for the transition to an 'open' prison. Despite their positive reports we remained doubtful as to the outcome of the review.

Around the middle of July 2000, Reg told me something I will never forget. He had felt very ill during the night at Wayland and had rung the emergency bell several times to ask for assistance. Nobody came. He continued to ring but nobody responded. Eventually, he gave up. Whoever was on duty that night had absolutely no interest in answering his calls for help. Reg was left alone, sick and in pain. It disgusted me at the time but in retrospect, looking at how close he was to becoming hospitalized, it was clearly a disgrace.

Reg rang me first thing on the morning of Thursday, 27 July to say he was being moved to the hospital wing of Norwich Prison for more tests. It was very sudden. For a couple of months he had suffered some bladder problems and now these were going to be investigated. He was supposed to see a urologist at the Norfolk and Norwich Hospital the following week. The doctor at Wayland had also suggested that he might be suffering from a kidney infection.

I arranged a visit at Norwich Prison for the next day. Reg looked terrible. He was in obvious pain and clutching his stomach for the entire visit. I went to the desk and asked if someone from the medical department could come down and give him some pain relief. I stressed that paracetamol was not adequate; he was obviously in need of something much stronger. Half an hour later a nurse came down with two paracetamol. Reg said he couldn't swallow them. I broke them up into small pieces and got him some water and he was finally able to take them. I was angry but knew I had to be careful. I didn't want to antagonize the staff. I wouldn't have to face the consequences if anyone took offence . . . but Reg might. He had enough to cope with as it was.

I was finally able to get hold of the Norwich Prison doctor on the Monday and she told me they thought Reg might have a urinary tract infection. He had been for tests at the hospital but nothing conclusive had transpired. He was due to return in a couple of weeks and in the meantime he'd remain at Norwich Prison. There was nothing obvious to cause alarm. I was relieved that Reg was away from Wayland and in close proximity to a proper hospital.

It wasn't long, however, before things took a turn for the worse. Reg became very sick on the Tuesday night, so ill that HMP Norwich had to move him back to the Norfolk and Norwich Hospital the following morning. Reg rang and told me what was happening: he said he'd been throwing up blood. I got a taxi and went straight to the hospital. We spent the morning together and in the afternoon he underwent an endoscopy, a camera in his stomach, to try to find out what was wrong. The results were inconclusive but a further X-ray revealed a large blockage in his small intestine and an operation was scheduled for the next day.

There was, of course, a prison escort with Reg at this time. Two officers from HMP Norwich remained with him constantly on twelve-hour shifts. He was cuffed and chained to one of the escort and they both accompanied him wherever he went. Despite his sickness and the obvious fact he wasn't going anywhere in a hurry, 'rules are rules' and they weren't going to be broken for anything as mundane as common mercy. He was wheeled through the hospital, down in the lift and along the corridors with a long chain pulling on his wrist, an additional discomfort to the awful pain he was already experiencing. Discretion was certainly not the order of the day; they couldn't have drawn more attention to him if they'd tried.

I stayed with Reg after the exploratory investigation. We were given a small room – Reg, myself and the prison escort. Reg was exhausted. I sat beside him on the bed and he fell asleep in my arms. I remember those hours very clearly. It was the first time I was ever really able to hold him.

Reg was taken down for his operation at about 10 a.m. the following morning. I was concerned but also hopeful. Perhaps after all this time, after everyone claiming he had IBS, they would finally be able to sort out his real problem. I sat alone in the room and waited. I paced the floor and looked out of the window. I felt sure he'd come through; Reg had always been so fit and strong. But as the hours passed by, one, two, three, four, it became increasingly obvious that something was seriously wrong. I was grateful when Reg's old friend Wilf Pine arrived. We sat together, both knowing there was bad news ahead. Eventually, almost six hours after he'd been taken into surgery, we were told we could see him.

But there were problems, as we suspected. The surgeon came to talk to us. He said that Reg had been through a long and difficult operation and had lost a lot of blood. He believed Reg had suffered heart failure during the operation. They had placed him in intensive care. The surgeon told us we shouldn't expect too much, that the next twenty-four hours would be 'telling'. He also said they had removed a large obstruction in his small bowel and that a sample had been sent to the pathology lab; he claimed it didn't look like a cancerous growth but couldn't be sure.

A nurse accompanied us to intensive care. Realization hit me in the lift – a bad dream become reality. It was impossible but it had happened. I am, and always will be, grateful to Wilf for all his help during this time. He drove from Dorset to Norwich when he knew that Reg was having an operation, a long journey despite the fact he was unwell himself. He was with us both at the very worst of times and I know that Reg was thankful, just as I was, for his support and friendship.

Reg was conscious but sleepy when we went into the room. Wired up to numerous monitors, surrounded by small flashing lights, figures, peaks and troughs, he seemed adrift in the monumental complications of modern medicine. I sat beside him and held his hand. He opened his eyes and smiled.

Wilf, who has been through numerous operations himself, interpreted the numbers on the monitors and tried to reassure me. He said Reg was quite stable and that the figures were good. We sat in semi-darkness while Reg slept. Our main concern was for his heart. We were not to know there was a much tougher enemy lurking in the shadows.

I stayed with Reg throughout the night. The doctors and nurses checked on him frequently. The prison escort sat outside the open door, the chains finally removed. From time to time Reg awoke and I told him it was all okay, he was doing well, there was nothing to worry about. We talked until he went back to sleep.

The next forty-eight hours were critical. Much to my relief, Reg was finally moved into a room on Horsford ward on the ninth floor. It was here that he began his temporary recovery. Horsford is a heart ward and the staff monitored his condition, doing regular ECT tests, over the following week. Their original worries were not proved and the tests seemed inconclusive as to whether he had actually suffered a heart attack or not.

Reg was not allowed any food at this time and the amount he could drink was minimal. He was very thirsty but only allowed 60ml of water every hour. Apart from this he was in reasonable spirits. We were both relieved he was out of intensive care and seemed to be over the worst. The results from the pathology lab could take anything from a few days to a week but I convinced myself that the news would not be bad.

Reg fought hard against his illness, determined he would get better. Every day a governor from HMP Norwich came over to the hospital to assess his condition and to make a decision as to whether the cuffs should go back on. He was given a temporary reprieve based on the number of drips and tubes that were already connected to him. It was made clear, however, that whenever the tubes were disconnected the cuffs would be put on again. I was told by an officer that there was pressure from 'above' (and he stressed *high* above) to chain him again as soon as possible.

I have no complaints against the prison officers who acted as bed-watch with Reg. The vast majority were kind and courteous. Some were indifferent but most were understanding and compassionate.

Even while Reg was trying to recover, he was always concerned he might be sent back to Wayland. He talked about it often. Just as he had been moved from prison to prison through the years, he was convinced they would shift him out of hospital as soon as they could. It preyed on his mind. The daily visits from Norwich Prison governors assessing his condition only increased his distress.

Trevor Linn had asked for a postponement of the Parole Board hearing just before Reg was admitted to hospital. He requested a temporary delay of not more than six weeks so Reg's medical condition could be properly assessed and a more accurate diagnosis and prognosis given. We both felt it was wrong for a decision to be made in the current circumstances. If the Board were to sit and turn Reg down again, it would be the final blow.

For a short while Reg seemed to be improving. He began to eat a little and to drink. The terrible scar on his stomach started to heal. And then the results from his tests came through. I knew as soon as the consultant entered the room. She was carrying a small sheaf of papers. She looked solemnly at us both and then sat down on the edge of the bed. It was obvious that the news was bad. I took Reg's hand. I could hardly bear to listen to her. She came straight to the point. The growth was cancerous. The pathology lab had given them confirmation. The cancer specialist, the oncologist, would come and talk to us soon. There were possibilities – chemotherapy or radiotherapy. There were chances.

When she left she asked the prison escort to stay outside and give us some time. I was grateful for that. Thinking he was over the worst, it was even more devastating to hear the truth. Cancer is a terrible word. There were things we both wanted to say but how do you talk when you know there are two people waiting to come back into the room, two captors whose very presence takes away any chance of privacy or confidentiality? We said what we could. We held each other. We made the most of the little time we had together.

I stayed with him overnight. While he slept I made some decisions. I was no good to him in pieces. We both had to be strong. We had a fight ahead, two fights in fact, one against his illness and the other against his continued imprisonment. If the former was out of my control then at least I could fight the latter. I knew I had to do anything I could to assure his compassionate parole.

Reg's anxiety increased over the following days. He found his own way to deal with his illness but found it increasingly hard to suffer the presence of strangers, of the prison escort, in his hospital room. He would wake in the middle of the night to their coughs or their talk or the rustle of their magazines. He remained convinced the authorities would send him back to prison, despite his condition. We talked to some senior staff from HMP Norwich and established that even if Reg was undergoing treatment for cancer he would still be returned to a prison environment as soon as he was fit to leave hospital. I tried to reassure him but we both knew the truth.

The prospect of Reg returning to prison was frightening. I thought of what it would mean for him – being sick, enduring cancer treatment alone, returning after each session to an empty prison cell. Most people facing such an illness at least have the daily comfort of their families to turn to for love, support and reassurance. Reg would only be allowed three visits a month. I couldn't see how he'd survive. He would go back to prison knowing he had cancer and that he was probably facing another parole knock-back and therefore another five to six years in prison minimum. There would be no reason for him to keep going or to keep fighting. Reg remained in pain and that pain was exacerbated by the uncertainty of his future.

Our close friends gave support at this time. Everyone knew someone who had cancer, someone whose story offered hope and encouragement if not of complete recovery then at least of temporary reprieve. It was something to cling to. I would like to say a special thank you to Donna Cox who kept in daily contact and offered endless support. Trevor Linn, Reg's solicitor, began the preparations for an application for compassionate parole. Reg saw a few people on visits, friends like Joe Martin, Bradley and Donna Allardyce, Tony and Tracey Mortimer, Johnny and Rose Squibb, Adam Myhill, Billy Knox, Richard Reynolds, Dave and Brenda Whitmarsh, and of course Wilf, who came as often as he could. Flowers, cards and letters poured in from all over the country. The newspapers followed his progress with daily reports from the hospital, and the hospital switchboard was swamped with calls.

Reg found it difficult to be confined to bed. He missed his daily showers but always insisted on keeping clean and shaving every day. He made a few phone calls and wrote some letters but most of his time was spent simply in recuperating and getting the rest he needed to build up his strength again. The consultants came to see him regularly and monitored his progress. For a short while things seemed to be going well with a gradual but steady improvement. Until Reg had recovered sufficiently from the operation he couldn't be properly assessed for whatever cancer treatment might follow. It was a matter of priorities.

Although sick and worried, Reg tried to keep a positive attitude. He appreciated the efforts of the medical staff, and the kindness of the nurses and the auxiliaries. He never complained. He faced his illness the same way he had faced his prison sentence. He tried to make the best of it.

One morning, desperate for a proper wash, Reg managed to persuade the nurses to take him for a shower. It was not an easy mission, attached as he was to so many drips and drains and tubes, but I think they realized how much it meant to him. They gently pulled and pushed and twisted, manipulating this, removing that. They disconnected what they could and water-proofed the rest. Eventually they gathered soap and tubes and towels and wrapped him in a dressing gown. Using all his strength Reg walked slowly and unsteadily down the corridor. Flanked by a couple of nurses, and followed by a bemused prison escort, he epitomized the victory of mind over matter. Ten minutes later he was back. Soaking wet and laughing, accompanied by a nurse almost as wet as her charge, he proclaimed himself clean and happy! I like to remember the way he was that day. The sheer physical effort exhausted him but mentally he was exhilarated, determined and hopeful. Suddenly anything seemed possible.

Frank Fraser arrived at the hospital one afternoon. Reg was pleased to see him. Frank was one of the few old faces that kept in regular contact and Reg enjoyed his company. He had always been vocal in his support of Reg's release and had often visited him in prison. They spent a couple of happy hours together.

Sadly, it soon became apparent that Reg's recovery wasn't progressing in the way it should. He began to eat less and his pain increased. The consultants came frequently; they looked, prodded and investigated. They talked. They made notes. It was all going wrong. Finally, they made the decision to operate again. We knew what they suspected . . . that the cancer had already spread. But nothing was certain. We tried to stay optimistic.

An operation was scheduled quickly. On the day it was carried out I remained in Reg's room with Wilf and Bradley. After a few stressful hours a prison officer put his head round the door. He told us that Reg had just left the operating theatre, that he was sitting up in bed and that he looked well. We all felt a rush of confidence. Perhaps things were not as bad as we'd imagined. Encouraged, we waited for one of the surgeons to come and talk to us.

Our expectations were soon dashed. Whatever we might have thought, whatever we might have imagined, the truth was ten times worse. We sat silently and listened. I can't even recall what he looked like . . . only his words remain in my head. What he said was brutal and terrible. There was no hope. There were no possibilities. There were no curative treatments. There was no further surgery, no drugs, no medication, no intervention that could prevent the inevitable. The cancer had taken hold. His kidneys were failing. Reg was dying.

It is impossible to describe what I felt at that moment. There are words – desolation, desperation, despair, panic, rage, anger, fear – but all of them are hopelessly inadequate. Alone they are useless, together they barely start to express the beginnings of grief.

It was a fight against time. Trevor was unable to submit the application for compassionate parole until the medical reports were given to him. These arrived on Friday, 25 August and, along with the legal representations, were faxed to the Home Office the same day. He was informed that we would probably get a response by the following Tuesday. It was a Bank Holiday weekend and everyone was away. We prepared ourselves for the wait.

On the Saturday morning, while a nurse was attempting to take yet another blood sample from Reg, the door opened and I was told I was wanted on the phone. I went to the reception area and picked up the receiver. It was the governor of Norwich Prison. He said that Reg had been granted his compassionate parole. I heard what he said but it seemed unreal. *Compassionate parole*. We had some kind of conversation, an exchange of words, but nothing I remember clearly. I thanked him. I put the phone down.

I went back to our room. The prison officers, already apprised of the situation, were standing outside. I opened the door and went in. The nurse was still there. I sat down beside Reg. I didn't want to tell him until we were alone. The next few minutes were an eternity. While I waited I tried to find the words. I tried to think of the right words.

Eventually the nurse was successful. She took the sample, packaged and labelled it, and left.

And then, as gently as I could, I told him. The phone call had come through. His compassionate parole had been granted. After thirty-two years, it was finally over. He was free. We looked at each other with incredulity. I could barely believe what I was telling him. He could barely believe what he was hearing. This was the moment he had waited for. We embraced and kissed. It seemed unreal, almost impossible. He was free. Nothing could detract from that simple single fact.

In reality the news was simultaneously wonderful and terrible, bittersweet, a great truth overshadowed by an awful certainty. We both knew it and we both made a choice; we chose to make the most of that single gratifying moment. To be free was everything. The rest was just the future. We were aware that Reg would never have got his compassionate parole unless the authorities were convinced his death was imminent. The medical reports had confirmed that fact. The Home Office had just reaffirmed it. Their gift was easily given. They thought it was finished. But nothing was over yet.

The prison escort left that afternoon. It was the first real symbol of Reg's freedom. He had finally gained not only his liberty but also some privacy. The relief was immense. We stayed up and talked for the rest of the day and half the night. I curled up in the chair beside his bed. I spent the next five weeks, day and night, beside him. I'm thankful for the time we had together. We had spent so long apart.

Reg had been moved on to a very busy post-operative ward. Instead of waiting for the nurses, we developed our own daily routine. Early each morning I would help him to wash and shave. He was losing weight and was often very tired. It was hard for him, as it would be for most of us, to find himself unable to do the simplest of tasks. I would make us both a cup of tea before the consultants came round. They would proceed with the same examination and ask the same questions to which they always got the same replies. There was no progress. Although Reg was able to drink, he still couldn't eat anything.

For the rest of the time, depending on X-rays and tests, Reg would sleep or talk or listen to music. Bradley and Donna often sat with us. On a couple of occasions someone came in to cut Reg's hair and give him a proper shave; it broke the usual routine and made the day a little different for him.

When he felt well enough Reg enjoyed having occasional

visitors although he tired quickly and found it hard to talk for long. The situation with visitors was to become a major problem over the next few weeks. A number of friends, acquaintances and complete strangers began turning up at the hospital on a daily basis. Although he would not see strangers, Reg found it hard to refuse anyone he knew. This put an additional strain on him. Although he appreciated their concern, he needed to rest. It was impossible to do this with a constant stream of people coming in and out of his room. I was worried and even the doctors expressed their concern over the situation.

In the end, we had to make an arrangement with hospital security that no visitors, unless previously arranged by Reg, would be allowed in to see him. His health had to take priority. We asked security to deal with any uninvited guests and to explain the situation. I know that most of them understood but a few took it as a personal slight. He had many friends and cared about them all but it wasn't possible to see everyone.

An interesting event occurred around this time. A photograph of our wedding was printed in a Sunday newspaper. As we were only in possession of ten prints ourselves, and this wasn't one of them, we were rather surprised. Where had the picture come from? The following week another paper published a spread of our wedding photographs. These were all pictures that the Prison Service had refused to give us and which they were supposed to be holding in 'safe-keeping'. We had been told we could acquire prints only on Reg's release. It was distressing that photographs of huge sentimental value to us both had found their way from the Prison Service to the *News of the World* and the *Sunday People*. Perhaps one day I will get an explanation from the Home Office.

As time passed it was obvious that Reg was not improving. Every movement became more of an effort. Although mentally he was still alert and lively, physically he was growing weaker.

One morning Reg told me he wanted to organize his funeral. It wasn't the first occasion he'd mentioned it. Months before, after Charlie's death, he had started to make arrangements. It was a hard thing to talk about but it was something he wanted and needed to do.

Shortly after this Reg expressed another wish. He wanted to go outside. Tired of his hospital bed, of being constrained, he longed to breathe fresh air again. It was not an impossible suggestion. We discussed it with the nurses and with security. The medical practicalities were surmountable but a more pressing problem would be the media. They had more or less surrounded the hospital.

We had to find a place where he was safe from intrusion and eventually we settled on the small internal courtyard, a peaceful area filled with flowers and plants. Plans were made and late one morning Reg was helped into a wheelchair. We went quietly through the corridors, down in the lift, through another ward and eventually arrived, without incident, at our destination.

It was the first time Reg had been outside in six long weeks. The courtyard was very still. It smelled of summer dust. For a moment it was possible to believe that we weren't in a hospital but in some secluded garden far away. No one spoke. Reg raised his face and closed his eyes. He breathed deeply. I knelt down beside him. I laid my hand on his arm. It was the last time he ever felt the sun on his face.

Over the next couple of weeks Reg didn't make the progress that was hoped for. He had gained his compassionate parole but still felt like a prisoner. Numerous tubes and wires anchored him to the bed and he continued to be fed and given fluids intravenously. They couldn't discharge him from the hospital in that condition. Everyone knew time was running out. They had to find a way to stabilize him.

It was essential to find somewhere, not too far from the hospital, where Reg could spend what remained of his life in comfort, privacy and freedom. A few people offered places but none was suitable. Eventually John Brunton, a local friend, suggested the Town House, a hotel about ten minutes' drive away. I went with him one morning to take a look. The manager showed us the room. It was the honeymoon suite, pleasant and with reasonable space, but what attracted me most was the view. The lawn ran directly down to the river, a wide expanse of silvery water with an occasional boat drifting by. It was an idyllic scene. If Reg was well enough he might even be able to sit outside in the gardens.

I knew that Reg's presence would bring a lot of publicity to the hotel but I was concerned that the seriousness of his condition might deter the manager from accepting the responsibility of having him as a guest. I was relieved when he agreed and with necessary optimism I booked the room, an open-ended agreement as I had no idea how long we might be there . . . or even if we would ever get there at all.

It was a relief to have some accommodation sorted. Now we had to get Reg well enough to be moved. The doctors and nurses, along with members of the administrative staff, the various specialists and the occupational therapist, all worked together to try to achieve the dream. I can't praise them enough for all they did. The ward sister, Sheila Ginty, was especially supportive; she helped with many of the arrangements and organized a local GP who could take care of Reg in the hotel, as well as the daily nursing visits he would need. She went through everything with me, forgetting nothing, making sure I was equipped in every way to cope with the move. Sandra, our Macmillan nurse, was also excellent. I will never forget her encouragement, understanding and compassion.

The following week was a frenzy of activity. It began with

a visit from a documentary team. Reg had agreed to give a final interview. He neither asked for nor received any money for this. There were simply things that he wished to say and to share before he died. Above all he wanted to make clear that the road he had taken was a terrible and painful one, and if, by speaking honestly, he could deter other people from making the same mistakes then perhaps something good could eventually come from it all. He was extremely honest in this interview and very open. For a few hours the room was full of people, lights and equipment. Despite his obvious exhaustion he battled to talk for as long as they needed and answered all their questions. It was a courageous act in terrible circumstances. One moment stands out for me above all others. He was asked if he was bitter about what had happened. Reg replied, simply, that he didn't have time to be bitter.

A few days later Reg was taken for another endoscopy and it was established that the artificial tube the surgeons had created remained unblocked. Our biggest fear, that the cancer had spread and closed it down, was unrealized. Certain muscles in the base of his stomach were simply not working properly. This was good and bad news. Good in that it wasn't the cancer causing the problem, bad in that there was little they could do to force the muscles to work. There was, however, one last chance.

The consultant came to see Reg. She said that in some cases if the patient simply ate something solid, anything they wanted, the muscles would begin to work of their own accord. It would, however, mean removing the tube that emptied his stomach, the tube that currently prevented him from being constantly sick. It was his decision. Reg didn't hesitate; he knew what he wanted. He didn't intend to die in hospital.

The tube was removed the next morning. At midday John Brunton drove from his pub and kindly delivered to Reg the lunch he had requested – a steak and all the trimmings! I sat and watched him eat. A part of me was terrified. If things went wrong now then Reg would never leave hospital. He ate his way through the whole steak and thoroughly enjoyed it. It was the first real meal he had consumed in quite a time. The next few hours were critical. We waited and waited . . . but there were no ill-effects. The night passed without incident. It was like a miracle. I knew then that, disasters permitting, we were finally on our way!

Within twenty-four hours the consultant had given Reg permission to leave. It was Friday, 22 September. They knew time was of the essence. By then everything, or almost everything, was in place. We only had to find a way of getting Reg out of the building without being besieged by the press.

The initial plan was for us to leave around midday. John Brunton had arranged for a white Rolls-Royce to take us from the hospital to the hotel. He wanted to do something special for Reg and was waiting for our phone call. He was going to drive the car himself. A hospital manager, the head of security and the communications manager, Mark Langlands, came to talk to me. We had gone through various 'escape routes' the previous day and made some decisions as to the best exits. All the staff had been extremely understanding throughout Reg's stay and helped to make things more tolerable, especially as regards the media. But now there was a problem. The press were gathering in the foyer and around the hospital; someone had leaked the news that Reg was leaving. At the moment there was only a handful but news travels fast. We knew we had to get out as quickly as we could.

Wilf arrived at round 10 a.m. with his friend Alex. They barely had time to get out of the lift and catch their breath before the situation was explained. The solution was obvious – we had to gather everything up and leave immediately. Wilf's car was waiting outside. We talked to various members of security and staff and started to reorganize. The exit was chosen and a new plan made. I gathered up all our possessions. It was not what we'd planned but we had no option.

There are many things I could say about the press, not all of them complimentary. I appreciate they have a job to do but sometimes their work seems to slip beyond the parameters of common humanity. It would be hypocritical of me to condemn them out of hand as a number of journalists and editors gave Reg and myself a fair hearing in recent years, but on *this* particular morning, with Reg as ill as he was, their presence was just another mountain to climb. All Reg wanted was to leave hospital quietly. He didn't want to be surrounded by journalists. He didn't want a thousand flashbulbs going off. He was dying and he knew it. His life was almost over. It was terrible for him to realize that someone close had sold him out – yet again. I hope that particular person appreciated their few sad pieces of silver.

I helped Reg to get dressed. He put on a new cream tracksuit that Tony and Tracey Mortimer had recently bought him. I packed the rest of our belongings. There was little time to say goodbye to anyone. It was one mad final rush. I threw everything into a bag: clothes, soap, toothpaste, books, razors, letters and cards. There was little time to think about anything. We helped Reg into a wheelchair. As we left the room I gave it one final backward glance; we had spent the last five weeks together there and it was full of memories. It seemed incredible, unbelievable that we were finally leaving. As always, it was not what we'd expected . . . but we were getting used to that.

We went down in the lift. Wilf and Alex left and went to collect the car. Reg and I, along with Sheila, Mark and a member of the hospital security, made our way through the bowels of the hospital. We seemed to walk for ever until we reached the pre-arranged exit. Wilf, thankfully, was waiting for us. We helped Reg into the back of the car and then loaded up the luggage. The next few minutes were frantic. Carrier bags, holdalls and cases were forced into every corner. We realized that the wheelchair would have to be dismantled but our need for haste made simple actions clumsy and we fumbled and fought with the basic mechanics for what seemed an eternity. Eventually we squeezed all the component parts into the limited space. Our final thanks and goodbyes to the staff were hurried and inadequate. I got into the back with Reg. Wilf started the engine and we pulled away.

We drove unnoticed through the hospital grounds and out through the exit. On reaching the main road there was a common exhalation of breath, a shared relief that we had avoided the worst. We didn't talk much. Reg was quiet. Occasionally he looked out of the window. I knew this wasn't what he'd ever imagined. His final freedom should have been a time of elation and hope. He should have been looking towards the future. I wondered how many times he had envisaged this day, this moment . . . but never like this. His thoughts were his own. None of us can know exactly what they were.

John Brunton had arranged for help at the Town House. As soon as we arrived Reg was assisted up the stairs and into the room. I think it was at that moment, as we passed through the door, that the truth really hit us all. Reg was out of prison and out of hospital. He was finally and absolutely free. As if the knowledge provided a surge of energy, Reg suddenly found the strength to move around alone. He walked unaccompanied to the window and looked out over the river. He was pleased with the room and the view. Wilf ordered champagne from the bar. We gathered chairs around the window and all sat down together. It was a very happy moment. Reg was in good spirits, more animated than he had been for many days. It was good to hear him laugh again.

That first day was wonderful. Reg was able to eat and drink a little. Bradley and Donna joined us for an evening meal and we sat around the bed talking and listening to music. The atmosphere was happy and relaxed. We could have been anywhere at any time. All our worries seemed to drift away. All our pain was temporarily lost. For a few hours we let ourselves forget.

Over the following week Reg's condition would worsen, but for a while he was able to savour the moment and enjoy himself. Our world at the Town House was tiny, caught within four walls. But it was more than enough. He was free and we were together. Our days and nights were our own. For what was left of his life he would never have to be alone again. Those first few days will always be precious to me. They were Reg's real days of liberty and he appreciated them. There was no more prison. There was no more waiting. For the first time in thirty-two years he was truly free.

One afternoon we heard a rumour, relayed on the radio, that Reg had somehow deceived the Home Secretary, the Prison Service and the specialists at the Norfolk and Norwich Hospital . . . and that he really wasn't seriously ill at all. It made Reg laugh. He said: 'Jack Straw must be having a few sleepless nights!'

We had several visitors over the weekend. Trevor Linn and Mark Goldstein, along with his wife Donna, came on the Sunday. It was good to see them. Reg had developed a close friendship with both over the previous few years. Trust and loyalty were very important to him. They had never let him down and he appreciated it. I was grateful too for everything they had done, for all their hard work and persistence. I was told later how shocked they were by Reg's appearance; he had become much thinner even since their last visit. They stayed for a few hours. When they left they knew they would never see him again.

In addition to close friends there were many people, some of them strangers, who helped Reg during his time at the hospital and at the Town House. It would be impossible to mention them all but special thanks should go to the doctors and nurses, to John Brunton and to John Ledgard, a local taxi-driver, for everything they did.

Some of Reg's old associates, Joe Pyle, Johnny Nash and Freddie Foreman, had made an arrangement to see him on the Tuesday after we moved into the Town House. By the Monday, however, Reg was already feeling very weak and tired. He said he couldn't cope with the visit and asked if I could cancel it.

Reg was extremely ill that evening, so bad that at around midnight I had to call the doctor. She came within half an hour and with competence and kindness dealt with all his immediate problems. Reg asked her some questions and she answered them honestly. He was aware that he had reached another crisis point; the cancer was spreading quickly. She asked him if he wished to be re-admitted to hospital. He said no. He wanted to die in peace with the people he loved beside him.

That evening was a turning point. Reg's condition worsened during the week. He became even weaker, unable to eat or even to drink very much. The one thing that never left him was his spirit. He knew that physically the battle was almost lost but his mind was very much alive. He had no self-pity and never complained. He appreciated the time he had and tried to make the most of it.

There was something about Reg that touched people deeply. It went beyond his name or his history. It was an inexplicable quality. Despite his reputation, despite his violent past, there was a curious vulnerability about him. He was often frighteningly open and trusting. Reg always believed in people until they gave him a reason not to, which was often sooner rather than later, but he never became cynical or disillusioned. When friends let him down he was more often sad than angry. He refused to be brought down or made bitter by deceit and deception.

By the end of the week Reg was very ill. Wilf Pine arrived on the Saturday. Joe Martin also came. He was an old friend of Reg's and Ron's, who had spent time with them both in Parkhurst and, later, in Maidstone with Reg. Joe had also visited several times at the hospital. Reg was hardly aware of our presence, lost in a morphine world, and barely conscious.

On the Saturday night, when we were alone, he was restless and didn't sleep. He was coughing badly. Occasionally he would grasp my hand and murmur a few words. Something would flicker in his eyes, a momentary recognition, there and then lost again. I lay on the bed and held him in my arms. I think he knew what was happening. I think he knew it was the last night.

I was surprised to be told on the Sunday morning that Freddie Foreman, Joe Pyle and Johnny Nash, despite Reg's wishes, were already on the train making the journey from London to Norwich. Joe Martin came again in the morning and sat with Reg for a few hours. I was sorry to see him go. He had always been a loyal friend to Reg. The others arrived just after Joe had left. They had been in the bar and came rather noisily through the door. They were accompanied by Wilf Pine. Donna was already in the room.

They gathered around his bedside. Reg was barely conscious and appeared unaware of their presence. He could not acknowledge or talk to them. I sat beside Reg on the bed. He seemed small and frail. He'd lost a lot of weight during his time at the hospital and the last of his strength had been ebbing away in recent days. There were some problems now with his right arm and he continued to worry at it, holding and stretching, sometimes grasping it with his other hand. I knew it was distressing him, that there was some pain. While the talk went on around us, I held his hand and stroked his arm.

I was relieved when, after about ten minutes, the district nurses arrived. They came every day to check on Reg's condition, to refill the pain-relieving syringes, to give advice and to adjust his medication if necessary. I asked our visitors if they would be kind enough to wait downstairs.

Shortly afterwards, the local doctor also arrived. It took over an hour for them to finish everything they had to do. They treated Reg, as always, with kindness and compassion. It was clear he was in some distress and they did their very best to help. Only Donna remained in the room with me. We sat close to Reg and waited. Although they moved him with the utmost gentleness it was apparent that any movement at all caused him pain. Reg's breathing had deteriorated. The doctor made a decision to increase the morphine and anti-sickness drugs.

After the doctor and nurses had left, Donna and I stayed alone with Reg. It was peaceful in the room. We sat quietly on the bed beside him. After a few minutes we were joined by Bradley. Gradually Reg's coughing subsided. He became less restless and more relaxed. He closed his eyes. He seemed to fall asleep.

By the time the others returned Reg had completely lost consciousness. His breathing was very bad. I thought they had just come to say a simple goodbye but they showed no inclination to leave. They stood around the bed and stared at him. I held Reg's hand. It became obvious what was happening and Wilf suggested it was time for them to go. Fred Foreman went instead to the en-suite bathroom.

It happened quickly. In a few seconds everything changed.

Wilf made a comment; it came back to me in a disconnected form. I felt a kind of dislocation, of incredulity. I looked around and then back at Reg. Donna stood up and tried to persuade Joe Pyle and Johnny Nash to leave. They were just outside the door when Wilf's voice called to me again. I heard him say 'That's it . . .' Reg's breathing stuttered, stopped and then suddenly started again – one last tiny half breath. And then there was nothing. Silence.

It was the worst moment of my life. I leaned over and took him in my arms. His skin was warm, his eyes closed as if he were still sleeping. I put my hand on his forehead and stroked his hair. I was aware of Wilf hammering on the bathroom door calling out to Freddie Foreman. I was holding Reg and crying.

What is grief – disbelief, loss, a holding of breath? A fierce angry impossible pain? Hopelessness? Emptiness? There are no good words. There is only a grasping, an absence of understanding. I held him in my arms and cried.

Reg was dead.

I spent the following days in a daze, struggling through the hours, hopelessly empty and alone. I didn't want anyone else with me. For the previous nine weeks I had been with Reg constantly. Without him I was lost. Friends and family were kind and supportive but they knew there was no consolation. Nothing can help you through that maze of despair. It was enough to know they were there for me, and always would be.

Reg's funeral took place on Wednesday, 11 October. Its organization was a mammoth task and I'm grateful to Wilf Pine and others for all their help. It was hard to cope with it and deal with my own feelings of grief at the same time. Fortunately, Reg had left very detailed instructions covering his choice of pall-bearers, church, hymns and songs, and that he wished to be buried in the same grave as his twin brother Ron. He had discussed these instructions with his solicitors and they were carried out to his exact specifications.

Back in the hospital, while Reg had been making the arrangements, a friend had suggested that his pall-bearers, like Ron's, should consist of his old associates. It hadn't even crossed Reg's mind. Although he was fond of some of them, there had been little contact in recent years. They didn't visit and he rarely talked to them over the phone.

Reg's final choice was never intended as a rejection of his old friends or his former life. It was a simply a matter of the heart. Through the difficult years, through the parole knock-backs, the disappointments and despair, it was mainly the love and support of his more recent friends that gave him the courage to continue.

The day was always going to be a difficult and emotional one. The level of media interest meant there would be cameras, photographers and journalists almost everywhere. It is hard enough to grieve in private but to have that grief made public only exacerbates the ordeal. I was glad our close friends were beside me. Their support gave me strength and courage. I would like to express my heartfelt thanks to all of them. I would also like to thank Richard Grayston who organized the security and all his men who acted with decorum and dignity.

It was alleged that I didn't want any gangsters at the funeral but this is not the case. I wanted exactly what Reg wanted – for everyone who had ever cared for him to be able to attend. Reg had a past and a present and the people at the funeral reflected that balance. It is well-known that I asked Wilf Pine to organize half the church and half the cars for Reg's former friends who, for the most part, had not been in recent contact with him.

Some of Reg's old associates refused to attend the funeral

because they had not been chosen as pall-bearers. It seemed sad that they had chosen to forego the opportunity to say goodbye. Whatever their feelings it was not the time for recriminations. There were many friends in the congregation, old and new, who said their farewells with genuine love and affection.

On the sides of the hearse the flowers I had chosen read *Free at last* and *Beloved husband*, one a public statement and the other private. There were twelve red roses as well, the flowers that Reg always sent to me. The streets were lined with people as we travelled towards Chingford. It was a long slow journey. It was hard to accept the finality of Reg's death. I would never hear his voice again or his laugh. I would never wake and see his face. He would never take my hand again or kiss me or hold me in his arms. There would be no more promises. The time for promises was past.

The cemetery was very crowded. We made our way forward to the graveside. It was heartbreaking to remember that only six months before I had stood beside Reg as Charlie had been buried. I felt overwhelmed by loss and loneliness. Reg was laid to rest with his twin brother Ron. Nearby lay the graves of his mother and father, his first wife Frances, Charlie and his son Gary. For the first time in thirty-two years they were reunited.

I do not believe that Reg deserved the relentless and unforgiving punishment he received. His continued imprisonment was not to do with justice or morality or decency. Many thousands of people convicted of more heinous crimes were released before him, among them terrorists, paedophiles and multiple killers. Reg watched them walk away. He always accepted his sentence. He never whined or complained. He had killed and he fully accepted the consequences. That his punishment bore no relation to that of others convicted of similar offences was something that he rarely mentioned. He knew his punishment was not simply a response to the crimes he was accused of in the dock. The Krays had jeopardized the old Establishment. They had mixed with lords, MPs and numerous social figures . . . and for *those* crimes they could never be forgiven.

In this country we offer most offenders, unless their crimes are particularly horrific, an eventual opportunity for redemption. Society needs its retribution but usually it also offers mercy and hope. Even after thirty-two years this was still denied to Reg. He received his freedom only because he was dying.

Much has been written, and will continue to be written, about Reg Kray. Most is untrue or grossly distorted, a mixture of half-truths, exaggeration and fantasy. It's not my intention to present an idealized portrait of him but perhaps to redress the balance a little.

There were many people who perpetuated the myth of Reg Kray through the years. It served a useful purpose to present Reg as a symbol, a one-dimensional figure, a personification of the 'glamour' of crime. That image helped to sustain and enhance the reputations of others who moved, or aspired to move, in the same world. Even after thirty-two years they could not acknowledge or accept the person he had actually become. There was no room in their minds, hearts or ambitions for a different Reg. He was cast in stone. Reg never attempted to deny who or what he had been. He never turned his back on the past but he no longer lived there; he had moved on and enthusiastically embraced the present. No one is unchanging.

The media also preferred its villains larger than life. Few newspapers or magazines were interested in the real Reg; the demonized version made much better copy.

The myth was useful for the Establishment as well; while it

continued to grow and to flourish, fed by the numerous books and articles of his former associates, Reg Kray could still be depicted as a potentially dangerous criminal and a threat to society.

The truth is that at the end Reg was not a gangster. He was no longer thirty-four. He was not a photograph or a piece of propaganda. He was not an image or a word. He was worth more than a mere commodity. Reg was a man who had survived over thirty-two years in prison and emerged, incredibly, without bitterness or self-pity. Although often portrayed as a caricature, he had reason, intelligence and warmth. He felt fear and doubt and had his share of regrets. He endured the gradual erosion of all his hopes but never gave up on life. Despite his circumstances, despite his own despair, he faced every day with enthusiasm, energy and gratitude. Above all, he never lost his capacity for love.

The past for Reg was a place of violence. As a young man he moved in unremittingly vicious circles and answered like with like. It was a brutal way of life, the appeal of which had begun to pall even before he went to prison. Reg's destiny was inextricably entwined with Ron's and their mutual fate was a terrible one. Reg Kray was no angel but he was not a devil either. He was simply a human being.

Reg wrote this book so that others would be deterred from travelling the same long and painful road. If there is to be an enduring legacy then Reg would wish it to be this. To say his life was wasted would be a denigration of his incredible spirit and of the joy he brought to me and to others, but there was so much more he wanted and desired. Prison did not take away his dreams; it simply made them impossible to achieve.

APPENDIX
REG'S PAPERS

REG KRAY

REQUEST/COMPLAINT FORM

ESTABLISHMENT	Wayland		CATEGORY	STATUS	DATE ISSUED
			C	Life.	30.9.98.
NAME	Kray		SERIAL No		DATE RECEIVED
			WLC 98 7976		5.10.98
NUMBER	LOCATION	DATE OF BIRTH	CROSS REF.		DATE REPLIED
058111	C.	24.10.33			6.10.98

GUIDANCE NOTES

(Further information is given in the booklet "How to make a request or complaint")

1. Please try to resolve your request / complaint informally if you can.

2. A written request / complaint should be made within 3 months of the relevant facts coming to your notice. A complaint about improper treatment should be made as soon as possible, giving full details. You should use this form within 3 months of the date issued.

3. Please limit your request / complaint to one subject. Ask for a separate form if there is something else you want to raise.

4. Please write clearly. Do not use abusive or insulting language.

5. Please write in ENGLISH if possible. (Welsh speaking inmates may write in Welsh). If you write in any other language this could lead to a delay

HAVE YOU DISCUSSED YOUR REQUEST / COMPLAINT WITH ANYONE? IF SO. WHOM?

Yes Listener. Inmate Bill Taylor.

REQUEST / COMPLAINT (give reason where appropriate): To Governor Oñsol.

I FEEL I AM ENTITLED To YOUr WATCH AFTER 30 YEArs AS CLEANGr - I AM SUre So. Po Burton will ENDORSE THis Req-est.

(You may continue on the back if necessary)

WHAT ACTION WOULD YOU LIKE TAKEN?

To Be giver A YOU WATCH.

VF007 (F2059A) 10/96 H M P Maidstone

302

SIGNATURE: DATE:

1998³

6th OCTOBER

REPLY:

There are no facilities or procedures for recognising long serving prisoners in this manner.

I fear that even if there were such arrangements, someone would wish to challenge your entitlement on the basis of:

    1) Not all time served with the same prison (firm)

or 2) Not technically an employee ? the Prison Service

I also suspect that any watch awarded in the present economic climate would be an economy model which may well act as a disincentive to others to undertake such long and faithful service.

I hope that the standard of your work is recognised in the less mercenary, but more worthwhile context of wing reports.

SIGNATURE: R M Orton DATE: 6 October 1998 R.M.ORTON

Number: O58111 Name: KRAY .... Location: B.H.2

Your cell was inspected on 7.2.98 ... by Officer POWELL / Jackson
SO
and failed to meet the required standard for the following reasons:

1. Lights: ....

2. Cell layout: TWO TABLES, Remove one

3. Observation Panel: ....

④ Other Remove Pictures / wallpaper on back of door and around Sink area Remove Shelf on back wall

Failure for the same fault on any future inspection or any previous warning of the same fault will result in you being placed on report.

H M PRISON WAYLAND

NO:	NAME:	LOC:	DATE:
	KRAY	B .	

APPLICATION:
You are now listed as RETIRED. and are not required for any Labour.

Reg Kray

CANTEEN SHEET

No.	Surname	Loc.	Amount	Date
058111	KRAY	C2-027	14.11	16/08/1999

Complete this form and return to the wing office as soon as possible

ITEM PRIORITY	QUANTITY	COST
1		
2		
3	1 Colgate	73.
4		
5	1 Pine Soap -	57.
6		
7	12 green tea	2·40·
8		
9	one Lighter	25
10		
11		
12		
13		
14		
15		
16		
17		
18		
19		
20		
21		

INMATES SIGNATURE _____ COST 3-95.

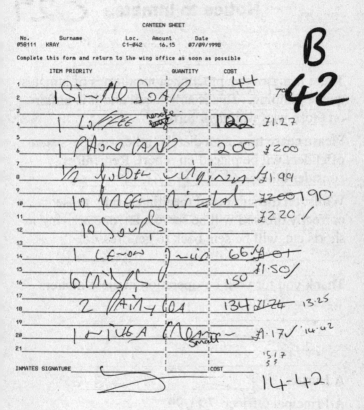

CANTEEN SHEET

| No. 058111 | Surname KRAY | Loc. C1-042 | Amount 16.15 | Date 07/09/1998 |

Complete this form and return to the wing office as soon as possible

	ITEM PRIORITY	QUANTITY	COST
1			44
2	1 Si~ME SOAP		7°
3			
4	1 COFFEE nescafe	122	£1.27
5			
6	1 PHONE CARD	200	£2.00
7			
8	1/2 GOLDEN Virgins		£1.99
9			
10	10 GREEN Nickls		£200 190
11			£220
12	10 SOUPS		
13			
14	1 LEMON Juic	66	
15			
16	6 MilkS	150	£1.50
17			
18	2 PAINY COA	134	£124 13.25
19			
20	1 ~iUGA CReam Small		£1.17 14.42
21			

INMATES SIGNATURE _____ COST

B
42

1517
55

14-42

Notice to Inmates

There is a growing practice at mealtimes of inmates queue jumping. This is anti-social and it is unfair on those who wait their turn.

Please cease this immediately, otherwise persistant offenders wil be placed on report. Remember, consider others.

Whilst on the subject of mealtimes, only those correctly dressed will be served, anyone arriving in shorts etc. will be sent back to get dressed.

Thank you for your co-operation in these matters

A Burton
A/Principal Officer 7/11/99

mealrule.doc

NORFOLK & NORWICH HEALTH CARE NHS TRUST

DEPARTMENT OF GASTROENTEROLOGY

WEST NORWICH HOSPITAL
BOWTHORPE ROAD
NORWICH NR2 3TU

Fax No: 01603 288368

Dr. Hugh Kennedy	Dr. Ian Fellows	Dr. Alison Prior	Dr. Richard Tighe	Dr. Andrew Hart
MD FRCP	DM FRCP	MD FRCP	MD MRCP	MD MRCP
Tel: 01603 288367	Tel: 01603 288356	Tel: 01603 288358	Tel: 01603 288230	Tel: 01603 288366

Our Ref: SG/JG/1136182   3rd February 2000
NHS No: Not known.

Mr. Reginald Kray
No: 058111
H.M. Prison
Wayland
Griston
Thetford
IP25 6RL

Dear Mr. Kray

When I saw you in clinic recently, you asked me for a letter verifying certain facts about your medical condition as you are concerned that there has been inaccurate reporting in the Press recently. I can confirm there is no reason to believe that you have stomach cancer, or indeed, cancer anywhere. We have never at any time considered or suggested an operation as there has never been any need for one.

I hope this is helpful.

cc: Mr. M. Langland
Press Officer
Norfolk & Norwich Hospital

REG KRAY

LICENCE

Crime (Sentences) Act 1997

The Secretary of State hereby authorises the release on licence within fifteen days of the date hereof of **REGINALD KRAY** who shall on release and during the period of this licence comply with the following conditions or any other condition which may be substituted or added from time to time.

1. He shall place himself under the supervision of whichever probation officer is nominated for this purpose from time to time.

2. He shall on release report to the probation officer so nominated and shall keep in touch with that officer in accordance with that officer's instructions.

3. He shall, if his probation officer so requires, receive visits from that officer where the licence holder is living.

4. He shall, on release, remain at the Norfolk and Norwich Hospital and shall not reside elsewhere without the prior permission of his probation officer.

Unless revoked this licence remains in force indefinitely.

J S PAGE
On behalf of the Secretary of State
26 August 2000

PDP/K 2234/5/23
Home Office
London SW1

Supervising probation officers:
Mr M Elliot and Mr H Matthews
87A Whitechapel High Street
London E1 7QX

INDEX

Index

INDEX

INDEX